Binzagr Institute for Sustainable Prosperity

"Sustainable prosperity" is a holistic notion encompassing the physical, mental, environmental, financial, educational, and civic wellbeing of all individuals, families, neighborhoods, and regions throughout the world. In this sense, sustainable prosperity requires the development of a multifaceted public policy framework addressing the root causes of global, national, and regional socioeconomic challenges. It must guarantee all individuals a decent quality of life with dignity and the opportunity to be a member of an inclusive, participatory, and just society. Sustainable prosperity means that every decision we make, individually or collectively, must take into account its direct and indirect effects on people, on the planet, and on the economy.

Crafting solutions to the complex challenges that confront us in the twenty-first century requires an interdisciplinary approach at the intersection of economics, ecology, and ethics. The Binzagr Institute for Sustainable Prosperity book series seeks proposals from a broad range of fields that encompass and further this philosophy. We welcome authored works or edited manuscripts that investigate socioeconomic inequality based on class, race, ethnicity, and/or gender, and that promote policies to further sustainable prosperity among marginalized groups. We especially encourage proposals that build on the Job Guarantee approach to full employment, financial sovereignty (functional finance), renewable energy, sustainable agriculture, environmental policies, local community development, local capacity building, social ecology, social venture partnerships, and social entrepreneurship.

More information about this series at
http://www.palgrave.com/gp/series/15386

Oren M. Levin-Waldman

Restoring the Middle Class through Wage Policy

Arguments for a Minimum Wage

palgrave
macmillan

Oren M. Levin-Waldman
Metropolitan College of New York
New York, NY, USA

Binzagr Institute for Sustainable Prosperity
ISBN 978-3-030-08994-8 ISBN 978-3-319-74448-3 (eBook)
https://doi.org/10.1007/978-3-319-74448-3

Printed on acid-free paper

This Palgrave Macmillan imprint is published by Springer Nature
The registered company is Springer International Publishing AG
The registered company address is: Gewerbestrasse 11, 6330 Cham, Switzerland

Preface

When the history of the 2016 election is written, there will no doubt be a number of interpretations offered for why Donald Trump, a politically inexperienced businessman and reality TV star who never held office, defeated former first lady, senator, and Secretary of State Hillary Clinton. As the left focuses on the anger of white blue-collar working-class America, an anger tinged with racism and xenophobia, the right is quick to point out that the electorate was simply sick of the identity politics being offered up by Democratic Party elites who felt they knew better than the public what was good for it. Perhaps the interpretation that will get the most attention is that this was the election in which the Democratic Party long the party of working-class Americans all but forgot about the middle class. It is true that Clinton's challenger in the primaries, Senator Bernie Sanders of Vermont, attempted to focus on the plight of those who have been forgotten by arguing for a $15 an hour minimum wage, a single-payer health-care system, and free college tuition. Still, during the campaign for the general election, nobody really discussed the middle class. During the primaries there had been some scant discussion about the rise in income inequality, but nobody really came out and explained why it was so significant. For the left, it simply meant that the wealthy were not paying their fair share, and therefore the way to redress the problem would be through more taxes on the wealthy to buy more programs for the benefit of the poor. For the right, of course, this only meant that we are in a dynamic global economy and further growth only requires greater flexibility on the part of workers.

What became clear is that much of the anger among those who voted for Trump was due to an economy that left them with little opportunity to live a middle-class lifestyle. Wages had been stagnant for decades. The manufacturing base had been decimated. The only jobs that were being created were either at the bottom of the income distribution in the low-skilled service sector or at the top of the distribution in the highly skilled technology sector, or among the professions. The rise in inequality, which could just as easily have been dismissed as nothing more than an oversupply of low-skilled workers driving down wage rates and indeed was by conservatives, really spoke to a reality that few wanted to address: the disappearance of the middle class. And yet, while Trump didn't really speak to the issue of the middle class and how best to shore up the middle class, he did seem to understand the issues facing blue-collar workers, or at least they thought he did.

Much has been made about how despite winning the Electoral College Trump still lost the popular vote. The three states that made the difference were the blue states of Wisconsin, Michigan, and Pennsylvania, which nobody could have imagined going to Trump. Clinton simply assumed that they were in the bag; so there was no need to go there and campaign. Trump actually campaigned there and talked about bringing back good-paying jobs. When the history of this election is written, what might stand out the most is that the pollsters got it wrong. Not only did they get it wrong, but candidates that base their campaigns on traditional polling so they can better target their stump speeches may actually be in for a rude awakening. The only data that was really important was the changing demographics of the labor market, particularly those labor markets in Wisconsin, Michigan, and Pennsylvania. All that the Trump campaign needed to do was to look at the changing labor market demographics in those states to know that good-paying jobs in manufacturing had disappeared and were replaced with lower-paying service jobs. The demographics told the story of a two-tiered economy with a middle class that was disappearing.

Still, despite a campaign that appeared to be speaking to the needs of workers even with the apparent disconnect between them and the billionaire candidate, there has been little discussion about the middle class. This book is about how one policy, the minimum wage, might just be one approach to shoring up the middle class. The minimum wage has long been a controversial issue in the economics literature. It has also been a hot political issue largely because its effects on certain groups, mainly employers and those earning around it, are greater than commonly supposed.

Those opposed to the minimum wage have long argued that a minimum wage results in lower employment because employers will either lay off workers, substitute technology for workers, or simply not hire new workers in the future. Therefore, a minimum wage particularly hurts low-skilled workers who are more likely to lose their jobs. Moreover, the percentage of the labor market that actually earns the statutory minimum wage is quite small, and those who do are primarily teenagers and/or other secondary earners. Since the majority of minimum wage workers are not primary earners or heads of households, it really is for all intents and purposes a non-issue.

Those who argue for the minimum wage focus their efforts primarily on the poor, arguing that a higher minimum wage will assist the poor by raising their wages. Moreover, it might reduce income inequality somewhat. And yet, if the minimum wage is such a non-issue, then why does it engender the degree of political opposition it typically does? Because the opposition only argues the benefits to the poor it is easy to ignore the beneficiaries because of a common tendency to stigmatize. But the opposition over a seemingly trivial non-issue would appear to be an acknowledgment that the minimum wage really does benefit more than simply those who earn the statutory minimum. Surely, it must benefit those who earn around the minimum wage—the larger low-wage labor market that we can refer to as the "effective" minimum wage labor market—because those earning in wage ranges immediately above those earning the statutory minimum will also need to get increases, as well as those in ranges above them. In other words, there may be ripple effects, or what we will in the pages to follow refer to as wage contour effects.

How the minimum wage and its effects are couched in many ways underscore E.E. Schattschneider's (1975) famous observation that politics revolves around conflict, of which there are two sides: actors and spectators. Some actors might seek to localize the conflict by narrowing the focus. This is precisely what opponents of the minimum wage do when they claim that only a small group earns the minimum wage and that they really aren't important. If one side is supposed to be localizing the conflict, the other should be seeking to tip the scales in its favor by socializing it. And yet, to date it is not clear that supporters have been doing a good job at it. By focusing on the benefits to minimum wage earners, they also maintain a narrow focus. Were they to view the statutory minimum wage as a reference point for the larger low-wage labor market, they would actually be talking about an effective minimum wage population, in which case the conflict will have been socialized. Of course, it might be that opponents understand that the effects are larger; otherwise why would they seek to keep the conflict localized.

If the benefits are larger than commonly assumed, then the minimum wage is either the most underrated policy utilized, or it is well understood by its opponents who are nonetheless adept at couching their opposition in the language of the public interest, that is, concern over adverse employment consequences. A policy that serves to effectively raise wages up the distribution is one with positive welfare effects and one that can serve the interests of the middle class. The minimum wage, as I will argue, is a middle-class issue and, as a traditional labor-management issue, always was. If a middle-class issue, is that it results in greater aggregate demand because of increased purchasing power, it also can serve as a foundation for job creation.

I am by no means suggesting that the minimum wage is a panacea for our economic woes or that it alone will restore the middle class. Raising the minimum wage is certainly not going to make us all equal, but it will reduce the growing gap between the top and the bottom in the distribution. It might slow down the rise in income inequality. Rather if a regular increase in the minimum wage might serve to exert an upward pressure on wages through the distribution, then its potential for positive welfare effects cannot be discounted. It is certainly a tool in the larger policy arsenal that should be included. And yet the larger issue is that public policy should be centered more on the middle class rather than simply assisting the poor. Because arguments for the minimum wage have long centered on aiding the poor, it has been easy to discount the minimum wage because, in the view of most neoclassical economists, most earners of the statutory minimum are not poor. Of course by focusing the debate so narrowly it has also been possible to obscure some of the larger benefits to society that would also certainly adversely affect the interests of those who would then be forced to pay their employees more.

In the public discourse, no employer, after all, is going to come out and say that he opposes the minimum wage because he wants to selfishly keep as much of his profits to himself. Rather, he will couch his selfish interests in terms of the public interest and argue that the minimum wage might therefore be harmful to the public interest because it will have employment consequences. Is it not more civilized to demonstrate your concern for the unemployed when the real concern is to maintain higher profits by paying workers as little as possible? For those who earn above the minimum wage, it is difficult to understand how the minimum wage can affect them. Therefore, their support for the minimum wage becomes an exercise in compassion for the poor. The political problem here is that policies intended to assist the poor do not garner as much support as those policies intended for the middle class. This may have something to do with a tendency to stigmatize the poor. And yet, when the neoclassical economist argues that the answer to low wages is for the poor to seek the education and training necessary to command higher wages, he is stigmatizing the poor. After all, it is the poor's fault that they lack the skills necessary to command higher wages. Therefore, the onus is on them to acquire those necessary skills. And if the onus is on them, there can be no justification for government imposing a mandatory wage floor, especially if it could in the process have adverse effects.

The minimum wage as a middle-class issue is also an example of what Martin Gilens (2012) calls "targeting within universalism." By couching an issue in broader terms, it will garner much more political support. But it isn't just about making an effective political argument. It is also about demonstrating with data that this is an issue that will indeed benefit the middle class. This is important because so little policy in recent years has been about the middle class. Even when policy is aimed at the economy, it assumes either fiscal or monetary form. With fiscal policy, policymakers are often offering tax cuts in order to stimulate investment. And with monetary policy, they are playing with interest rates ostensibly for the same purpose. None of these policies focus on the middle class per se because neither one includes the need for a serious wage policy to keep wages rising.

If the middle class is in decline it may be for several reasons: First, there have been economic transformations whereby manufacturing has been replaced with services with highly skilled and educated workers at the top and an oversupply of low-skilled and poorly educated workers at the bottom. Second, labor market institutions that served to bolster middle-class wages and in fact created the blue-collar middle class, like unions, have been in decline. The minimum wage is also a labor market institution whose value has deteriorated due to inaction. Third, wages have been stagnant for more than four decades now, in part because of declining labor market institutions and also in part because of rising health insurance premiums that have eaten into the wage bill. There is a school of thought that maintains that the decline in the middle class is the result of public policies that have resulted in the wealthy becoming even wealthier at the expense of everybody else. It may be too extreme to say that policymakers set out to target the middle class, but in allowing certain labor market institution, like unions and the minimum wage, to deteriorate policymakers may have in effect aided and abetted those forces that contributed to the middle class' decline. That is, certain so-called natural market forces were exacerbated by public policy decisions.

This book has been many years in the making. It now represents the fifth book that I have written on wage policy. It has been more than 16 years since I published my first book (2001) on the minimum wage where I argued that the minimum wage is at root a political issue and has tended to increase when there was a strong constituency supporting its increase. That constituency was organized labor and when organized labor declined in terms of union membership, the minimum wage effectively stagnated. Although I (2011) introduced the idea of wage contours and positive welfare effects a decade later in *Wage Policy, Income Distribution, and Democratic Theory*, the main premise of the book was that a wage policy would be in keeping with democratic theory. In this book I am specifically pulling together bits and pieces of work I have done, mostly since *Wage Policy, Income Distribution, and Democratic Theory* and arguing that in the end the minimum wage would do more than commonly supposed to restore the middle class. Not only would it boost the incomes of many throughout the distribution through wage contour effects, because it would increase aggregate demand for goods and services, it also serves as a foundation for job creation. I realize that I am making an argument contrary to the neoclassical orthodoxy, but it is only when we view the issue through a different prism can we see what is really at stake. Also the orthodoxy reigns supreme because not enough people challenge it, largely because the conflict is viewed within the prism of those interests that are served by localizing the conflict.

I have benefitted from conversations with many people over the years. Portions of the manuscript were read by my friend and colleague the late Robert Prasch. Charles Whalen read portions and offered many suggestions, and indeed these were issues we discussed greatly over the years. Also anonymous reviewers offered their comments which surely improved this manuscript. All comments received have no doubt made this a better manuscript, but I bear sole responsibility for the errors or omissions remaining. I want to thank the editor of the *Journal of Workplace Rights* (Sage Open)—Joel Rudin—for permission to reprint pieces that appeared in those pages: "Wage Policy as an Essential Ingredient in Democratic Society" 17, 1 (2014), and "Is Wage Inequality Designed or Preordained?"

(April–May 2017). I also thank Taylor and Francis and the editor of the *Forum for Social Economics* for permission to reprint pieces of "Refocusing the Minimum Wage Debate: Overcoming Management Failure and Achieving the High Road." I thank Taylor and Francis and the editor of the *Journal of Economic Issues* for permission to reprint pieces of "Policy Orthodoxies, the Minimum Wage, and the Challenge of Social Science" 38, 1 (March 2004). Lastly, I thank Taylor and Francis and the editor of *Challenge*—Jeff Madrick—for permission to reprint pieces from "Wage Policy as an Essential Ingredient in Job Creation" 55, 6 (November 2012) and "A Conservative Case for the Minimum Wage" 57, 1 (January 2014). Over the years, I have published many pieces on the minimum wage in *Challenge*, and Jeff has always been receptive, I think, precisely because I have been arguing against the orthodoxy. Lastly, I thank my family for their support. My children, Avi and Ariel, are grown and out of the house now, but they continue to inspire. Of course, my wife Renee provides the love and support necessary to see things through.

New York, NY, USA Oren M. Levin-Waldman

Contents

List of Tables

CHAPTER 1

Introduction

On Labor Day 2013 fast-food workers all over the US went out on a one-day strike for a $15 an hour minimum wage. Since then, fast-food workers have continued to engage in sporadic daily strikes for a minimum of $15 an hour. Meanwhile, over the last several years several states have either adopted a minimum wage higher than the federal minimum wage of $7.25 an hour or have raised their existing ones. Currently, at least 29 states have minimum wages that are higher than the federal minimum, and of them 16 have adopted a mechanism for their automatic adjustment so that they can keep up with inflation and no longer lose value. Additionally, several localities have legislated $15 an hour minimum wages, which in many cases will fully take effect by 2020. All of this clearly speaks to three trends. The first is that the minimum wage has failed to keep pace with inflation. Historically the minimum wage tended to be set at 50 percent of average annual hourly earnings. In 2015 it was only 28.9 percent of an average annual hourly wage of $25.08. In 1968 the minimum wage adjusted for inflation was the equivalent of $10.97 an hour in 2015 dollars. In 1968 a minimum wage earner was at 106 percent of the federal poverty level, but in 2015 it is below 80 percent.

The second trend, and not unrelated to the first, has been increasing income inequality. Nobody believes that an increase in the minimum wage will make us equal by any stretch, nor is that really the goal. And it certainly won't address what many have observed as the pulling away of the

O. M. Levin-Waldman, *Restoring the Middle Class through Wage Policy*, Binzagr Institute for Sustainable Prosperity,
https://doi.org/10.1007/978-3-319-74448-3_1

top from the rest of us in recent years (Piketty 2014; Stiglitz 2012; Hacker and Pierson 2010). But the rate of increase would clearly be less. Much of the literature suggests that wage inequality will be less, specifically in the lower tail of the distribution—the 50/10 percentile ratio (Belman and Wolfson 2014). Even those who reject the revisionist literature that the decline of labor market institutions has contributed to growing inequality because of the pulling away of the top do acknowledge that they do affect the lower tail of the distribution (Autor et al. 2008).

The third trend is that wages overall, especially among the middle class, have been stagnating for more than three decades. If nothing else the protests for a $15 an hour minimum reflect a level of frustration with an economic system that appears to reward CEOs with compensation packages worth millions while workers struggle to make ends meet. But it also appears to reflect a level of frustration with a political system that often seems helpless if not totally oblivious to the concerns of not only low-wage workers but the middle class generally (Bartels 2008; Gilens 2012). These protests, then, need to be placed within the context of a growing "chasm" between the very top and the rest of us (Smith 2012), or what some refer to as increasing polarization due to rising inequality and the skewed politics toward the extreme wealthy that has come from that inequality (McCarty et al. 2008).

State of the Current Minimum Wage Debate

Much of the current debate over the minimum wage has revolved around employment consequences. Critics of the minimum wage have tended to focus on the employment side while supporters of the minimum wage have focused on the benefits of pay increases specifically for those in poverty. The debate in short has amounted to a contest between those arguing the employment consequences versus the anti-poverty benefits. Moreover, those arguing the employment consequences have focused specifically on teenagers, largely because for many years they constituted the majority of minimum wage workers, or at least those earning the statutory minimum. While this may have been true at least as late as three decades ago, it is less so today. Nevertheless, since the report of the federal Minimum Wage Study Commission was published in 1981, it has been the conventional wisdom that a 10 percent increase in the minimum wage results in a 1–3 percent reduction in employment among teenagers.

The same commission did find employment consequences to be considerably less among adults.

Still, much of the literature on the employment consequences focused specifically on teenagers. Beginning in the mid-1990s, however, following studies of the fast-food industry by David Card and Alan Krueger (1995a, 1998), and particularly after 2000, with the New Minimum Wage Research, as Belman and Wolfson (2014) call it, much doubt has been cast on the conventional wisdom. It isn't that all studies have been found to be incorrect, rather because the focus has only been on teenagers, the data on the minimum wage has been skewed when applied to older workers and when factoring in issues of heterogeneity (Dube et al. 2010; Allegretto et al. 2011). Because the data only focus on specific segments of the labor market, the overall conclusions that can be drawn from them are ambiguous. That is, the effects are incomplete. While we are told that some groups may bear costs in the form of job loss, we are being told that other groups may derive benefits and that on the whole in a calculus could outweigh the costs. Critics claim that there is no reason to look at adults when most minimum wage workers aren't adults, but are teenagers. To the New Minimum Wage Research they respond that the minimum wage is so much below a market-clearing wage that it could not possibly have an effect. Those that argue for the minimum wage often assert that the minimum wage is too low because it has failed to keep pace with inflation. The critics who acknowledge that higher minimum wages haven't had an effect on employment because they are still below market-clearing wages are ironically acknowledging the supporters' point that the minimum wage is too low.

Still, critics maintain that the minimum wage is a poor tool for assisting the poor because most minimum wage earners are not poor (Burkhauser and Finegan 1989; Sabia and Burkhauser 2010). On the contrary, they are secondary earners in that they are either teenagers in their parents' households or spouses of primary earners. And yet to refer to them as secondary effectively trivializes them because they are now placed in a category of other whereby their contributions are deemed to be unimportant (Schneider and Ingram 1993). If they are unimportant or only contributors to a household rather than principal household supporters, then there is no need to raise their wages, especially if there may be negative employment consequences.

The more poor people who can be categorized as unworthy, the less responsibility society has to care for their well-being. The neoclassical synthesis, in short, assumes a minimum wage to be inefficient, in part, because it isn't necessary. If the minimum wage was primarily benefitting teenagers and not benefitting those working to support a family, what was the logic of the minimum wage at all? It was simply irrelevant. At the same time, it was irrelevant because it did not bear on the poverty rate. Moreover, for those minimum wage earners who are poor, the minimum wage will only hurt them because employers will likely respond by substituting technology for low-skilled workers, who are disproportionately among the ranks of the poor. Of course, all of this makes sense if these are indeed the demographics of the low-wage labor market. But by focusing on this narrow construction, we are missing the larger low-wage labor market that may also be affected by the statutory minimum wage.

The narrow focus of the debate has really obscured what the minimum wage is really about, and that is the middle class. This book is about the minimum wage and the middle class. To suggest that the minimum wage is ultimately a middle-class issue would strike most as rather counterintuitive. After all, how can a wage that is so far below that of most middle-class workers really affect them? Although the minimum wage was certainly intended to raise the wages of those at the bottom of the distribution, it was also intended to be more. At a minimum, it was intended to give low-wage workers a measure of bargaining power they otherwise lacked because of the asymmetrical power imbalance between them and their employers. Because there was now a floor, there was also a limit to how much they could be exploited. But it was also viewed as a means to expand purchasing power, which would also be good for the economy. Historically, however, the minimum wage was a labor-management issue whose expected benefits would be increased efficiency, an expansion of purchasing power, and ultimately greater demand for goods and services.

One wonders how it is that a non-issue like the minimum wage which only 2 percent of the labor market actually earns could ruffle the number of feathers it does whenever the issue comes up for public debate. The issue often elicits the most intense animosity from its opponents. In this book, I argue that the effects are much larger than the current debate would suggest. To relegate the minimum wage labor market to the 2 percent that actually earns the statutory minimum wage is to obscure a growing problem in the USA. That is, the "effective" minimum wage labor market—those that earn in wage ranges around the statutory labor market—has grown considerably over the last three decades and now comprises almost a fifth of the American labor market. Although this "effective" minimum wage labor market is still dominated by those lacking in skills, their levels of educational attainment are higher now than they were more than 30 years ago. Moreover, these workers are also older.

That a growing segment of the American labor market is now among the ranks of the effective minimum wage population no doubt speaks volumes to the changing economic base of the economy. What has often been missed here is that with increased globalization and the emergence of a two-tiered economy with highly educated and highly paid workers at the top of the wage distribution and poorly educated and poorly paid workers at the bottom, the growth of this "effective" minimum wage population has to be seen as a manifestation of the disappearing middle class. In recent years various authors have written about the business community's assault on the middle class through deliberate public policy decisions that have resulted in a widening inequality gap between the top and the bottom (Smith 2012; Stiglitz 2012; Hacker and Pierson 2010). I am not as concerned about how we reached this point as I am about where we go from here. In the pages that follow I intend to show how the minimum wage, as but one tool in a larger arsenal of public policy revolving around middle-class economics, can be used to help restore the middle class. But this requires taking a broader view of the minimum wage.

In making this argument am I suggesting not only that economic policy models based on the neoclassical economic synthesis have been wrong, but that progressive policy that has animated much of the political left—indeed the contemporary Democratic Party—has been misguided. If we as a nation want to close the income gap, create a higher wage economy, and restore the middle class—which is also an essential ingredient in the maintenance of strong democracy—then we need policies that are based on what Martin Gilens (2012) calls "targeting within universalism." This means that policy has to be couched in a way that it appeals to a broad spectrum of voters. The minimum wage can only have broad appeal if it is couched as a middle-class issue. If it is only an issue that affects teenagers who are not considered to be poor, it simply won't resonate with most voters.

Middle-Class Economics?

The public debate in recent years has been witness to voices about what best to do for America's middle class. On the one hand, there is the argument that policy skewed toward the interests of the wealthy has effectively resulted in what journalist Hendrick Smith (2012) calls the stealing of the American dream. Policies have been pursued that have effectively redistributed wealth and income to the wealthy at the expense of the middle class. There may be another school of thought that the decline of the middle class has been due to deteriorating families and values (Murray 2012). Some might, of course, take issue with this and maintain that at the end of the day it is about income.

Discussions about how to rebuild the economy and the middle class have revolved around the standard boilerplate solutions. The political left focuses on new programs financed through higher taxes on the rich while the political right recycles the standard laissez-faire policies of the past: lower taxes and reduced regulation. If government would simply unleash the marketplace, everyone would prosper. That everyone has not despite the Bush tax cuts and financial deregulation dating back to the Clinton administration is only taken as further evidence that government still regulates too much, the welfare state is still too big, and these two together have contributed to the moral hazard of workers being rigid when it comes to wage rates. Wage rigidity, in other words, and not market failure, is the reason for unemployment and the declining fortunes of the middle class. But it isn't just wage rigidity; it is wage rigidity in a global marketplace where new technologies are demanding that workers come to the table with advanced skills.

Low wages speak to the growth of the low-skilled labor market, which itself is the result of economic transformation. For this, market purists offer the explanation of a skills mismatch biased toward technical change. Rather than requiring employers to pay higher wages, workers should obtain the necessary training and skills in order to command higher wages. This, however, conveniently shifts the onus onto the workers. Worse, if workers are responsible for their lack of skills, then job creation isn't nearly as important as training and retraining. But as Gordon Lafer (2002) has argued, this has become a charade unto itself which has served to deflect attention from the real problem—that no serious policies aimed at job creation have been pursued. This would also appear to be a catch-22. Market purists argue that high wages hamper job creation. But more jobs created would exert upward pressure on wages. It isn't hard to see, then, that for those who prefer a low-wage economy that job creation is really not a desirable goal. Better, then, to deflect criticism by shifting the discussion over to job training and worker deficits. At the same time, the political class that buys into the education and training argument often misses that more workers attaining more education and training may also, according to the same supply and demand forces that pushed down the wages of those at the bottom, similarly push down the wages of those at the top.

The political left responds that public policies favoring the wealthy have only made the rich richer at the expense of the poor. Capital mobility in an ever increasingly global economy has resulted in the flight of good-paying manufacturing jobs from first unionized states to right-to-work states where wage rates have been lower and second to developing countries where wage rates are only a fraction of what they are in the USA. Meanwhile, these high-paying jobs have been replaced with low-paying and low-skilled service sector jobs. As a result, we have a two-tiered or dual economy with highly paid and highly educated and skilled workers at the top of the wage distribution, and poorly educated and poorly paid workers with little if any skills at the bottom. And as a nation we are witnessing the disappearance of the middle class. Attendant to that disappearance has been a widening of the wage gap between the top and the bottom. In other words, increased income inequality, which can be attributed to a variety of factors, including both global market forces and the decline of American labor market institutions, has to be viewed as symptomatic of the new dual economy in which the middle class is ever becoming less of a presence.

From a policy stance, the Fed has been pursuing the standard monetary response of pumping money into the economy through a combination of lower interest rates, bond buying, and quantitative easing. Democrats in Congress have been pushing the standard fiscal policy model of economic stimulus either through increased public spending, through one-time tax rebates, or through extended unemployment insurance. Absent in all this has been a serious discussion of the role of labor market institutions in bolstering the wages of the middle class so that they can continue to demand goods and services in the aggregate. What has received short shrift, in other words, is a wage policy, which at a minimum needs to be pursued, alongside monetary and fiscal policy, if the middle class is to benefit.

Perhaps most disconcerting about the current debate is that there is really very little daylight between the right and the left. Both assume that the answer to the nation's economic woes is the same top-down approach that has traditionally been taken. Whereas the right assumes that the Fed will continue to pump money into the economy through reductions in interest rates, the left assumes that the same effect can be had if only government invests more in the private marketplace. Both rely on massive investments to come from the top and flow down. Often overlooked, however, is that what drives an economy is aggregate demand for goods and services, and this requires that individuals have purchasing power that will enable them to demand goods and services in the aggregate. If workers cannot afford to purchase goods and services because their wages are too low, it matters little how low interest rates fall. Businesses are not going to simply create new jobs if there is no demand for their goods and services. An economy, in other words, grows from the bottom up, not the top down. Raising workers' wages will do more to grow the economy than either tinkering with interest rates or spending massive amounts of federal dollars on new programs. Moreover, it would be consistent with the grassroots spirit that built up the nation in the first place.

It would also decrease dependency on government programs. In a report from the Center for Labor Research and Education at the University of California at Berkeley, Ken Jacobs et al. (2015) observe that low wages cost the country $152.8 billion a year in social expenditures—subsidies to the working poor via food stamps, housing vouchers, and other supports—paid for by taxpayers. Although paying workers low wages means reduced prices for consumers, we all ultimately pay for it through increased taxes for government programs. Another way to look at this is that subsidies to low-wage workers are effectively subsidies of their employers' profit margins. Minimum wage supporters during the early part of the twentieth century made a big deal out of what were referred to as parasitic industries. Progressive reformers maintained that firms paying less than that which was necessary to support their labor in dignity were essentially parasites on the community because the difference ultimately came from someplace (Lehrer 1987).

The parasitic-industry argument proved to be a powerful tool for those seeking to establish a minimum wage specifically for women. By adopting this analysis, reformers were able to offer two separate explanations for the existence of low wages. The first explanation had to do with the comparative disadvantage that unorganized individual workers had with their employers when it came to bargaining. The second explanation was that employers paying low wages were simply taking advantage of their workers' vulnerable position, which made them parasites on society because they were effectively receiving a subsidy from the community. Parasitic employers who paid less than the true social costs of labor could undersell their competition. Moreover, they would not be motivated to lower their costs through innovation or organization or production techniques (Power 1999). But studies like the one from the Center for Labor Research and Education only demonstrate in stark economic terms how much these employers are parasites on the body politic.

The question that arises is why Americans don't see that they are really subsidizing the profits of low-wage employers. That we are all paying to subsidize low-wage workers could be said to fall into Theodore Lowi's (1964) definition of distributive politics, whereby each group in society gets something and we all pay for it. Ironically, however, it isn't so much that the poor are deriving benefits from these subsidies as it is that their employers, who now have further incentive to pay low wages because they know that their low-wage workers will indeed be subsidized. But the report also suggested that it was a $15 an hour minimum which was the point at which dependency on those subsidies would be diminished. When coupled with the New Minimum Wage Research that suggests the negative employment consequences predicted by the standard model aren't really there, this perhaps ought to be the point where we as a society seriously question the direction of economic policy in recent years.

For some, middle-class economics is about reducing income inequality, especially by imposing new taxes on the wealthy. This issue isn't nearly as monolithic as is often presented. Income inequality is an amorphous concept here. Wages and income are not the same. While income may include wages, income can include dividends and savings at the upper end of the distribution and income supports at the bottom of the distribution. Therefore, when comparing top wages to bottom income the ratio may not be nearly as great as the ratio between top wages and bottom wages because those at the bottom are receiving supports. But a comparison of the top to bottom shows the ratio to be larger still because those at the top have income from stocks, bonds, and other investments. Another issue is before-tax income and after-tax income. Overtaxing income at the top of the distribution may reduce the ratio between the top and the bottom, only because the after-tax income of those at the top has been reduced, but this does not mean that the after-tax income of those at the bottom has risen. In other words, reducing inequality may not necessarily be the same as assisting the middle class.

While the political left will no doubt argue that the wealthy have benefitted at the expense of the poor and the middle class, there is some truth to what they are saying. First, they point to the growth in the economy during the 25-year period following World War II when marginal tax rates were 90 percent. Second, they argue that income inequality has resulted in a political system skewed to the interests of the wealthy—only resulting in policies that tend to be less favorable to the middle class—and the only way to address this problem is to take steps to redress this imbalance. Since many of the wealthy became wealthy due to tax cuts that effectively redistributed income from the bottom and middle to the top, it only makes sense to redistribute from the top to the bottom through higher taxes on the wealthy. But this approach might also assume too much.

Taxing the top will reduce income inequality in that the ratio between after-tax income of the top and after-tax income of the bottom will now be less, but it doesn't follow that this will necessarily benefit those at the bottom. Unless, it is assumed that higher taxes imposed on the top will go to fund more programs that can boost the incomes of those at the bottom. But if the reduction of after-tax income of the wealthy intended to reduce inequality results in greater dependency on public supports at the bottom, is that really a socially desirable outcome? The goal of middle-class economics should be the boosting of incomes of the bottom and the middle. In other words, a rising tide that lifts all boats will also assist those at the bottom of the distribution. Let's assume for a moment that taxing the top can fund programs to assist—subsidize the low incomes of—those at the bottom. Contrary to fostering self-esteem, we are only deepening dependency. The American middle class was in part built on the American work ethic. But it was also built by labor market institutions that bolster wages. The first institution that made a difference was the trade union. Factory work in the late nineteenth century was no more skilled and dignified than many of the service jobs performed by low-wage workers today. Labor unions sought to give their members dignity in their work by fighting for wages that would be considered respectable. Prior to the advent of labor unions, there was little that wage labor did that was considered respectable (Glickman 1997).

Core to middle-class economics is shoring up the middle class by raising wages and creating jobs through the increased purchasing power that will attend to higher wages. The approach to job creation over the last few decades has done anything but. On the contrary, it has been assumed that money pumped into the economy through monetary policy would result in jobs flowing down from the top. During the Great Depression of the 1930s, there were jobs programs to put people back to work. But these programs were augmented by other programs intended to provide individuals with greater purchasing power. The purpose of Social Security was to provide the elderly with purchasing power so that they could demand goods and services. Even the objective of public assistance, virtually, non-existent before the 1930s, was to provide poor people with purchasing power. With the National Labor Relations Act of 1935 Congress legitimized collective bargaining on the understanding that workers who could negotiate better wages would have greater purchasing power. And the Fair Labor Standards Act (FLSA) of 1938 which created the nation's first federal minimum wage was similarly intended to boost the purchasing power of workers, thereby enabling them to demand more goods and services.

Economic policy during the 1930s was built on the assumption that for the economy to grow individuals needed purchasing power so that they could afford to buy things. Since the Reagan revolution beginning in 1981 and following the stagflation of the 1970s when a consensus seemed to emerge that Keynesian economics wasn't working, it has become the accepted wisdom that workers demanding higher wages actually hurt the economy rather than help it. Increasingly manufacturing left the country in search of lower wage rates. The term "wage rigidity" emerged to explain the failure of the economy to grow—workers were simply being inflexible in their wage demands. After all, the neoclassical synthesis always posited that in competitive markets there really was no such thing as unemployment because workers could always lower their demands to the point where employers would demand their labor services.

Keynes himself had been clear that it mattered little how low workers' monetary wage demands fell; their services would not be demanded if nobody was demanding their potential employers' goods and services. The apparent paradox here no doubt parallels Keynes' paradox of thrift. Workers will naturally not consume all of their income but will put some into savings for a rainy day. But the more they put away, the less they spend, which in turn will lead to a slowdown in the economy, inevitably resulting in their own layoff. In other words, the idea of putting away for a rainy day is that one won't really need it, but because everybody is doing it, it becomes inevitable that they will need it which in the end will only deplete their savings. This certainly applies to the logic of paying low wages.

Employment policy in recent years has essentially revolved around two main approaches. The first has centered on the assumption that the Fed would pump money into the economy by tinkering with interest rates. The second has centered on fiscal stimuli, whether it has been through tax reductions, rebates, or even big stimulus packages like the one passed in 2009. Nowhere in these approaches has there been a corresponding assumption that wages really need to rise. Consider for a moment Sidney Weintraub's (1972) argument that economic management without an "incomes policy" is simply insufficient to seriously create jobs. Fiscal policy, which often involves huge expenditures of public monies, often will not have the desired effects if not properly targeted. As an example, in 2003 Congress authorized $300 tax rebates to individuals and $600 rebates to married couples. To give a rebate to all taxpayers certainly fits the definition of equality as each receiving the same thing. From an efficiency stance, this stimulus was poorly targeted. Those at the lower end of the distribution into the middle no doubt spent the money, which was precisely the intent of the rebate. But those at the upper end of the distribution were less likely to spend the money. Many of them may have tossed the checks into savings. Although various interests will benefit from grants and contracts, the impact is not widely dispersed. Moreover, increased spending only necessitates new taxes.

Monetary policy by itself also has costs. The Fed by law serves the banking interests and its primary responsibility is to ensure the solvency of banks. As inflation rises, the Fed typically applies the brakes with higher interest rates and reserve requirements, which produces unemployment. At the same time, increased taxes due to increased spending will only lead workers to seek higher wages to pay the higher tax, thereby exacerbating inflation. For economists to apply the breaks, but who themselves would not be affected, was in Weintraub's view immoral. Rather the unemployed were essentially innocent lambs being led to their slaughter through otherwise conventional tactics. But if wages could be stabilized, price stability would then avert the economic damage otherwise occasioned by conventional stabilization tools. In other words, if the traditional tools of fiscal stimulus and monetarism were to be used, they then needed to be complemented with an income policy.

As radical as this might have sounded, it really wasn't that far removed from Milton Friedman's assumption about an "incomes policy," which for him was really a euphemism for wage restraint. Friedman actually advocated a steady growth of roughly 3 percent in the money supply to maintain a balance because he also assumed that money wages would be constrained. Wages, in short, would increase to match productivity, which was roughly 3 percent per year overall. In other words, Friedman's advocacy of monetarism also assumed a commensurate increase in wages. Weintraub, however, was suggesting that the two traditional tools of fiscal and monetary policy without an active policy to ensure that wages will also rise simply do not work. Rather, a wage policy would need to be the third side of the triangle. Nevertheless, a wage policy can stand on its own merit. Whatever form it takes it is an essential component if we as society seek to achieve a more equitable distribution of income and shore up the middle class.

Minimum Wage and the Middle Class

To argue that the minimum wage is really about the middle class requires viewing the issue through a different set of lenses. First of all, those who earn the statutory minimum wage are not nearly as important as those who earn around the minimum wage. In other words, the minimum wage is a reference point for the larger low-wage labor market which now comprises close to a fifth of the overall American labor market. Second of all, the question that needs to be addressed is what the impact of an increase in the statutory minimum wage is on wage rates around the statutory minimum wage. This requires viewing the minimum wage through the prism of wage contours.

Not much research has been done in this area since the pioneering work of John Dunlop (1957), but the essence of wage contour theory is that workers with similar characteristics in similar industries earn similar wages. Each group of workers has a reference wage, and it is then essential to look at various wage ranges around those reference wages. A change in the reference wage, then, is going to lead to changes in the ranges around that reference wage. When wage contour theory is applied to the minimum wage it can help us sort out several thorny issues. It would imply that workers earning wages in ranges above the statutory minimum wage, and those earning above those ranges, will also see their wages go up as well. This must be happening; otherwise how do we explain the level of opposition to an otherwise non-issue? The problem, however, is that we do not have much data on wage contour effects. We do have inconclusive data on employment effects but nothing really on this question of wage contour effects. We do, however, have some hints that provide a reasonable basis for intelligent speculation.

Data from the Current Population Survey (CPS) for the years 1962–2008 show that in years when the statutory minimum wage increased, the median wages in ten constructed contours also increased. And in years when the statutory minimum wage did not increase, neither did the median wages in any of the ten constructed contours. Because these ten contours together constituted up to 70 percent of the workforce, and those earning at the top of the tenth in 2008 were earning around $100,000 a year, it became apparent that the minimum wage did indeed have welfare effects for the middle class (Levin-Waldman 2011). At best this data is suggestive because CPS data is really individual-level data which at best can show a correlation; it cannot demonstrate a causal relationship. We really do not know how employers behave in response to increases in the statutory minimum wage. Do they raise the wages of those earning above the statutory minimum wage? But if the minimum wage is a key rate, do employers who don't employ minimum wage workers tend to increase the wages of their workers in response to an increase in the minimum wage because their workers are in a group of wages around that key rate? In other words, is the impact of an increase in the minimum wage only internal to a firm, or is it external as well? Again the data from the CPS may be suggestive. And yet, when data is anything but definitive, then the policy arena ought to be ripe for experimentation, which no doubt will lend itself to politics. In other words, policies aren't pursued because of the strength of the models behind them but the relative interests behind them.

Adding to this suggestive data is the report of the Congressional Budget Office (CBO) on the minimum wage issued in early 2014. The CBO concluded that an increase in the minimum wage to $10.10 an hour once fully implemented in 2016 (if passed then which it wasn't) could have resulted in a reduction in employment of 500,000. Still, the CBO concluded that on balance an increase in the minimum wage would be good for the economy because more than 16 million workers would see their pay increased and that these workers would spur further growth because they would spend their higher wages. The 16 million workers that the CBO was talking about certainly exceeded the number of workers earning the statutory minimum wage, which was less than four million. That more than four times the number of minimum wage workers were projected to get a pay increase would again suggest that there are wage contour effects. Also suggestive of wage contour effects are the findings through their meta-analysis of the various minimum wage studies, particularly since 2000, that increases in the minimum wage do result in increases in average wages, especially among workers in the lower tail of the distribution (Belman and Wolfson 2014).

If not for wage contour effects, how do we explain that this seemingly non-issue as the critics claim is so contentious politically? Also if not for wage contours, how do we explain a CBO report that on the face of it would appear to be contradictory? If an increase in the minimum wage results in the loss of up to 500,000 jobs, then the critics would appear to be correct when they suggest that the costs outweigh the benefits. This, however, assumes that employment consequences should be the determining measure of whether a policy's benefit outweighs its costs. But as will become clear in the next chapter, the data on the employment effects are ambiguous at best. In most cases, the data does not really support the claims of critics that the minimum wage does more harm than good. If an increase in the minimum wage results in more than 16 million workers getting pay increases despite 500,000 fewer jobs, then there are other measures of the minimum wage that we as a society need to be mindful of. If the welfare effects are larger than commonly supposed, then the minimum wage needs to be viewed as a critical policy tool in the broader arsenal intended to restore the middle class. What an examination of the minimum wage through the prism of wage contours can surely show is that the effective minimum wage population is not only larger but that its demographic profile in no way reflects the claims of minimum wage critics that minimum wage earners are not primary earners but secondary ones, and mostly teenagers.

This is a critical piece of information because if the effective minimum wage population is really larger than the critics claim, then the problem of the low-wage labor market cannot simply be ignored. To a certain extent, defining the minimum wage labor market is critical to arguing the middle-class benefits of the minimum wage as a policy tool. But it also cuts to the heart of how agendas are set in American politics. Peter Bachrach and Morton Baratz (1962) famously argued that it was the agenda setters that really had power because by setting the agenda they are the ones who determine the decisions that will ultimately be made. Similarly, E.E. Schattschneider (1960) argued that politics was about the ability to mobilize bias. In a standoff over an issue, one party would seek to socialize the conflict while the other side would seek to localize it. All conflicts consisted of actors—those actively engaged in the conflict—and spectators—those not actively involved but sitting on the sidelines. The object of some actors would be to get spectators involved through the mobilization of bias. It isn't hard to see how this typology applies to the minimum wage debate. Critics and those who oppose increases—primarily business interests—will no doubt seek to localize the conflict by maintaining the minimum wage in its narrow focus. Supporters, however, have an opportunity to socialize the conflict, and very much in the spirit of Gilens' targeting within universalism, and demonstrate the broader reach of the minimum wage, which is that it affects the middle class.

The Broader Impact

This book argues that there are positive welfare effects for the middle class.

An increasing minimum wage, and one that can keep pace with either inflation or productivity gains, can benefit the middle class. Consequently, it can also provide a foundation for jobs creation because the higher wages that workers throughout the distribution will receive will enable them to demand more goods and services in the aggregate. To talk about the minimum wage as a middle-class issue is to talk more about its macroeconomic benefits rather than the demand-side effects in most of the economics literature.

Nevertheless, I am not suggesting that the neoclassical model of competitive markets is completely wrong; only that it has limited application in the real world. As I will show in the next chapter, there is a quality of the tragedy of the commons at work here because what is really happening is a collision between the tenets of microeconomics and macroeconomics. In micro-theory at the level of the firm it makes perfect sense to pay workers as little as possible. In this vein, it is logical that employers will respond to workers lowering their wage demands by demanding more of their labor services. But if all employers were to pay their workers as little as possible, there would be no demand for firms' goods and services because workers wouldn't have the wherewithal to purchase them. To talk about the minimum wage as a middle-class issue is to present it in macroeconomic terms. And to talk about it in macroeconomic terms is to return the minimum wage to where it was originally supposed to be when the FLSA was enacted in 1938. When initially passed, the minimum wage was intended as a measure to advance the interest of workers who were not otherwise covered by collective bargaining agreements. The two together were intended to stabilize labor-management relations. By inflating wages in a depression where wages were already depressed, the minimum wage would assist recovery efforts by offering low-wage workers enhanced purchasing power. The minimum wage was initially conceived of as a labor-management or human resources issue, and it can be restored to its rightful place if we emphasize its middle-class value.

Finally, in this book I argue that as a middle-class issue the minimum wage can not only provide a foundation for job creation but also serve to redress increasing income inequality and achieve greater democracy. As a middle-class issue, I argue that the minimum wage affords workers, especially those at the low end of the wage spectrum, greater dignity in their work. Any policy that in any way enhances autonomy, by at a minimum conferring dignity on individuals, is in keeping with a democratic society. Ironically, these are the same values the political right espouses. So a wage that in any way enhances self-sufficiency and personal responsibility and reduces the need for public subsidies ought to be in keeping with conservative principles as well. Moreover higher wages that enable more autonomous individuals to participate more fully as full-fledged citizens only enhances democratic society.

A minimum wage, then, can be said to be critical to the ends of democracy for the following reasons: First, through the additional security it may afford workers through higher wages, especially at the bottom of the distribution, it enhances personal autonomy, and enhanced personal autonomy can allow for greater participation in the public sphere. Individuals living above the poverty line will feel better about themselves and feel more inclined to become more productive. They will be more productive by virtue of their ability to better maintain themselves. Second, to the extent that a minimum wage reduces income inequality, it should result in less strife and fewer threats to democratic society. Third, a minimum wage that becomes a foundation for job creation through its contour effects becomes part and parcel of economic development. Economic development is central to democracy because it is the basis for a broad middle class, which, in and of itself, militates against the dual distribution composed of those at the very top and those at the very bottom.

In the pages that follow, I argue that the minimum wage is really a middle-class issue that can not only help to restore the American middle class but also be a positive foundation for economic growth and job creation. In Chap. 2, I review the various studies of the minimum wage and its effects. There are plenty of studies, but nothing is definitive. Far from settled, the wealth of studies suggests that the data on the minimum wage is ambiguous at best. This has no doubt made it easier for the issue to be laden with politics. Because the data which isn't clear cut is coupled with microeconomic arguments against and macroeconomic arguments for, both opponents and proponents alike can cloak their interests in sound economic theory and present themselves as speaking in the name of the public interest. And yet, from a policy standpoint, the implication could not be more clear, which is that in the face of ambiguity there should be room for policy experimentation based on the needs of the community.

Chapter 3 introduces data from the CPS to not only show the welfare effects of increasing the minimum wage for the middle class but also give us a sense of the labor market earning the effective minimum wage. In this chapter I also situate the minimum wage within the context of rising income inequality. What the CPS data shows, consistent with other studies, is that following increases in the minimum wage, there often tended to be decreases in income inequality. To the extent that the minimum wage does reduce income inequality it again serves as a tool to bolster the middle class. In other words, institutions do matter and that in order for income inequality to be reduced, the wages of those at the bottom and those in the middle must rise in relative terms as well as absolute terms.

Chapter 4 argues that based on the positive welfare effects of the minimum wage for the middle class, the minimum wage can serve as a foundation for jobs creation. I review the standard models for job creation that have been pursued to date based on both monetary and fiscal policies and argue that a wage policy in the form of a minimum wage also needs to be a critical component in the mix. By demonstrating that the minimum wage is about job creation which could reduce reliance on the welfare state and foster greater self-sufficiency, our basic assumptions are turned on their head, which only illustrate further how the minimum wage is ultimately the most conservative approach to assisting the middle class.

In Chap. 5, I argue that to the extent that the minimum wage can reduce income inequality and benefit the broader middle class, it may challenge some of the fundamental assumptions of the median voter theorem—the model developed by Anthony Downs to show that as income distributions are skewed to the right, the preferred amount of redistribution is a function of the relative position of the median voter on the income scale. The greater the distance between the median voter's income and society's average income, the greater is society's preferred amount of redistribution. The fundamental assumption being that redistribution will take place through taxation. In this chapter, I argue the opposite that the minimum wage's welfare effects potentially mitigate the need for redistribution because the distance between the median voter's income and the average of society is effectively narrowed. Once it becomes clear that the minimum wage is indeed about the middle class, the traditional partisan and ideological battle lines ought to break down. Although a minimum wage may be taken as a form of redistribution, it is not the same as taxing one group more to give another something else. Firms are paying their workers more, but they are still receiving value in the form of work in return.

In Chap. 6, then, I explore how various thinkers have come up with yet other theoretical approaches to the minimum wage, which might make more sense once we are able to get beyond the narrow parameters of the debate as it exists currently and see it in a much broader light. One approach might be to ask whether the minimum wage can be conceived of as an efficiency wage which will achieve greater productivity. Is it simply employers' responsibility to pay efficiency wages, or is society as a whole responsible? Another approach is to ask whether the minimum wage could be viewed as conferring property rights in a job, and if so does the absence of one amount to stealing? This raises the possibility that the minimum wage could be a civil rights issue. If the minimum wage is about civil rights because it is about conferring a property right to a job, does that effectively imply a positive right to work? What exactly is it that opponents of the minimum wage, on a philosophical level, are concerned about?

The minimum wage might be a necessary ingredient in the development of personal capabilities, and to the extent that higher wages will enable more workers to be autonomous and self-sufficient, there is a conservative argument to be made for the minimum wage. Not only might such a conservative argument turn thinkers like Milton Friedman on his head, but it would be consistent with early republican values of free labor. Another, and even more revolutionary approach, is to ask whether government should bolster the middle class by being an employer of last resort, where the government wage would effectively be the new minimum wage. Could government as a matter of policy mitigate the concerns that some might have about the minimum wage implying a positive right to work by replacing the minimum wage with a public works program that would become the employer of last resort? Lastly, there is the question of whether a minimum wage puts us on a path toward a universal basic income (UBI). If the critics are correct that raising the minimum wage might result in the substitution of technology for labor, especially in an increasingly global economy, might that not render a UBI inevitable? Politically, these approaches may be problematic. When presented in the form of a trajectory, it becomes clear that the minimum wage as a means of assisting the middle class is really the more conservative approach. Consequently, the middle-class approach would appear to represent a middle of the road, and perhaps the most feasible politically.

Finally in Chap. 7, I argue that a minimum wage that enables individuals to live in greater dignity will enable them to be more autonomous. In lines with Amartya Sens' (1999) notion of developing capabilities, I argue that a minimum wage that enables individuals to be autonomous does indeed enable them to develop their capabilities. Autonomy is certainly a prerequisite for democracy. A minimum wage that reduces inequality and contributes to economic development by serving as a foundation for job creation also makes for greater democracy. But a minimum wage which increases on a regular basis may also lead to greater democracy to the extent that it may serve to develop the social capital of low-wage workers. Various studies show that those with higher incomes are more likely to be engaged in the civic affairs of their communities. This chapter ultimately demonstrates why a minimum wage is an essential ingredient in achieving greater democracy.

Bibliography

Allegretto, Sylvia, Arindrajit Dube, and Michael Reich. 2011. Do Minimum Wages Really Reduce Teen Employment? Accounting for Heterogeneity and Selectivity in State Panel Data. *Industrial Relations* 50 (2): 205–240.

Autor, David H., Lawrence F. Katz, and Melissa S. Kearney. 2008. Trends in U.S. Wage Inequality: Revising the Revisionists. *The Review of Economics and Statistics* 90 (2): 300–323.

Bachrach, Peter, and Morton S. Baratz. 1962. Two Faces of Power. *American Political Science Review* 56: 947–952.

Bartels, Larry M. 2008. *Unequal Democracy: The Political Economy of the New Gilded Age*. Princeton: Princeton University Press.

Belman, Dale, and Paul J. Wolfson. 2014. *What Does the Minimum Wage Do?* Kalamazoo: W.E. Upjohn Institute for Employment Research.

Burkhauser, Richard V., and T. Aldrich Finegan. 1989. The Minimum Wage and the Poor: The End of a Relationship. *Journal of Policy Analysis and Management* 8 (1): 53–71.

Card, David, and Alan B. Krueger. 1995a. *Myth and Measurement: The New Economics of the Minimum Wage*. Princeton: Princeton University Press.

———. 1995b. Time Series Minimum Wage Studies: A Meta-Analysis. *AEA Papers and Proceedings* 85 (2): 238–243.

———. 1998. A Reanalysis of the Effect of the New Jersey Minimum Wage Increase on the Fast-Food Industry with Representative Payroll Data. Working Paper No. 6386. National Bureau of Economic Research.

Dube, Arindrajit, T. William Lester, and Michael Reich. 2010. Minimum Wage Effects Among State Borders: Estimates Using Contiguous Counties. *The Review of Economics and Statistics* 92 (4): 945–964.

Dunlop, John T. 1957. The Task of Contemporary Wage Theory. In *New Concepts in Wage Determination*, ed. George W. Taylor and Frank C. Pierson. New York: McGraw-Hill Book Co.

Gilens, Martin. 2012. *Affluence & Influence: Economic Inequality and Political Power in America*. New York/Princeton/Oxford: Russell Sage Foundation and Princeton University Press.

Glickman, Lawrence B. 1997. *A Living Wage: American Workers and the Making of Consumer Society*. Ithaca/London: Cornell University Press.

Hacker, Jacob S., and Paul Pierson. 2010. *Winner-Take-All Politics: How Washington Made the Rich Richer – And Turned Its Back on the Middle Class*. New York: Simon & Schuster.

Jacobs, Ken, Ian Perry, and Jennifer MacGillvary. 2015. *The High Public Cost of Low Wages*. University of California Berkeley Center for Labor Research and Education. Research Brief, April.

Lafer, Gordon. 2002. *The Job Training Charade*. Ithaca/London: Cornell University Press.

Lehrer, Susan. 1987. *Origins of Protective Labor Legislation for Women, 1905–1925*. Albany: State University of New York Press.

Levin-Waldman, Oren M. 2011. *Wage Policy, Income Distribution, and Democratic Theory*. London/New York: Routledge.

Lowi, Theodore J. 1964. American Business, Public Policy, Case-Studies, and Political Theory. *World Politics* 16 (4): 677–715.

McCarty, Nolan, Keith T. Poole, and Howard Rosenthal. 2008. *Polarized America: The Dance of Ideology and Unequal Riches*. Cambridge, MA/London: MIT Press.

Murray, Charles. 2012. *Coming Apart: The State of White America 1960–2010*. New York: Crown Forum/Random House.

Piketty, Thomas. 2014. *Capital in the Twenty-First Century*. Cambridge, MA/London: Belknap Press of Harvard University Press.

Power, Marilyn. 1999. Parasitic Industries Analysis and Arguments for a Living Wage for Women in the Early Twentieth-Century United States. *Feminist Economics* 5 (1): 61–78.

Sabia, Joseph J., and Richard V. Burkhauser. 2010. Minimum Wages and Poverty: Will a $9.50 Federal Minimum Wage Really Help the Working Poor? *Southern Economic Journal* 76 (3): 592–623.

Schattschneider, E.E. 1960. *The Semisovereign People: A Realist's View of America.* New York: Holt, Rinehart.
Schneider, Anne, and Helen Ingram. 1993. Social Constructions and Target Populations: Implications for Politics and Policy. *American Political Science Review* 87 (2): 334–347.
Sen, Amartya. 1999. *Development as Freedom.* New York: Anchor Books.
Smith, Hendrick. 2012. *Who Stole the American Dream?* New York: Random House.
Stiglitz, Joseph E. 2012. *The Price of Inequality.* New York: W.W. Norton.
Weintraub, Sidney. 1972. Incomes Policy: Competing the Stabilization Triangle. *Journal of Economic Issues* 6 (4): 105–122.

CHAPTER 2

Unsettled Findings

The data on the minimum wage has never been conclusive but ambiguous at best. On the one hand we have the standard model steeped in neoclassical economics that predicts that increasing the minimum wage will result in lower employment. But on the other hand, we often have data from the real world which doesn't always support the standard model's predictions. To a large extent, our findings on the minimum wage are unsettled because the data that we have is simply poor data. Much of it is based on individual-level data from the Census Bureau's Current Population Survey (CPS), which at best will give us employment figures before and after a minimum wage increase. But this cannot establish a causal relationship between the minimum wage and changes in employment. Also most minimum wage increases are enacted during periods of employment growth, but their implementation could be several months later, by which time the economy is experiencing a rise in unemployment. Again, the data cannot establish that rising unemployment was due to the increase in the minimum wage, rather than other factors. Whatever correlations that can be shown, even those that appear to be strong and statistically significant, become spurious (Allegretto et al. 2011).

The data also says nothing about firm behavior. We simply do not have data that informs us about how firms respond to increases. At the same time, confusion over the effects, even from the predictive models, may arise from two models that are at cross purposes with one another. That is,

O. M. Levin-Waldman, *Restoring the Middle Class through Wage Policy*, Binzagr Institute for Sustainable Prosperity,
https://doi.org/10.1007/978-3-319-74448-3_2

the standard model that predicts unemployment is in part based on a microeconomic understanding of how firms behave when external forces affect their internal wage structures. Nevertheless, there are also macroeconomic arguments for why a minimum wage may be beneficial to the economy.

The minimum wage debate in recent years has in large measure come to mirror the tragedy of the commons. The confusion would appear to be a function of the distinction typically made between microeconomics on the one hand, and macroeconomics on the other. The competitive market model is clearly a micro-model: when workers lower their wage demands, employers will hire more workers. The idea that workers whose wages are increasing will be able to demand more goods and services in the aggregate because they have greater purchasing power is a macro-model. When the two collide, the result in many ways resembles the tragedy of the commons.

In an 1833 pamphlet, William Forster Lloyd told the story of those who would bring their cattle to the common grazing area, which was free. Therefore, it was in their self-interest to do so as rational human beings who were able to understand their interests and then find the best and most efficient way to achieve them. And yet, when everybody else did exactly the same thing because they were each just as rational, the common grazing area was destroyed. As a result, they no longer had any place to bring their cattle to graze that was free. Now they would have to pay. In popularizing this story, Garret Hardin (1968) called this the tragedy of the commons to demonstrate that individual rationality could lead to collective irrationality. When individuals act on their own and rationally according to their self-interests, the shared resource of the community will be depleted. By depleting the common resource the group's long-term interests will be undermined.

We can see the same thing happening with the minimum wage. In micro-theory at the level of the firm it makes perfect sense to pay workers as little as possible. In this vein, it is logical that employers will respond to workers lowering their wage demands by demanding more of their labor services. But if all employers were to pay their workers as little as possible, there would be no demand for firms' goods and services because workers wouldn't have the wherewithal to purchase them. In the typical macroeconomics text, this is often referred to as the fallacy of composition. The fallacy of composition occurs when one believes something is true of the whole just because some part of the whole is true. The classic example of this in economics is what is referred to as the paradox of thrift, which is the belief that if one person can save more money by spending less, then an entire economy can save even more by spending less. But if everybody spends less, there is less consumption which will result in layoffs, which will then force those who were laid off to eat into their savings. The same applies to the minimum wage. A firm can no doubt increase its profits by paying workers less, but if every firm does the same thing, the absence of aggregate demand for goods and services will result in an economic slowdown. In the end, firms will only have less profit.

What typically happens, however, is that economists often take the micro-model and attempt to couch it in macro-terms: if all workers lower their wage demands, more employers will hire them and the result will be the absence of unemployment, or so that is the case in a purely competitive market. What about the fact that workers who have now agreed to accept lower wages will have less purchasing power, which will result in shrinkage of aggregate demand? The model simply assumes that prices will readjust themselves downward so as not to have that shrinkage in demand.

The problem with this assumption is that there is a limit to how low prices can fall because most employers have fixed costs. Moreover, the fundamental assumption of the competitive market model that the cause of unemployment is wage rigidity—the refusal of workers to accept lower wages, which is only hardened by a minimum wage that creates a floor—is just flat out wrong. Unemployment is caused by the absence of demand for goods and services. As workers forced to accept lower wages demand less, the result will be unemployment as other businesses are forced to lay people off. A worker could theoretically accept a wage of zero and still be unemployed if the would-be employer has no need for him or her because nobody is demanding that employer's goods. Therefore, a general reduction in wages and prices is not likely to lead to a readjustment; rather it will only make things worse. Even if it is assumed that the demand for labor is inversely related to the real wage, an exogenous decline in the level of money wages cannot increase employment even if the price of wage-goods declines proportionately. Moreover, if wage-deflated wages lead to a redistribution of income from wage earners to non-wage earners, it will also result in less spending. An episode of deflation could also result in a decrease of net financial wealth (Brown 1992). At the same time, there is also a limit to how much prices can be reduced following wage reductions. Employers still have fixed costs, and if they cannot reduce their prices to meet the new lower wages, the result will be a drop-off in demand because of reduced purchasing power.

This tragedy of the commons, however, appears to have had two results. First it has allowed two opposing sides on the political debate over the minimum wage to cloak their respective positions in economic terms. Those who oppose the minimum wage can always point to the micro-model to justify their position. In terms of the economist's approach to the minimum wage, the data often revolves around a couple of themes. The minimum wage leads to lower employment, either through disemployment because workers were fired or because fewer low-paying jobs were created following an increase. Also there may be lower employment because the new minimum wage attracted more people into the market in search, in which case there are now more people chasing fewer jobs. Or the minimum wage does not really assist the poor, and if it doesn't how much of a benefit is there to justify lower employment? More recently, however, a new political economy of the minimum wage has emerged to demonstrate that the minimum wage does not have adverse employment consequences. From the perspective of larger political economy the implications would appear to be clear. Whereas one set of findings leads to the conclusion that the minimum wage is bad policy and should not be pursued, the second set of findings almost implies that in the absence of hard-core data that the minimum wage is detrimental to the economy, then perhaps policymakers ought to be free to experiment.

In the next couple of sections, I want to review the two sets of findings and show why ambiguity ultimately should lead to policy experimentation. Part of the problem, as we will see, resides in what Thomas Piketty (2014), in his study of income inequality in both the USA and France, has called the economic discipline's "childish passion for mathematics" (p. 32). This obsession has only served to create the appearance of being scientific, without having to answer the far more complex questions posed by the real world in which we live. And yet, this childish obsession has also bolstered a minimum wage orthodoxy that has become well entrenched.

The Standard Model

The competitive model, often referred to as the neoclassical synthesis, holds that the costs to society of raising wages to be greater than any benefits. In perfectly competitive markets, market-clearing wages are achieved when the demand for labor is exactly equal to the supply of labor. In such a market, there is no such thing as unemployment because wages either rise or fall until the demand for labor is exactly equal to the supply of labor. At the wage at which demand equals supply, all those willing and able to work at that wage will be employed. If more people are willing to work, the wage will fall further, thereby inducing firms to hire more workers, with the result being that the supply of labor once again equals the demand. Conversely, when firms are unable to hire as many workers as they would like, the wage rises to induce additional people to enter into the workforce until supply and demand are once again equal.

A wage floor, such as a mandated minimum wage, prevents the cost of labor from dropping below that minimum. When the minimum wage is higher than the equilibrium wage, fewer workers will be hired than are willing to work, with the result being unemployment. In a competitive market, each worker receives the value of his or her marginal revenue product, which is the amount of increase in the output that results from an increase in say a unit of labor. If adding an additional worker results in a rise in total revenues, the firm's output will rise as a result. Firms typically use the marginal revenue product of labor as a criterion for determining how many more workers to hire because they are able to calculate how much more output can be expected based on how many units they add. Therefore, a minimum wage, if it is effective, will do one of two things: it will either result in the layoff of those workers whose value is less than the minimum or it will result in an increase in productivity among low-efficiency workers (Stigler 1946; Ehrenberg and Smith 1997).

Consequently, the minimum wage ends up hurting low-wage workers—precisely those whom it was intended to help. As the cost of labor is increased (due to a mandated minimum wage that is higher than the market-clearing wage), firms are willing to hire fewer workers and employment drops. Only if the demand for goods and services on the part of consumers is increased, can it be expected that there will be an increased demand for labor that will effectively bid up wages. A minimum wage, then, benefits some—those who will be paid more money—at a cost to others—those who will either lose their jobs and/or not be able to find other jobs because employers do not believe their value to be worth the new minimum wage. A policy that artificially raises wages to help some at the expense of others is simply inefficient because an economy forced to lay workers off as a function of artificially inflated wages isn't utilizing its full labor capacity. Even if there is some outward appearance of benefit to be derived from an increase in the wage floor, there will invariably be a cost to be borne whether in the form of job loss, lost opportunity for jobs, lost benefits, or increased output per man hour—the demand for higher productivity.

The problem with this model is that it represents a theoretical construct with characteristics that simply do not exist in the real world. Although the minimum wage is assumed to be inefficient because it leads to an underutilization of labor in the aggregate, the competitive model fails to address the consequences of a world where wages could be allowed to drop to a level whereby demand would be equal to supply. In the real world, the minimum wage is likely to affect different people differently (Brown et al. 1982; Belman and Wolfson 2014). More to the point, the model of perfect competition assumes the minimum wage to be beside the point because the source of low wages is not a function of distorted market power, but the failings of individuals. They simply are not worth more than the low wages they have been receiving. Therefore, it is up to them to improve themselves, and a minimum wage cannot solve this problem; rather all that it can do is artificially inflate wages, thereby absolving low-wage workers of their responsibility for themselves. As the locus of the model is on the individual, it totally negates structural variables that may affect individual behavior.

The neoclassical ethos simply assumes a good and efficient outcome to arise from individuals freely making choices and pursuing their interests. This emphasis on free choice and efficiency, however, may also mask the particular vision of society contained in the neoclassical ethos's normative conception of the economy. In this vision, workers can always determine whether they will be employed by virtue of their willingness to be flexible when it comes to their wage demands. Deborah Figart et al. (2002) call this conception the wage as price—what one in an exchange relationship is going to pay for one's labor services. But it fails to take into account that there are other conceptions: mainly wages as living—the notion that the purpose of wages is to provide an adequate level of support for workers—and wages as social practice, which emphasize the socially and historically specific process of wage setting. That worker flexibility may be efficient for the overall market place does not mean that it is for the needs of individual workers. Although a minimum wage is assumed to be inefficient because it leads to an underutilization of labor in the aggregate, the neoclassical vision, as it expresses itself through competitive markets, fails to address the consequences of a world where wages could be allowed to drop to a level whereby demand would be equal to supply. Just how low do wages have to drop in order for the supply and demand for labor to intersect? What happens, after all, when wages completely bottom out? Is this not ultimately the cause of labor market instability? Is this not the source of poverty—that people do not receive sufficient wages to provide for themselves, and in turn are unable to demand goods and services? And is this not ultimately the source of a depression? In other words, might this not be another source of inefficiency?

This model does not posit the source of low wages to be the result of, for example, distorted market power, but failings of individuals. On the contrary, neoclassical economics holds there to be no difference between labor and other goods and services. According to the neoclassical ethos, both firms and individual workers in competitive markets are considered to be "wage takers," and are therefore assumed to have no bargaining power. This means that in theory, neither one has the ability to exploit one another. Institutional economists, however, especially those writing during the Progressive period categorically rejected this analysis. On the contrary, workers faced a marked inequality of bargaining power and consequently suffered from the exploitive and otherwise unjust wages that were offered them (Kaufman 2005).

Early institutional labor economists emphasized that the labor market imperfectly gave employers superior bargaining power relative to individual employees. Because of the inequality in bargaining power, there really was nothing to prevent the economic coercion of workers. Among the early Progressive thinkers, Robert Hale reformulated the problem of coercion to demonstrate that the sphere of private "voluntary" market relations was indistinguishable from public power exercised in a direct fashion. Capitalists especially, through their state-conferred property rights, enjoyed coercive power through their ability to compel exchanges on terms that they would consent to. By virtue of their ability to threaten to withhold their capital or the products of their capital from those who required them, they would be able to compel. The one who did not own property, that is, the typical low-wage worker whose only option was to bargain with say the one main property owner for a job in order to attain subsistence, was essentially being coerced. If background circumstances were such that individual choices were effectively circumscribed, then there was no question that coercion was ubiquitous and that workers, especially those that did not own property, really did not enjoy the same freedom as those with property, that is, employers. As far as Hale was concerned, absolute freedom wasn't really possible, and that all one could really hope for at best was relative freedom (Fried 1998).

Robert Prasch (1995) argues that the neoclassical model is really an idealized view of the market which assumes one market place, but fails to take into account different markets for different goods. Theories of competition assume a specific type of market, but they don't allow for the fact that other types of markets may exist. Rather there are two characteristic types of market participants: those who trade in the market to fulfill their needs and those who trade in the market in order to fulfill their wants. Crucial to the success of neoclassical theory is the assumption that everybody who enters into an exchange is fully constituted independently of the market. Hence they are all equal in their bargaining power, with each participant able to in effect determine under what conditions to enter into an exchange. Because of their bargaining power, employers do not have to be conscious of their bargaining power; rather they simply maximize their profits in a manner indicated by standard theory. Therefore, a wants trader has the option of withdrawing from the market if the proposed exchange fails to meet his/her profit-maximizing criteria.

The wants trader is by definition, then, less dependent on the market due to his or her ability to withdraw at any time. This also implies that the wants trader possesses other resources that can be relied upon until such time that the trading conditions are to the wants trader's advantage. The needs trader, however, does not enjoy the same luxury and may be forced to accept an exchange that is less than ideal, and which in some cases may be considered exploitive because it meets a basic need such as eating. As most minimum wage earners are essentially needs traders without real bargaining power, they are in reality forced to in effect accept whatever conditions are offered at the lowest wage rates because they don't really have the ability to hold out for something better. Consequently, they don't enjoy the same freedom as those with greater bargaining power.

In the world of asymmetrical power, only employers are wants traders where workers are needs traders. They need to work in order to survive. Kristian Braekkan and Victoria Sowa (2015) argue that more attention needs to be paid to exploitation because capitalism is a disciplinary system in which workers are perpetually disciplined by their need to work in exchange for wages that enable them to subsist. And as globalism required that wages fall in order to be competitive and that social programs be cut so that business environments would be attractive to investment and economic growth, the effect has been to only discipline workers more. Exploitation, as they define it, can be a state of mind—that workers perceive themselves to be exploited. This refers to what they call "psychological contracts," which are the expectations workers have based on the employer's explicit and implicit promises communicated prior to hiring. The neoclassical model assumes that workers who are exploited can simply leave and take another job elsewhere, but this is only true in a slack labor market. A worker with few options for survival but to remain in an employment situation where psychological contract violations occur would effectively be forced to be in a situation where they will continue to be exploited. And if workers perceive themselves to be exploited, there may be less organizational commitment. They found that perceived contract violations led to decreased organizational commitment and to decreased trust in the employing organization. It then follows that technological change which forces down the wages of low-skilled workers is effectively exploiting them, and that income inequality is simply a manifestation of that exploitation.

The neoclassical economist will of course respond that the needs trader is still able to negotiate and hold out for better terms. Even if holding out for better terms means starving, a choice has been made. Higher costs of doing so does not necessarily negate freedom of choice. But the neoclassical argument more fundamentally misses the point: it isn't the wage demands that workers make that determine whether they are employed; rather it is the aggregate demand for goods and services (Minsky 1986, pp. 123–124). In a survey of business executives during the 1930s and 1940s, Richard Lester (1946), a later institutional economist, observed that business executives tended to think that costs and profits were contingent on the rate of output, and not the other way around. As far as these executives were concerned, employment levels were not determined by wages rates but by the rate of output. This would, of course, suggest that no matter how low workers are willing to reduce their wage demands, if there is no demand for their firms' goods and services, they simply will not be employed.

The principal focus of much of the empirical literature has been on the youth labor market. Since the Minimum Wage Study Commission (MWSC) report came out in 1981, it has been the prevailing wisdom that the minimum wage takes its greatest toll on the youth labor market, that a binding wage floor reduces employment for younger and less-skilled workers. The Commission staff estimated that a 10 percent increase in the minimum wage would reduce teenage employment by about 1 percent. Other estimates have placed the disemployment effect even higher (MWSC 1981, pp. 35–38). Following this report, a consensus emerged among mainstream economists that a 10 percent increase in the minimum wage will result in a 1–3 percent reduction in teenage employment (Kosters 1996; Kosters and Welch 1972; Welch 1974, 1978; Meyer and Wise 1983). At the same time, effects are judged to be proportionately smaller among adults aged 20–24 years (Neumark and Wascher 1992), and that adults on balance appear to be better off under a wage floor.

Although the MWSC too noted the smaller effects among adults, they have not been the focus of much of the research. Herein lies a problem, for there have not been many studies estimating just how many people might be attracted to the labor force. On the one hand, the absence of data for the latter does strengthen the position of the former. On the other hand, the data on the former has not been all that comprehensive that there isn't room to consider the latter. The key point, however, is that there is no uniformity of findings, which ultimately makes the use of economic models a political act unto itself. The data is also demand-side oriented; not supply-side oriented. In attempting to estimate how much fewer workers will be hired following a minimum wage increase, that is, their labor services being demanded, it misses how many more workers might be attracted into the labor market in search of higher wages, that is, their labor services being supplied. Still, it is worth mentioning that the lower employment predicted by the standard model is in part due to the supply-side effects arising from a higher wage.

Ironically, however, the MWSC report implies supply-side effects. By distinguishing between reduced employment and higher unemployment, the Commission effectively acknowledged that a higher wage would effectively attract people into the labor market. Because workers actively looking for work constitute the formal definition of unemployment, the official unemployment rate would increase due to an expanded market of job seekers. Most studies that suggest lower employment usually mean that fewer workers will be hired as a result of higher wages and that in some cases there will be an increase in unemployment due to a potential layoff of existing minimum wage workers. But to formally acknowledge that unemployment will rise because more workers may look for jobs at higher wage rates is to acknowledge that there are supply-side effects.

The principal focus on the teen labor market, at least in the past, may have been because most minimum wage earners tended to be younger. Most minimum wage earners were either teenagers or secondary earners in their households. Therefore, it was argued, because they weren't primary earners, the costs to society in terms of higher unemployment were simply not worth the costs. The principal argument for not focusing on the potential benefits to the poor, however, is that most minimum wage workers are not adults. Much of the data on who earns the minimum wage shows that only a small fraction of the labor force earns it and that most of them are teenagers. Earners of the minimum wage are for the most part teenagers or contributing members of a household budget (Brown 1996; Burkhauser and Finegan 1989). The MWSC estimated that 68 percent of minimum wage earners were in families headed by married couples. Of these, 1.5 million were the only earners in their families, thereby making up 14 percent of low-wage workers. Fifty-four percent of all minimum wage workers were in families with two or more earners. Still, the Commission made it clear that minimum wage earners were not the primary earners in families with more than one earner (MWSC 1981, p. 13).

On these grounds, it is often concluded that raising the minimum wage would not greatly help the poor. On the contrary, raising the minimum wage is more likely to hurt the poor because at a higher wage, employers are more likely to hire more skilled labor as a substitute for unskilled labor. Because low-skilled individuals are heavily overrepresented among the ranks of welfare recipients, minimum wage increases will effectively result in employers discriminating against recipients (Finegold 1998). These studies, however, might well miss the point. Even if most minimum wage earners are not the primary earners in their households, it does not follow that the income of those earners isn't necessary for the sustenance of the family unit. Moreover, it misses the wage's potential for redistribution. Gramlich (1976), for instance, has pointed toward evidence that minimum wage increases primarily benefit adult females and that whatever disemployment effects may result among low-wage adults are not strong enough to make them worse off on balance.

Bruce Kaufman (2003) points out that a minimum wage as a macro-tool does have roots in institutional economics. John R. Commons, in particular, took the view that a decline in prices and wages during recessions and depressions would only aggravate them by reducing purchasing power and in turn leading to bankruptcy. For Commons, the answer lay in redistributing income from profits to wages through collective bargaining agreements. Collective bargaining would both prevent over-savings and underconsumption, thereby assisting in maintaining purchasing power and aggregate demand. Although he recognized that unions do have defects that might hinder economic efficiency in various ways, he also believed that in most cases the benefits to society would outweigh their costs. The same argument could easily apply to the minimum wage, as money to pay higher wages to workers is effectively being redistributed from profits. But it isn't redistribution in the classic sense of taking from one party to give to another. Those receiving higher wages are still working.

Still, another variation of the model holds that it simply contributes to wage rigidity that not only affects short-term unemployment but long-term as well. Mark Partridge and Janice Partridge (1999) argue that the minimum wage is positively related to long-term unemployment rates. Because, according to the standard model, a minimum wage prevents workers from lowering their wage demands, employers will demand less labor. If low-skilled workers with a low value of marginal product cannot take a job below the minimum wage, the probability of them being offered a job at all will only diminish and the duration of their unemployment will increase. And yet, it is also possible that a minimum wage might have very little impact on long-term unemployment if the industries that employ a disproportionate share of minimum wage workers have almost no unemployment to begin with.

The neoclassical model has nonetheless found a home in conservative political circles. During the 1980s the nature of the political debate over the minimum wage did begin to change. With the election of Ronald Reagan to the presidency came a whole new outlook on the economy. For neoclassical academics like Milton Friedman, the White House finally had an occupant who viewed government as the problem, rather than the solution to the nation's economic and social problems. Summing up the goals of economic policy, George Stigler (1986), from the same Chicago school of thought as Friedman, argued that "The supreme goal of the Western World is the development of the individual: the creation for the individual of a maximum area of personal freedom, and with this a corresponding area of personal responsibility" (p. 93). As noble as policies intended to provide a safety net or reduce income inequalities might be (which would also include the minimum wage), they were fundamentally at odds with the tenets of freedom. Consequently, the older institutionalist arguments emphasizing the role of government, to the extent they had been listened to at all during the 1970s, had lost their voice.

The Reagan administration made no secret of its views that too much interference in the economy was the principal reason the economy had been in a recession during the 1970s. Moreover, inflation was by and large a product of workers demanding too much from their employers, without returning sufficient productivity, which meant that labor unions were as much part of the problem. Although the number of workers associated with unions never exceeded 30 percent during the 1950s, it dipped below 19 percent during the 1980s (Goldfield 1987). Many states passed right-to-work laws following the Taft-Hartley Act, but it was Reagan's firing of the Professional Air Traffic Controllers Organization (PATCO) air traffic controllers that signaled to private employers that they too would be within their rights to do so as well. This sent a clear message to labor unions across the country that any form of union militancy would not be tolerated (Dubofsky 1994). But packing the National Labor Relations Board (NLRB) with people hostile to the interests of labor also meant that the NLRB could no longer be used as an instrument of union growth (Moody 1988, p. 142). Meanwhile, the minimum wage was stagnating. The decline of unions and the stagnation of the minimum wage really cannot be separated, because with the decline of unions the minimum wage lost its biggest political base of support. Historically, the minimum wage in the USA tended to be increased when there was a political constituency to lobby for it. That constituency was organized labor. But as union membership declined, so too did the political constituency that could lobby on its behalf (Levin-Waldman 2001).

The standard model along with these findings has become an orthodoxy unto itself. The orthodoxy, however, is not without its flaws. First and foremost, it assumes competitive markets and that in competitive markets workers can determine the overall demand for labor simply by adjusting their wage demands. But in the real world, the demand for labor is based on output and aggregate demand for goods and services (Lester 1946, 1947; Palley 1998). Employers do not demand more labor because the price of labor has decreased but because consumers demand more of the goods and services that they produce. It is this need to produce more that leads employers to hire additional workers. Secondly, the orthodoxy is predicated on problematic data. Much of the data is based on time-series data which merely looks at changing employment rates at various points in time, usually around when a minimum wage increase has occurred. Then through statistical testing, attempts are made to establish a correlation between an increase in the minimum wage and a change in employment. Statistical tests at best show correlations, and even strong ones, but they do not necessarily establish causal relationships. In the end, it cannot be established with authority that a particular minimum wage increase results in a disemployment effect—that it was specifically that increase that caused the disemployment effect, as opposed to other circumstances, that is, an economic downturn, the loss of markets, and so on. It does not tell us anything about the behavior of firms per se; rather it provides a basis upon which their behavior can be inferred.

Michael Reich (2010) argues that much of the CPS data suggesting large negative effects due to minimum wage increases only show these large negative effects to be among teenagers. One typically looks at trends prior to minimum wage increases and then trends following minimum wage increases, but if one only looks at trends following increases a negative trend may be found. Still in light of a negative pre-minimum wage trend, it is incorrect to attribute a post-minimum wage trend to minimum wage policy. This statement has to be understood within the larger context of 16 minimum wage increases between 1955 and 1996, which were also more likely to occur in times of relatively strong employment growth. But it is also in the context of more and more states raising their minimum wages above the federal level, beginning in the late 1980s. Moreover, these states with higher minimum wages are not limited to areas above-average living costs, or those that necessarily tend to be more liberal. But instead of taking the standard position that one possible reason for this may be that the minimum wage is still much lower than market-clearing wages, he suggests that it may be that higher wage floors can significantly reduce employers' recruitment and retention costs. Low-wage employers typically experience above-average turnover and job vacancy rates. Therefore, it is likely that job vacancy rates would fall if a higher wage served to make those jobs more attractive. While it may still reduce the desired level of employment, it might still leave the actual level of unemployment unchanged. Which is to say that minimum wages do not kill jobs; they kill job vacancies. Put another way, minimum wage increases do not necessarily lead to disemployment because workers were fired; rather they decrease the number of jobs created in the future for low-wage workers.

Even attempts to get around the inherent weaknesses of time-series data have their limitations. Using individual-level data from the National Longitudinal Survey of Youth (NLSY), Janet Currie and Bruce Fallick (1996), for instance, examined disemployment effects of minimum wage increases in 1979 and 1980. They also examined the effects of the minimum wage on individual year-to-year changes. Their approach was specifically to measure the effects by identifying a group of workers that would most likely be directly affected by the minimum wage and then compare their employment to the employment of a group of workers who were least likely to be affected. Affected workers were found to be 3 percent less likely to be employed a year later. At the same time, no evidence was found that minimum wage increases affected the wages of those workers who remained employed a year later. Still, they were not able to establish that it was the increase in the minimum wage that was a direct cause of their not being employed a year later as opposed to other factors. In the end, all that can be made are inferences, and to the extent that it provides the basis for inference, it serves to support the theoretical construct contained in the traditional textbook. On the contrary, all that can be made is a plausible inference based on statistical tests bound to show a high likelihood. And yet, based on changes in employment patterns following say a minimum wage increase, a further inference is made about the behavior of firms, which only reinforces the reigning orthodoxy.

All of this raises the obvious question: why despite these flaws has the orthodoxy been so entrenched? There are several possible explanations. The first has to do with the composition of the minimum wage labor market itself. Because only a small fraction of the labor market actually earns the statutory minimum wage, the potential benefits are presumed to be so small that they could not possibly offset the more likely larger costs. Moreover, the benefits are presumed to be smaller still because most minimum wage earners are not the primary earners in their households, but are secondary earners and by and large teenagers (Brown 1996; Burkhauser and Finegan 1989). So because these incomes are considered to be less consequential to the maintenance of their households, the potential benefits given the costs are considered to be yet smaller.

The first reason the orthodoxy is so entrenched is because of our commitment to a particular definition of efficiency, one steeped in the utilitarian calculus of maximizing utility while minimizing costs.

There are several other explanations for the neoclassical orthodoxy being so entrenched, which are by no means unrelated to the efficiency claim. The second reason for the prevalence of this orthodoxy has to do with ideology and a general anti-labor bias built into economics models generally. Thomas Palley (1998) suggests that the political dominance of business and the intellectual dominance of laissez-faire have meant that economic policy since the 1970s has consistently favored business at the expense of labor. Because the economics profession produces what society takes for economic knowledge, it has assumed the role of determining society's vision of how the economy works. Moreover, the economics profession has adopted an intellectual view that is implicitly anti-labor and pro-business. Economic theory is often considered anti-labor because the reigning economic model of competitive markets assumes unemployment to be caused by high and rigid wages. Because labor market institutions like the minimum wage serve to raise wages, they too are presented as forces driving up unemployment (pp. 19–20).

Competitive market theory, however, is generally viewed as being anti-labor because it treats labor as a commodity. Workers are simply inputs in the production process and as such have no personalities of their own. But this view also appears to have some grounding in the Progressive period. Consider for a moment Max Weber's (1947) understanding of bureaucracy as an efficient means for administration in both the public and private sectors. In the public sector it would enable the efficient administration of government through the impartial application of rules and procedures. Organizations based on division of labor, hierarchy of command, span of control, and credentials as the basis for staffing would be able to dispassionately apply rules. The purpose of the organization, then, wasn't for workers to socialize, as that assumes individuality, but to strip workers of their individuality—their personalities—for the purpose of achieving greater efficiency (pp. 330–335). Therefore, as competitive labor market theory assumes a full-employment economy, the minimum wage orthodoxy is not only a product of those assumptions, but it nicely serves the interests of those who believe that all government interferences—whether in the form of regulation, public programs, and other interventions—greatly undermine free-market ideology and free choice.

A third reason has to do with the composition of the minimum wage labor market itself. Because only a small fraction of the labor market actually earns the statutory minimum wage, the potential benefits are presumed to be so small that they could not possibly offset the more likely larger costs. These benefits are presumed to be smaller still because most minimum wage earners are primarily secondary earners in their households. So because these incomes are considered to be less consequential to the maintenance of their households, the potential benefits given the costs are considered to be even smaller. This too contributes to the sense that they are inefficient—they are unnecessary. And yet, this misses the fact that so-called secondary earners may in fact be necessary to the maintenance of the household. By describing them as "secondary earners," the effect is to cast the minimum wage population—what some would describe as a "target population"—as other, with the purpose being to delegitimize them.

The use of the term "secondary" effectively represents a negative social construction of the target population, and one very much based on a particular societal ethos (Schneider and Ingram 1993). Because they are unimportant, the minimum wage couldn't possibly be used as a positive policy tool. They are cast as being unworthy of wage increases on the grounds that such increases are not necessary to the maintenance of their families. This construction is very similar to the centuries-old distinction between the "worthy" and "unworthy" poor. Those who were poor through no fault of their own—widows, the disabled, the elderly, and orphans—were considered to be worthy and were to be treated with compassion and charity. The unworthy were those who were simply lazy and lacked "moral character" and thus were to be treated harshly (Katz 1989). The more poor people who can be characterized as unworthy, the less responsibility society has to care for their well-being.

To a large extent, the appeal of the neoclassical ethic regarding the minimum wage may have as much to do with how the minimum wage population is constructed. Similarly if low-wage workers can be conceived of as unworthy of higher wages because of their attributes and perceived failings, society again then bears no responsibility for their low wages and is thus under no obligation to ensure that their wages rise above a certain level. The point is that it has been entrenched precisely because it has served a particular ideological position. This in no way diminishes the importance of the efficiency consideration. Rather, neoclassicals have been able to rely on this type of empirical research to demonstrate how the minimum wage is simply inefficient. The neoclassical ethic, in short, assumes a minimum wage to be inefficient in part because it isn't necessary. Obscured here, however, is the normative theory that social welfare is maximized from an efficiency standpoint when as many teenagers are employed at low wages, even if it is at a cost of their parents earning wages sufficient to support themselves and their families.

A fourth reason has to do with what David Card and Alan Krueger (1995) refer to as publication bias. Because journals will not publish results that are not statistically significant, with significance generally defined as a t ratio in excess of 2, there is a natural tendency for editors and reviewers to look more favorably on those studies with statistically significant results. In the case of the minimum wage, this has only been compounded by the strong theoretical presumption of the economics profession that minimum wage increases will have employment effects.

This in turn may lead to further biases because editors and reviewers may be predisposed to accepting only those papers that can show a "significant negative effect," and it is this "significant negative effect" that ultimately guides the choice of empirical specifications. The choices made in this regard are then intended to ensure that the results are statistically significant. And lastly, the orthodoxy may be so entrenched because of what Robert Heilbroner and William Millberg (1995) refer to as a crisis in vision. Modern economic thought simply lacks a sense of how society ought to be ordered and how modern scientific analysis ought to be put in the service of that vision. Because of this, we may miss the potential for the minimum wage to serve other policy interests, such as making a more just and democratic society (Levin-Waldman 2000c, 2003, 2009, 2011). The persistence of the orthodoxy would appear to bear out Piketty's observation about the profession's childish obsession with math.

The New Political Economy of the Minimum Wage

Researchers in recent years have actually addressed the data issue by collecting new data with results that not surprisingly have called into question the efficacy of the orthodoxy. The principal challenge to the reigning orthodoxy usually came from studies of the fast-food industry conducted by Card and Krueger (1995, 1998) and others (Katz and Krueger 1992). Specifically in studies of the fast-food industry in New Jersey with Pennsylvania serving as a control group, Card and Krueger found the minimum wage to have no disemployment effect at all. On the contrary, employment in New Jersey restaurants was actually found to have increased. There was also no substitution effect, and even though the minimum wage increase did lead to price increases for meals, there was no evidence that prices rose faster in New Jersey stores that were most affected by the wage increase. Moreover, the minimum wage increase did not negatively affect the number of store openings. In a follow-up study several years later, Card and Krueger only confirmed their earlier results (1998).

These studies, however, were controversial and have raised a whole host of other research questions. Much of the criticism centers around the issue of measurement and the quality of available data. The basic problem is that just because no adverse effects were observed, it doesn't necessarily follow that there wouldn't be were the minimum wage raised beyond a certain point (Kennan 1995). These increases may not have had the consequences predicted by the competitive model because the minimum wage has been so far below a market-clearing wage (Freeman and Freeman 1991).

Perhaps more than anything else, these studies demonstrate that a major limitation of the orthodoxy is that it only predicts unemployment in competitive labor markets. By Card and Krueger's (1995) own admission, the fast-food industry is a monopsony to the extent that it is the principal employer of minimum wage workers, and therefore it is not representative of most industries. Because they are the only firms willing to employ minimum wage workers, these workers have no other choice but to accept those low wages that they are offered. In a monopsony market, minimum wage increases may actually result in employment gains, largely because the market-clearing wage is still below that of a perfectly competitive market. As an increase in the minimum wage is still likely to be less than the market-clearing wage of a perfectly competitive market, the minimum wage in a monopsony is likely to result in greater employment and efficiency because it will still be less than the equilibrium wage in a perfectly competitive market. Even subscribers to the model of competitive markets recognize that minimum wage increases in a monopsony labor market will lead to both greater employment and efficiency (Brown et al. 1982; Houseman 1998). Kevin Lang and Shulamit Kahn (1998) even go so far as to suggest that higher minimum wages, contrary to the effects claimed by those who argue the youth disemployment effects, actually shift employment toward youth and students, especially in the fast-food industry.

Employment may also increase because employers engage in rescheduling. While wage increases will lower employment in the standard model, minimum wages in an alternative model can actually increase employment because the wage floor actually increases the relative costs of hours, in which case the employer has greater incentive to increase the mix of jobs relative to hours. The key point being that the wage rate is used to determine hours, as opposed to clearing the labor market. Therefore, the minimum wage can increase employment (Palley 1995). Employment can increase because the number of hours per worker may actually decline. As the cost of employing hours per worker increases, employers have greater incentive to reduce the workweek and hire more workers. This is simply another form of substitution.

Thomas Michl (2000) explores this rescheduling scenario by presenting a simple model of the demand for workers and weekly hours per worker in which wage increases in principle induce firms to hire more workers while simultaneously reducing the workweek. Using data from both Card and Krueger and also from David Neumark and William Wascher (2000)—which was initially employed in an attempt to discredit Card and Krueger—Michl suggests that a case can be made that to the extent that the New Jersey minimum wage increase had any impact on labor demand, it was to reduce the number of weekly hours per worker. Hours in New Jersey restaurants were found to have declined by around 6 percent or by about an hour and 15 minutes per week. But in later work, Allegretto et al. (2011) observed that higher minimum wages may lead the workers themselves to reduce their hours.

An important, but often neglected, subtext to the whole minimum wage debate is that there isn't any conclusive data to make any definitive statements about any effects at all, whether they be positive or negative. In effect the issue becomes the model and its legitimacy, with different groups having to varying degrees a stake in it. This became all too apparent when, after the Card and Krueger studies came out, the fast-food industry financed its own studies, using its own data in an attempt to discredit Card and Krueger. Ironically, those studies conducted by David Neumark and William Wascher only confirmed Card and Krueger's findings. In addition, as John Schmitt (1996) points out, the economics profession also began to show signs of accepting that moderate increases in the minimum wage may have little, if any, effect on employment. In the end, this ought to confirm the argument that the model which is adopted will affect different people differently. That there is this level of ambiguity in the data might suggest that a more political model informs us more about how the minimum wage debate will be resolved than does the traditional normative economics textbook analysis.

Still, there have been other studies that only support the Card and Krueger studies of no disemployment effects. In a survey of small business, Levin-Waldman (2000a) found that not only had the minimum wage increase, which took effect in September 1997 and increased the minimum wage to \$5.15 an hour, not affected most small businesses but at least 79 percent still would not be affected had the minimum wage increased again to \$6.00 an hour. And in a follow-up study, it was observed that more than 86 percent of small business would not be affected by an increase to \$6.00 and that still 64 percent of small businesses wouldn't be affected by a further increase to \$7.25 an hour (Levin-Waldman 2000b).

Adding to this, Arindrajit Dube et al. (2007) looked at the effects of a minimum wage law that was enacted by a public ballot measure for the city of San Francisco in 2003. While the federal minimum wage was still \$5.15 an hour, San Francisco's was now \$8.50, which was still 26 percent higher than California's minimum wage of \$6.70. Looking at primarily the restaurant industry because it was considered to be the primary employer of fast-food workers, they found that the benefits to the increases did outweigh the costs. The city wage floor did significantly raise the wages of those at affected restaurants and compressed the wage distribution among restaurant workers and increased the average wages of fast-food workers twice as much as those at sit-down restaurants. And yet, there was no increase in business closure or employment loss detected. To the extent that such findings undermine the traditional orthodoxy, they also add to the ambiguity surrounding the effects of the minimum wage. Moreover, they reinforce some of the evidence that suggests that we may know very little about the minimum wage or its actual effects. Still, that new studies show that the traditional orthodoxy may not be accurate doesn't mean that the earlier studies which held there to be disemployment effects were wrong. Clearly, the findings from those studies are what researchers observed. The problem may have been the prism through which they were viewing the data. Dube et al. (2010) argue that a major problem with the data is that economists have been taking two different methodological approaches. Traditional national-level studies use all cross-state variation in the minimum wage over time to estimate the effects. Meanwhile, case studies typically compare adjoining local areas with different minimum wages around the time of the policy change. They specifically compare all contiguous county-pairs in the USA that are located on opposite sides of a state border, in an attempt to generalize the case study approach by all local differences in minimum wages in the USA over a 19-and-a-half-year period. Because the restaurant industry is the most intensive user of minimum wage workers, it is the prime focus, although other low-wage industries are considered too. In 2006, they employed 29.9 percent of all workers paid within 10 percent of state or federal minimum wages, thus making them the single largest employer of minimum wage workers. Also the proportion of workers at or close to the minimum wage is similar among all restaurant workers. What they found was that employment effects vary substantially among specifications. The estimated earnings effects were positive and significant for both limited-service and full-service restaurants, with the earnings effects being somewhat greater among limited-service restaurants than among full-service restaurants. For cross-state contiguous counties, they found strong earnings effects and no employment effects. When looking at local comparisons while also controlling for heterogeneity in employment growth, they found no detectable employment losses from the types of minimum wage increases that have been taking place over the years in the USA.

In a subsequent study, Dube and Reich along with Sylvia Allegretto (2011) examined whether minimum wages really reduced teen employment. Using CPS data from 1990 to 2009 they controlled for both heterogeneity and selectivity. Here their central argument concerns confounding effects of heterogeneity patterns in low-wage employment that are coupled with selectivity of states that have implemented minimum wage increases. There was little difference in employment effects between male and female teens. Rather many minimum wage studies probably overstate their precision due to the use of conventional standard errors, which may also lead them to incorrectly reject a hypothesis of no employment effect. But minimum wage studies that have used local employment data generally don't find disemployment effects. In this particular study, they focus their estimates on the effects of minimum wage increases on wages, employment, and hours of work for teenagers. Their evidence does not support disemployment effects associated with minimum wage increases. Nevertheless, there may still be an effect on hours. Although firms may not decrease their demand for workers, they may nonetheless decrease their demand for the number of hours that are worked by teenagers. Or teenagers themselves may opt to work less following minimum wage increases, thereby supplying fewer hours of their labor services. All in all, their findings added to those of the previous study that minimum wage increases, again in the range that have been implemented in the USA, do not reduce employment among teens.

We can also draw on the evidence from minimum wages in other parts of the world as well. In 1999, for example, the British Parliament passed the National Minimum Wage (NMW) which effectively supplanted the Trade Boards Act of 1909 that would attempt to establish minimum wages on an industry/occupational basis. Now there would be a uniform minimum wage covering the entire country. A key feature of this act was the establishment of the Low Pay Commission (LPC), which would be an independent body that would report on the state of the low-wage labor market and make periodic recommendations for wage increases. The LPC effectively removed the issue of the minimum wage from the political will of Parliament. By creating the commission, the Parliament would be forced to publicly respond to the LPC, which also ensured that the minimum wage could not be kept off the political agenda at times the Parliament might be dominated by those who weren't as friendly to the minimum wage. But Jerold Waltman (2008) also notes that not only did the NMW raise wages, it did so with no negative effects. It certainly raised the wages of the less well-off, although their income gains were modest. But the result was that more people in Britain had more discretionary income as a result. And because of wage compression engendered by the NMW, there was a slight reduction in income inequality. At the same time, studies of the NMW have repeatedly failed to turn up evidence of disemployment effects. On the contrary, employment levels actually rose following the introduction of the minimum wage. Moreover, objective observers even attributed recent increases in unemployment to increased supply factors rather than increases in the minimum wage.

Meaning of Unsettled Findings

It should be clear that the data with regard to effects of the minimum wage on employment are ambiguous at best. This reality was underscored by a report of the Congressional Budget Office (CBO) in early 2014 that suggested that a minimum wage increase to $10.10 an hour as proposed in President Obama's State of the Union address would lead to a total reduction in employment of 500,000 jobs by 2016 once fully implemented. Despite this, the economy was still going to be better off. Citing the conventional economic analysis, employment would be reduced because an increase would force employers to pass some of the increased costs onto consumers, which in turn would lead consumers to purchase fewer goods and services. As they would then produce fewer goods and services, they would hire fewer workers. Therefore, employment might be reduced through the "scale" effect. Or a minimum wage increase would raise the costs of low-wage workers relative to other inputs, which would lead some employers to respond by reducing their use of low-wage workers toward other inputs. In this case, employment would be reduced by the substitution effect. At the same time, the report suggested that the conventional analysis might not apply in certain circumstances. As an example, a firm hiring new workers finds that it has to increase the wages of existing workers doing the same work. An increase in the minimum wage then means employers have to pay existing workers more. Consequently, it lowers the additional cost of hiring a new worker, thereby leading to increased employment.

Still, the report was unclear about what it meant to talk about a reduction in total employment. A disemployment effect occurs when employers respond to increases in the minimum wage by laying off existing workers. Nowhere in the report, however, is the term disemployment effect used. Rather the term used is reduction in total employment, which is significant. This could occur in three different ways. The first is for employers to lay off workers. The second is for low-wage employers not to hire in the future, in which case total employment is reduced. And the third, which the report does not really get into, is that a higher wage will attract back into the labor market those who may have shunned work because the prior minimum wage was considered to be too low. Now there are more people in the labor force, which means that employment on the whole is lower. Even though the CBO report does not come out and say it, it is nonetheless alluding to a very important distinction, which is that there is a difference between rising unemployment because of disemployment and lower total employment because fewer low-wage jobs will be created in the future. The CBO report seemed to be implying the latter.

Nevertheless, the CBO went on to say that at least 16.5 million Americans would see their incomes increase and that on the whole a minimum wage increase would be good for the economy, and that it would potentially lead to some economic growth. This would be because some of the people earning slightly above the new minimum wage of $10.10 an hour would also receive pay increases. Moreover, a few higher-wage workers would owe their jobs and increased wages to the increased demand for goods and services that would result from a minimum wage increase. Here the CBO was offering the standard macro-argument for increasing the minimum wage: more people earning higher wages have greater purchasing power which enables them to demand more goods and services. In time, this might lead to job creation. Of course, as I suggested in the beginning of the chapter, the reverse is the tragedy of the commons. But the CBO suggested that there would be even larger macro-benefits from its impact on the federal budget deficit. On one level, federal spending and taxes would be affected by increases in real income for some people and the reduction in real income for others. One group of workers with higher income would then pay more in taxes and receive less in various types of federal benefits than they otherwise would have. Another group of workers who become jobless because of increases or because higher prices reduce consumption would see a reduction in real income, meaning that they would pay less collectively in taxes and receive more in federal benefits.

Here the CBO concluded that the net effect of raising the minimum wage would most likely be a small decrease in budget deficits for several years to come, but a small increase thereafter.

On the whole though, the CBO concluded that the benefits outweighed whatever costs. By the CBO's own admission, it was not basing its analysis on new data, but on a meta-analysis of studies that have been around. Undoubtedly, this study appeared to suffer from the same methodological flaws that Dube et al. (2010) identified as being the primary problem with most of the data. But the other problem the study might have suffered from was essentially Piketty's (2014) criticism of the economics profession's childish obsession with math. In this case, it was like many other studies based on econometric modeling, which may not prove to be true in the real world.

And yet, the claim that more than 16 million Americans would get pay raises was also hinting at another macroeconomic argument that is often dismissed in the typical minimum wage debate between those who argue the disemployment effects among teenagers versus the anti-poverty effects. That is, the minimum wage is really about the middle class. In earlier work I (2011) found that in ten constructed contours beginning with the statutory minimum the median wages in each contour increased in those years there was an increase in the minimum wage. Those earning at the top of the tenth contour in 2008 were earning around $100,000 a year. Moreover the ten constructed contours encompassed close to 70 percent of the labor market. This would suggest that through contour effects that the minimum wage benefits the middle class.

Without going into contours, the CBO was suggesting that there are clearly ripple effects for those wages around the minimum wage. The suggestion of 16 million benefitting would be consistent with the idea that those earning just above the old minimum wage would also be getting pay raises because those earning the new minimum are now approaching the wages of the next interval. The more people who received wage increases, the more demand for goods and services, which in turn would drive the economy. But there was something else about the CBO report, which is who earns the statutory minimum wage may not be as important as who earns around the minimum wage. Here is where the concept of wage contours is so vitally important because the statutory minimum is nothing more than a reference point for the low-wage labor market. In other words, there is nothing natural about wage rates. On the contrary, wage rates are determined more by institutions than the natural market place.

Role of Social Science

There are perhaps two directions that unsettled findings can take us. The first is to conclude that we still do not know enough about the effects of the minimum wage, and given the potential for unintended consequences, that is, disemployment effects, we should not have one. The other is that given that the data does not absolutely establish a causal relationship between minimum wage increases and adverse employment consequences, there should then be room for policy experimentation. This would appear to flow logically from the role that economics as a social science should be playing, which is mainly to provide information to policymakers that they can use in the public policy decision-making process serving the collective will of the communities they serve. But there is another aspect that lends itself to the tragedy of the commons. In part, these unsettled findings, and in some cases their total disconnect from the theoretical models, stem from the problem of empirical findings grounded in solid social science methodologies challenging theoretical models also grounded in the social sciences (Levin-Waldman 2004).

Charles Lindblom (1959) observed a long time ago that policy is made on the basis of incrementalism. Instead of a comprehensive model, otherwise known as the root model, whereby goals are identified, and alternatives are evaluated on the basis of costs and benefits, and choices are made, we make policy through successive limited comparisons—what he refers to as the branch model. Here we begin with policies that are already there and compare them to possible alternatives or perhaps limited changes. It is the idea that in a slow cumbersome system, at best we can get a foundation upon which improvements can be made through incremental steps. As those foundations are built upon gradually in increments, the cumulative effect is to develop policy. To a large extent, this model of policymaking which Lindblom refers to as the science of muddling through is similar to Thomas Kuhn's (1970) notion that scientific revolutions don't occur through one-time findings or experiments but through a succession of experiments over time whose cumulative effect is revolutionary when compared to findings many years before. The minimum wage orthodoxy would imply that public policy is driven by a model. But policy is not formed on the basis of single models, but results from a mix of variables along with the mix of interests and actors involved (Stone 2002; Kingdon 1995). In other words, policy is a function of a bargaining process where different groups have different stakes in the process.

An appeal to models, however, can serve the interests of elites who can use the language of the public interest to cloak their self-interests. When there is no good research to contradict the model, the appeal to the model becomes a strong argument unto itself. This then raises the question of what happens when new social science research emerges to challenge the reigning models that have become their own orthodoxy. The purpose of social science ought to be the provision of information useful to the debate over policy; not that it would necessarily drive the direction of policy. That ultimately is a political question. In theory then, data collected in accordance with rigorous scientific methodology should be apolitical. If anything social science would ideally remove politics and ideology from the policy process. Social science is supposed to generate definitive facts, that is, observable data, that are more or less value-free for use in the public decision-making arena. And yet, in the real world different interests will use this value-free data for their own purposes. Policymaking in the real world has less to do with formal techniques of rational problem solving as suggested in Lindblom's root model and more to do with the selective use of information by the different actors in the process based on how that information best serves their respective interests (Johnson 1994). Policy actors construct arguments to justify and persuade others, which may be based on data or anecdotal stories (Stone 2002). The link between research and action, then, is not as tight as an analytic model might suggest.

Although the idea that social science ought to be used for social action and social reform has a long-standing tradition in the social sciences, social scientists and policymakers often have different perspectives. Social scientists generally believe that the sole source for policy decisions should be the information derived from social science methodologies. Policymakers, however, tend to take social science information as only one source among many different and often competing sources of information. Social scientists and policymakers often do not share the same philosophical viewpoints. Moreover, the basic logic of social science and politics also differs. Social science rests on the logic of science, which is internal. Politics, however, rests on a logic which is external in that ideologies and outside pressure groups are also considered important. That is, in the former it is the experiment itself that produces results whereas in the latter it is the actors and what they bring to the bargaining table that produces results. Because the social scientist is wrapped up in theory, she/he has the luxury to think in terms of the idealized and perhaps well-reasoned general good. The policymaker, however, is more often than not, only interested in the specific needs of certain groups. This is because the policymaker's position is contingent on satisfying the interests of competing constituencies. Consequently social science ends up being only one of many forces attempting to influence policymakers in the decisions (Nelson et al. 1987).

If public policy isn't made on the face of social science, then how is it made? One model of policymaking is the garbage can model, in which the policy process is a garbage can and into it are dumped various problems and solutions by a variety of different actors. Moreover, the different actors themselves move in and out of the process. "The mix of garbage in a single can depend on the mix of cans available, on the labels attached to the alternative cans, on what garbage is currently being produced, and on the speed with which garbage is collected and removed from the scene" (Cohen et al. 1972, p. 2). As different people move in and out of the process they throw different ideas into the mix, in which case the outcome is affected not only by the mix within the can but by a host of variables outside the can, such as the types of pressures that different actors in the process are responding to. Among those things that can be dumped into the can is selected data.

Policy outcomes are the product of policy streams and political streams coming together when they are able to take advantage of new policy windows. John Kingdon (1995), for instance, refers to the garbage can as the policy primeval soup in which there is a mixture of policy and political communities, each of which creates the different streams. Policy communities tend to be composed of specialists in a given area who operate independently of political changes or pressure from voting constituents and interest groups. But they are also comprised of legislators and other public officials who do respond to political pressures whether it be from their constituents or interest groups that otherwise have a vested interest in the policy outcome. In the case of the minimum wage, the policy community would obviously include labor economists who either cling to the theoretical constructs of the model or those who have done considerable empirical work on the matter and are then in a position as a result of their work to generalize and make broader claims, that is, policy prescriptions. The minimum wage policy community would also be comprised of legislators both for and against, interest groups that have a stake in the outcome, and think tanks and academics that have been writing on this issue. Then there is the political stream, which is independent of a specific problem and is made up of things such as public mood, campaigns mounted by interest groups, recent election results, and ideological and party composition of legislative bodies and composition of the executive. In other words, the political stream is comprised of a variety of different factors that will influence how some in the policy community respond to a specific issue. New findings could certainly affect how some in the policy community will respond, but so too could the changing nature of the economy. It is when the policy and political streams are coupled, which usually occurs when a policy window opens—an opportunity that can really be taken advantage of—that policy is made.

New findings challenging a reigning orthodoxy do not mean that there will suddenly be new policy outcomes. There are still the same entrenched interests with a stake in maintaining the status quo. And yet, new findings can open a new policy window, thereby allowing the streams to mix. The Card and Krueger studies certainly gave ammunition to politicians who had long supported an increase in the minimum wage (Reich 1997). How much of an effect the new findings had on the debate is not entirely known, but it can be inferred that there were groups that felt that their interests were now threatened. That is, when an orthodoxy is challenged, it no longer provides policymakers the convenient hook upon which to hang their opposition. If anything, a weakening of an orthodoxy makes it all that more difficult to dodge the issue by deferring to the orthodoxy, especially in a policy process laden with interest groups. Now they are put in the uncomfortable positions of having to defend their positions and justify why they think that increasing the minimum wage would be a bad idea. If the argument that a minimum wage increase will have employment consequences is sufficiently weakened, a new justification will need to be found. The reigning orthodoxy does not have to be completely discredited; rather a sufficient weakening of it can pave the way for new research to form the basis of a more complete paradigm shift.

New data may not prove conclusively that a policy like the minimum wage is not completely without unintended consequences, but it does cast some doubt on the authority of the model that so far has appeared to be driving public policy. This should open up the door for policymakers who were previously afraid to explore the use of the minimum wage as a tool for achieving other societal objectives to experiment. Perhaps the new political economy, as exemplified by recent research on the minimum wage, demonstrates that instead of a reigning orthodoxy, we are really left with incomplete information, which is subject to interpretation. How that information is interpreted is then a function of how it can be put in the service of those interests that have a particular agenda (Levin-Waldman

2001; Schram 1995). Moreover, policymakers no longer enjoy the political cover that effectively absolved them of having to justify their position. Instead they have greater room to experiment because the glue that opponents of the minimum wage have used to hold them in place has effectively been broken. New research, then, has the value of furthering the democratic nature of the policymaking process by forcing policymakers, especially elected representatives, to justify their positions (Levin-Waldman 2004). This also opens up new possibilities because if policymakers no longer feel bound by the rigid orthodoxy that increases in the minimum wage will yield employment consequences, they now have opportunities to consider other policy goals for which the minimum wage might serve as a tool.

Conclusion

How, then, do we undo the tragedy of the commons? At the end of the day, unsettled findings allow each side of the debate to advance its interests. If there are studies demonstrating that minimum wage hikes are harmful, we are no longer forced to confront the larger question of why the market place fails to create decent paying jobs. If this data then suggests that the minimum wage population is inconsequential, the issue is effectively trivialized. Hence low-wage workers are at fault for the low wages they earn. But if we have data that shows that there really are no serious disemployment effects and that the minimum wage population is much larger than opponents would like us to believe, then the minimum wage is indeed a consequential issue for helping people. It has the potential to help people and perhaps correct certain pathologies. This requires looking more at the macro issues and less at the micro issues. Policymakers should be concerned with what is good for the economy as a whole, not just a narrow segment of the labor market. Of course, this may also entail revisiting our models based on observation in the real world. The nature of interest group politics demonstrates that there are interests that clearly understand this.

That there are unsettled findings also enables us to see that the issue is very subjective in that it reflects competing visions of what we want society to be. The minimum wage might ultimately speak to the type of wage structure we would like to achieve in society. In the *Wealth of Nations*, Adam Smith (1976) suggests that the wages that workers earn, especially relative to those of other countries, reflect the wealth and overall strength of the economy. A nation that pays its workers poorly may in part be symptomatic of a nation that stands still or is in decline. It is possible that Smith was merely commenting on appearances rather than the policy choices societies and their governments effectively make. But Smith also recognized that employers would collude with one another in efforts to drive down wages, in which case the forces of natural market place were really not in play.

In the next chapter I will argue that the minimum wage is anything but inconsequential. While not a silver bullet for addressing low wages, stagnating middle-class wages, and rising income inequality, the minimum wage has nonetheless been underrated. And yet, it speaks to the very meaning of what it means to talk about free markets and the type of society we wish to live in. What the data will show is not only the impact of wage contours but also the composition of the "effective" minimum wage labor market. When these two sets of data are juxtaposed together, there is a very powerful argument for the minimum wage as a tool for restoring the middle class.

Bibliography

Allegretto, Sylvia, Arindrajit Dube, and Michael Reich. 2011. Do Minimum Wages Really Reduce Teen Employment? Accounting for Heterogeneity and Selectivity in State Panel Data. *Industrial Relations* 50 (2): 205–240.

Belman, Dale, and Paul J. Wolfson. 2014. *What Does the Minimum Wage Do?* Kalamazoo: W.E. Upjohn Institute for Employment Research.

Braekkan, Kristian, and Victoria Sowa. 2015. Exploitation by Economic Necessity: Using the Marxist Conceptualization of Exploitation to Investigate the Impact of Workplace Violations. *Journal of Workplace Rights* 5: 1–10.

Brown, Christopher. 1992. Commodity Money, Credit, and the Real Balance Effect. *Journal of Post Keynesian Economics* 15 (1): 99–107.

Brown, Charles C. 1996. The Old Minimum-Wage Literature and Its Lessons for the New. In *The Effect of the Minimum Wage on Employment*, ed. Marvin H. Kosters. Washington, DC: AEI Press.

Brown, Charles, Curtis Gilroy, and Andrew Kohen. 1982. The Effects of the Minimum Wage on Employment and Unemployment. *Journal of Economic Literature* 20: 487–528.

Burkhauser, Richard V., and T. Aldrich Finegan. 1989. The Minimum Wage and the Poor: The End of a Relationship. *Journal of Policy Analysis and Management* 8 (1): 53–71.

Card, David, and Alan B. Krueger. 1995. *Myth and Measurement: The New Economics of the Minimum Wage*. Princeton: Princeton University Press.

———. 1998. A Reanalysis of the Effect of the New Jersey Minimum Wage Increase on the Fast-Food Industry with Representative Payroll Data. Working Paper No. 6386. National Bureau of Economic Research.

Cohen, Michael D., James G. March, and Johan P. Olsen. 1972. A Garbage Can Model of Organizational Change. *Administrative Science Quarterly* 17 (1): 1–25.

Congressional Budget Office. 2014. *The Effects of a Minimum Wage Increase on Employment and Family Income*. Congress of the United States, February. Downloaded from http://www.cbo.gov/publication/44995

Currie, Janet, and Bruce C. Fallick. 1996. The Minimum Wage and the Employment of Youth. *Journal of Human Resources* 31 (2): 404–428.

Dube, Arindrajit, Suresh Naidu, and Michael Reich. 2007. The Economic Effects of a Citywide Minimum Wage. *Industrial and Labor Relations Review* 60 (4): 522–523.

Dube, Arindrajit, T. William Lester, and Michael Reich. 2010. Minimum Wage Effects Among State Borders: Estimates Using Contiguous Counties. *The Review of Economics and Statistics* 92 (4): 945–964.

Dubofsky, Melvyn. 1994. *The State & Labor in Modern America*. Chapel Hill: The University of North Carolina Press.

Ehrenberg, Ronald G., and Robert S. Smith. 1997. *Modern Labor Economics: Theory and Public Policy*. 6th ed. Reading: Addison-Wesley.

Figart, Deborah M., Ellen Mutari, and Marilyn Power. 2002. *Living Wages, Equal Wages: Gender and Labor Market Policies in the United States*. London/New York: Routledge.

Finegold, David. 1998. Is the Fair Labor Standards Act Fair to Welfare Recipients? *Journal of Labor Research* 19 (2): 245–262.

Freeman, Alida Castillo, and Richard B. Freeman. 1991. Minimum Wages in Puerto Rico: Textbook Case of a Wage Floor? NBER Working Paper No. 3759, June.

Fried, Barbara H. 1998. *The Progressive Assault on Laissez Faire: Robert Hale and the First Law and Economic Movement*. Cambridge, MA: Harvard University Press.

Goldfield, Michael. 1987. *The Decline of Organized Labor in the United States*. Chicago: University of Chicago Press.

Gramlich, Edward M. 1976. Impact of Minimum Wages on Other Wages, Employment, and Family Incomes. *Brookings Papers on Economic Activity* 2: 409–451.

Hardin, Garret. 1968. The Tragedy of the Commons. *Science* 162 (3589): 1243–1248.

Heilbroner, Robert L., and William S. Millberg. 1995. *The Crisis of Vision in Modern Economic Thought*. Cambridge/New York: Cambridge University Press.

Houseman, Susan N. 1998. The Effects of Employer Mandates. In *Generating Jobs: How to Increase Demands for Less-Skilled Workers*, ed. Richard B. Freeman and Peter Gottschalk. New York: Russell Sage Foundation.

Johnson, Bob L. 1994. The Politics of Research-Information Use in the Education Policy Arena. *Education Policy* 13 (1): 23–36.

Katz, Michael B. 1989. *The Undeserving Poor: From the War on Poverty to the War on Welfare*. New York: Pantheon Books.

Katz, Lawrence, and Alan B. Krueger. 1992. The Effect of the Minimum Wage on the Fast-Food Industry. *Industrial and Labor Relations Review* 46 (1): 6–21.

Kaufman, Bruce E. 2003. John R. Commons and the Wisconsin School of Industrial Relations Strategy and Policy. *Industrial and Labor Relations Review* 57 (1): 3–30.

———. 2005. The Social Welfare Objectives and Ethical Principles of Industrial Relations. In *The Ethics of Human Resources and Industrial Relations*, ed. John W. Budd and James G. Scoville. Champaign: Labor and Employment Relations Association.

Kennan, John. 1995. The Elusive Effects of Minimum Wages. *Journal of Economic Literature* 33 (December): 1950–1965.

Kingdon, John W. 1995. *Agendas, Alternatives, and Public Policies*. New York: Addison-Wesley Longmn Inc.

Kosters, Marvin H., ed. 1996. *The Effects of the Minimum Wage on Employment*. Washington, DC: AEI Press.

Kosters, Marvin H., and Finis Welch. 1972. The Effects of Minimum Wages on the Distribution of Change in Aggregate Employment. *American Economic Review* 62 (3): 323–332.

Kuhn, Thomas S. 1970. *The Structure of Scientific Revolutions*. Chicago: University of Chicago Press.

Lang, Kevin, and Shulamit Kahn. 1998. The Effects of Minimum-Wage Laws on the Distribution of Employment: Theory and Evidence. *Journal of Public Economics* 69: 67–82.

Lester, Richard A. 1946. Shortcomings of Marginal Analysis for Wage-Employment Problems. *American Economic Review* 36 (1): 63–82.

———. 1947. Reflections on the 'Labor Monopoly' Issue. *Journal of Political Economy* 56 (6): 513–536.

Levin-Waldman, Oren M. 2000a. The Minimum Wage Can Be Raised: Lessons from the 1999 Levy Survey of Small Business. *Challenge* 43 (2): 86–96.

———. 2000b. The Rhetorical Evolution of the Minimum Wage. *Rhetoric & Public Affairs* 3 (2): 131–153.

———. 2000c. Minimum Wage and Justice? *Review of Social Economy* 58 (1): 43–62.

———. 2001. *The Case of the Minimum Wage: Competing Policy Models*. Albany: State University of New York Press.

———. 2003. The Minimum Wage and the Cause of Democracy. *Review of Social Economy* 61 (4): 487–510.

———. 2004. The Living Wage Movement: Its Significance to Urban Politics and Citizenship. *Perspectives on Work* 8 (1): 40–42.

———. 2009. The Minimum Wage and Competing Ethical Conceptions. *Advances in Industrial and Labor Relations* 16: 181–210.

———. 2011. *Wage Policy, Income Distribution, and Democratic Theory*. London/ New York: Routledge.

Lindblom, Charles E. 1959. The Science of Muddling Through. *Public Administration Review* 17: 79–88.

Meyer, Robert H., and David A. Wise. 1983. The Effect of the Minimum Wage on the Employment and Earnings of Youth. *Journal of Labor Economics* 1 (1): 66–100.

Michl, Thomas R. 2000. Can Rescheduling Explain the New Jersey Minimum Wage Studies? *Eastern Economic Journal* 26 (3): 265–276.

Minsky, Hyman P. 1986. *Stabilizing an Unstable Economy*. New Haven: Yale University Press.

Moody, Kim. 1988. *An Injury to All: The Decline of American Unionism*. London/ New York: Verso.

Nelson, Carnot E., Jeanne Roberts, Cynthia Maederer, Bruce Wertheimer, and Beverly Johnson. 1987. The Utilization of Social Science Information by Policymakers. *American Behaviorist Scientist* 30 (6): 569–577.

Neumark, David, and William Wascher. 1992. Employment Effects of Minimum and Subminimum Wages: Panel Data and State Minimum Wage Laws. *Industrial and Labor Relations Review* 46 (1): 55–81.

———. 2000. Minimum Wages and Employment: A Case Study of the Fast-Food Industry in New Jersey and Pennsylvania: Comment. *American Economic Review* 90 (5): 1362–1396.

Palley, Thomas. 1995. Labor Markets, Unemployment, and Minimum Wages: A New View. *Eastern Economic Journal* 21 (3): 319–326.

———. 1998. *Plenty of Nothing: The Downsizing of the American Dream and the Case for Structural Keynesianism*. Princeton: Princeton University Press.

Partridge, Mark D., and Janice S. Partridge. 1999. Do Minimum Wage Hikes Raise U.S. Long Term Unemployment? Evidence Using State Minimum Wage Rates. *Regional Studies* 33 (8): 713–726.

Piketty, Thomas. 2014. *Capital in the Twenty-First Century*. Cambridge, MA/ London: Belknap Press of Harvard University Press.

Prasch, Robert E. 1995. Toward a 'General Theory' of Market Exchange. *Journal of Economic Issues* 29 (3): 807–828.

Reich, Robert B. 1997. *Locked in the Cabinet*. New York: Alfred E. Knopf.

Reich, Michael. 2010. Minimum Wages in the United States: Politics, Economics, and Econometrics. In *Labor in the era of Globalization*, ed. Clair Brown, Barry Eichengreen, and Michael Reich. Cambridge/New York: Cambridge University Press.

Report of the Minimum Wage Study Commission. 1981. Vol. 1. Washington, DC: Government Printing Office.

Schmitt, John. 1996. *Cooked to Order*. American Prospect, pp 82–85, May–June.

Schneider, Anne, and Helen Ingram. 1993. Social Constructions and Target Populations: Implications for Politics and Policy. *American Political Science Review* 87 (2): 334–347.

Schram, Sanford F. 1995. *Words of Welfare: The Poverty of Social Sciences and the Social Science of Poverty*. Minneapolis: University of Minnesota Press.

Smith, Adam. 1976. In *An Inquiry into the Nature and Causes of the Wealth of Nations*, ed. Edwin Cannan. Chicago: University of Chicago Press.

Stigler, George. 1946. The Economics of Minimum Wage Legislation. *American Economic Review* 36 (June): 358–365.

———. 1986. The Goals of Economic Policy. In *The Essence of Stigler*, ed. Kurt Leube and Thomas Moore. Stanford: Hoover Institution Press.

Stone, Deborah. 2002. *Policy Paradox: The Art of Political Decision Making*. New York/London: W.W. Norton & Co.

Waltman, Jerold L. 2008. *Minimum Wage Policy in Great Britain and the United States*. New York: Algora Publishing.

Weber, Max. 1947. *The Theory of Social and Economic Organizations*. Trans. A.M. Henderson and Talcott Parsons. New York: Free Press of Glencoe.

Welch, Finis. 1974. Minimum Wage Legislation in the United States. *Economic Inquiry* 12 (3): 285–318.

———. 1978. *Minimum Wages: Issues and Evidence*. Washington, DC: American Enterprise Institute for Public Policy Research.

CHAPTER 3

Middle Class Welfare Effects

The argument that the minimum wage is beneficial rests on the assumption that the welfare effects are broader than simply raising incomes of the poor. In this chapter, I present data addressing three related issues: the data on the first demonstrates that there are wage contour effects to increases in the minimum wage, and that through these contour effects, a larger segment of the population will derive benefit from increases in the minimum wage. And the data on the second shows the demographics of what can be referred to as the "effective" minimum wage population—those earning in wage contours around the statutory minimum. Therefore, if the minimum wage labor market is constructed in terms of who earns around the minimum wage because we are viewing the minimum wage through the prism of contours, and if because of those contour effects the benefits accrue to a population larger than the "effective" minimum wage population, it then stands to reason that the minimum wage is indeed a middle-class issue. The data on the third, then, shows the effect of the minimum wage on income inequality, which is also related to the health of the middle class.

The biggest problem with the minimum wage debate to date is that it has been limited in scope. Much of the research, as we saw in the last chapter, has focused on a limited sub-segment of the labor market: those specifically earning the statutory minimum wage. And yet, if the statutory minimum wage can be viewed as a main reference point for wage setting

O. M. Levin-Waldman, *Restoring the Middle Class through Wage Policy*, Binzagr Institute for Sustainable Prosperity,
https://doi.org/10.1007/978-3-319-74448-3_3

in the larger low-wage labor market, the minimum wage assumes a larger dimension. The minimum wage then becomes about the "effective" minimum wage population, which is now comprised of low-wage workers who earn around the statutory minimum. But this can only be understood if we examine the minimum wage through the prism of wage contours: the intervals workers are earning in above the statutory minimum wage. Small businesses often claim that increases in the minimum wage will hurt them (Haarlander and Tan 2004). In other words, the genuinely political opposition would appear to be alluding to the effects of wage contours.

The 2014 CBO report appeared to allude to wage contour effects when it suggested that as many as 16 million Americans were going to see their pay, despite the fact that no more than 3.6 million hourly wage earners were getting paid at or below the statutory minimum wage. Clearly if only 3.6 million hourly workers were paid the statutory minimum, then the benefits were accruing to more than those earning the statutory minimum. It then had to follow that more than 12 million of these workers were earning wages in contours above the minimum. The implication appeared to be clear: an increase in the statutory minimum wage would force employers to raise the wages of their workers who weren't earning the statutory minimum, but who were earning around the minimum. Although the CBO report did not address itself to the issue of rising income inequality, much of the literature touting the possible welfare benefits of the minimum wage note that one benefit would at least be a decline in the rise in income inequality. Why is income inequality so critical to the discussion of larger benefits to the middle class? Because the growing gap between those at the bottom, mostly low-paid and low-skilled workers, and those at the top, mostly highly paid and highly skilled workers, speaks to a significant issue: the disappearance of the middle.

Wage Contours

The classic model of the wage contour was developed by John Dunlop (1957) to explain how a firm's internal wage structure might be as much affected by external forces as internal ones. Wage contours were to be defined as a group of workers with similar characteristics working in similar industries and earning similar wages. For each group there would be a group of rates surrounding a key rate and these key rates would be affected by changes in the key rate. Within an industry, the key rate would essentially be defined as any rate serving as the reference point for that industry. Since key rates were specific to industries, they could also vary from industry to industry. This would appear to imply that there is nothing natural about wage rates. On the contrary, wage rates are determined more by institutions than the so-called natural marketplace. But it also suggests that the minimum wage could be regarded as the key rate for what we commonly refer to as the low-wage sector, which means that a larger segment of the actual labor market is earning an "effective" minimum wage.

William Spriggs and Bruce Klein (1994) found that the minimum wage's greatest import was that it functioned as a reference point for wages around it. Despite changes in the statutory minimum wage, firms merely maintained their internal wage structures. In some cases there may have been employment consequences as a result of minimum wage increases, but these effects were not found to be significant. Rather firms simply viewed the minimum wage as a reference point for what starting wages should be. Which is to suggest that a statutory minimum wage at the current \$7.25 an hour would be a reference point for other firms in the low-wage industry—those opting to pay more than the statutory minimum wage. As a reference, then, they might opt to start their workers off at say \$8.50 an hour. Building on this construct, David Gordon (1996) later argued that a decline in the real value of the minimum wage would also affect those earning in between the point where the statutory minimum wage used to be and where it was at the end of the dip. Therefore, an increase in the minimum wage might lead to an upward pressure on wages because employers would feel compelled to pay higher wages even to those earning the statutory minimum (pp. 214–215).

The real importance of the minimum wage, then, lies in its impact on wages from the statutory minimum to some point above. Moreover, one would not be able to begin accurately measuring the size of the minimum wage population until the minimum wage was looked at in real terms rather than statutory terms. This, of course, would imply that as the statutory minimum wage increases, so too would the starting wages in other firms within the industry, thereby shifting upward the general wage structure. Using a wage contour construct similar to Spriggs and Klein (1994), Deborah Figart and June Lapidus (1995) estimated that an increase in the minimum wage from \$4.35 to \$4.75 during the 1990s would then have resulted in an increase in women's average wages from \$9.79 to \$10.00, although the effects of those earning less than the previous average would have been larger.

More recently, the issue of contours has been looked at from a more empirical standpoint. David Neumark et al. (2004) did acknowledge that the minimum wage might have wage contour effects, particularly for those earning immediately above the minimum wage. They concluded the effects of the minimum wage for those throughout the distribution to be negative because low-wage workers were bound to be hurt through a reduction in hours. Still, the fact remains that as workers' wages fall into wage ranges or contours, a shift in one will result in a shift in others. Looking at state minimum wages from 1960 to 2000, Thomas Volscho (2005) estimated that each $0.81 increase in the minimum wage would result in a 35.5 percent reduction in the Gini coefficient ceteris paribus. Moreover, state wages on average had the effect of reducing the degree of income concentration in the top quintile, thereby lending support to the "ripple effect," or what we might otherwise refer to as wage contours.

In earlier work (2010), using data from the Integrated Public Use Microdata Series-Current Population Survey (IPUMS-CPS) from 1962 to 2008, I constructed ten wage contours. The first contour in each year ranged from the statutory minimum wage to 25 percent above. Each successive contour ranged an additional 25 percent. During this period, median wages in each contour increased in years when there was an increase in the federal minimum wage. In years when there was no increase, median wages remained unchanged for the most part. These trends alone suggest wage contour effects, and that the reach of the minimum wage extends far beyond the sub-market that actually earns the statutory minimum wage. Arguably there may be other factors to explain increases in median wages, especially in the upper contours, but whatever those factors may be they appear to be noticeably absent in those years when there was no increase in the minimum wage.

According to these earlier findings, beginning in 1964 more than 57 percent of the labor market was earning through the ten contours and in 2008 more than 70 percent were earning through the ten contours. Although there was fluctuation, the share of workers earning at the bottom—the first three contours—was around 20 percent, which is by no means an insignificant share of the labor market. This certainly is consistent with estimates that by any reasonable definition that close to a quarter of the American labor market is low wage. In 2005, the incidence of low-wage work was 25 percent in the USA; 22.1 percent in the UK; 20.8 percent in Germany; 18.2 percent in the Netherlands; 12.7 percent in France; and 8.5 percent in Denmark. To the extent that median wages in all ten contours were rising following increases in the statutory minimum wage, 62.8 percent of the labor market was seeing their wages rise during this 46-year period. Between the 1960s and the 2000s, the percentage of the labor force earning through these contours increased by 32.1 percent (Solow 2008). There might be two ways to interpret this. One is that wages, in absolute terms, did creep up, as evidenced by the shrinkage in the first two contours and the increase in the eighth through the tenth contours. The other is that more people earning in the top two contours may be a function of fewer people earning above those contours, which might also be indicative of stagnant wages.

The neoclassical model, of course, touting the expected disemployment effects of increases in the minimum wage, would posit that those most likely to be adversely affected will be low-wage workers. As the most vulnerable group, low-wage workers—those in the bottom contour—are most likely to be unemployed than those in the middle and the top. In both non-minimum and minimum wage years, unemployment was higher among the bottom contour than among the middle and the top contour for the exception of the 1970s. Unemployment in the bottom contour was generally higher in non-minimum wage years than in minimum wage years. In other words, the data for the 46-year period appears to contradict the effects predicted by the neoclassical model. With few exceptions, most notably during the 1970s when the nation was plunged into recession, the unemployment rate tended to be lower in those years when the minimum wage was increased than in those years preceding an increase. The same pattern held true for low-wage workers in the bottom contour. Moreover, unemployment among the bottom contour tended to be lower than in all ten contours. This would seem to be counterintuitive because we would expect unemployment to be higher among those with lower educational attainment.

The conventional wisdom has long argued that the absence of employment consequences would most likely have been due to the new minimum wage rates still being considerably lower than market-clearing rates. Raising the minimum wage beyond a certain point—the tipping point—could still have adverse consequences (Freeman and Freeman 1991; Gordon 1995). Even Card and Krueger (1995) acknowledged that there was a tipping point, but that if there were no observed employment consequences it was most likely because minimum wage increases, where they occurred, had not reached that point. Intuitively, however, especially given the language of tipping points, one would expect that following large percentage increases in the minimum wage for there to have been increases in unemployment due to disemployment effects.

It should be recalled that predicting unemployment the neoclassical model is focused exclusively on demand-side effects—the impact that an increase will have on an employer's demand for labor. It does not pay nearly as much attention to supply-side effects—the impact that an increase will have on labor seeking to enter the labor market and find jobs. Relative to employment, unemployment may be lower because minimum wage increases have attracted more workers into the labor market. Neoclassical theory, however, calls this scenario into question on the assumption that fewer jobs available because of disemployment effects due to increases will result in higher unemployment as more workers, that is, those just attracted into the labor market, chase those fewer jobs. The plausibility of the neoclassical assumption in the USA lies in how unemployment is officially defined: individuals who recently filed a claim for unemployment insurance and/or were actively looking for a job in the last four weeks. And yet, if we were to focus on demand-side effects in terms of the demand for goods and services, a higher wage resulting in more purchasing power will ultimately lead to greater employment. The focus on demand-side effects usually focuses on employers' demand for workers rather than the macroeconomic demand for goods and services that higher wages will generate more of.

During the 46-year period unemployment could have risen in particular years because of downturns in the business cycle. Unemployment during this overall period increased. That it fluctuated during this period means that it cannot be stated with any certainty that there are adverse employment consequences. To the extent that unemployment was lower in years that the minimum wage was increased than in years that it was not, it would appear that these increases really had no effect on employment. And this was particularly true in the bottom contour among those workers we would expect to bear the greatest brunt of the increases. This data, however, did not measure changes that might have a greater impact on employment than wage rates. Nevertheless, I did test the effects on employment by conducting a logistical regression analysis. With each variable set to a value of 1 or 0, the minimum wage variable was set to a value of 1 in each contour if it exceeded the median hourly wage of that contour in a given year. These regressions were only done for each year that there was an increase in the minimum wage. As the question was which factors were more likely to result in an individual being unemployed, it made sense to test for the effects of having low educational attainment—with less than a 12th grade education—gender, race, age—specifically the 18–24 age cohort—and being in the bottom contour (first two). I also tested for the effects of years when there was a recession, either for the whole year or part of it.

In most cases, the minimum wage variable was not statistically significant. Both during the 1960s and the 1970s the minimum wage was not statistically significant. During the 1980s where it was statistically significant, there was a very negative effect that those earning a wage higher than the median wage of the first contour were more likely to be unemployed. During the 1990s, where it was again statistically significant, the effect, although positive, was small relative to the other variables. During the 2000s, the positive effect of the minimum wage variable was smaller than during the 1990s, but it was statistically significant. On one level, these findings may be irrelevant because the objective of economic analysis ought to be to provide policymakers with information that they can in turn use to make policy decisions. The data is certainly ambiguous enough that there is sufficient wiggle room for policy experimentation. Given that much of economic policy has centered around the assumption that growth will more likely occur when there is less regulation and less wage rigidity, these data would appear to suggest an alternative. That is, economic growth may occur when more attention is paid to wage rates and the impact that changes in wage rates at the bottom may have on wage rates throughout the distribution.

In the pages that follow, I look at the wage contour effects from 2002 to 2015 on the basis of data from the IPUMS-CPS. This time period is significant for a variety of reasons. First, at the federal level, with the exception of 2007–2009, the federal minimum wage had not increased. The three-stage increase that began in 2007, which brought the minimum up to its current $7.25 an hour level, was due largely to a political sea change in Congress following the 2006 midterm congressional elections. The Democrats took control of both chambers of Congress, which they had not had since the 1994 midterm election, and passed an increase in the minimum wage as part of its first 100 days—a throwback to the first 100 days of the New Deal in 1933. Second, many states during this period, especially following the 2008 election, either increased existing state minimum wages or passed them for the first time. This too was significant because it was a response to the failure of the federal minimum wage to keep up.

Building on this earlier work, Table 3.1 shows the contour distribution from 2002 to 2015. As was the case earlier, the first contour begins with the statutory minimum wage in each year and ranges to 25 percent above. Each successive contour ranges an additional 25 percent.

From 2002 until 2015, median wages in ten contours increased during those years that the minimum wage increased and remained flat during those years that the minimum wage did not. That there were no increases in median wages during those years when there was no increase in the minimum wage, and there were long periods of time when there were no increases in the minimum wage, suggests that wage stagnation may be attributable to the failure of the minimum wage to keep up. Moreover, increasing median wages through all ten contours suggests middle-class welfare benefits, especially when somebody earning at the top of the tenth contour in 2015 was earning around $124,000 a year. These ten contours also comprised close to 70 percent of the labor market. Again it is possible that the median wages in the upper contours could have been increasing due to other factors, but the question nonetheless remains as to why the median wages in those upper contours do not increase during years that there is no increase in the statutory minimum wage.

The drawback to this approach is that we do not really know how firms respond to minimum wage increases. These observations would lend themselves to the following hypothesis: When firms are compelled to raise the minimum wages of those at the very bottom, they will feel compelled to raise the wages of those workers in the contour immediately above. But they might also feel compelled to raise the wages of those in a third contour if they felt compelled to raise the wages in the second contour following the minimum wage increase. Depending on how high and tight the wage structure goes in a firm, it is not too difficult to see how they might feel compelled to increase the wages of those throughout the wage structure in their firms. Still, this doesn't address the question of why the wages in other firms may also be rising.

We would have to assume that in most firms that hire low-wage workers, the wage structure, for the exception of a few managers, is most likely not going to reach the tenth contour, if it goes much above the fifth or sixth. Does this mean that we are seeing some type of spillover effect? Do workers who see workers in another industry getting raises in turn demand wages for themselves? And if they do, and their respective wage structures begin at a higher point, does that mean we will see the contour effects in those industries as well? These trends do lend themselves to the

Table 3.1 Wage contours: 2002–2015

	MW	*1st*	*2nd*	*3rd*	*4th*	*5th*	*6th*	*7th*	*8th*	*9th*	*10th*
Year											
2002	$5.15	$5.77	$7.21	$9.13	$11.54	$14.42	$17.31	$22.16	$27.40	$33.65	$40.87
2003	$5.15	$5.77	$7.21	$9.13	$11.54	$14.42	$17.62	$22.16	$27.40	$33.65	$40.87
2004	$5.15	$5.77	$7.21	$9.13	$11.54	$14.42	$17.79	$22.17	$27.40	$33.65	$40.87
2005	$5.15	$5.77	$7.21	$9.19	$11.53	$14.42	$17.62	$22.12	$27.40	$33.65	$41.35
2006	$5.15	$5.77	$7.21	$9.23	$11.54	$14.42	$17.69	$22.12	$27.40	$33.65	$40.87
2007	$5.85	$6.97	$8.50	$10.10	$12.50	$15.87	$19.71	$24.04	$31.25	$38.46	$48.08
2008	$6.55	$7.21	$9.62	$11.92	$14.42	$17.79	$22.36	$27.88	$34.62	$44.23	$55.29
2009	$7.25	$8.17	$10.00	$12.50	$15.55	$19.28	$24.04	$30.77	$38.46	$48.08	$60.10
2010	$7.25	$8.17	$9.86	$12.46	$15.63	$19.23	$24.04	$30.77	$38.46	$48.08	$60.10
2011	$7.25	$8.17	$9.62	$12.50	$15.39	$19.23	$24.04	$30.77	$38.46	$48.08	$60.10
2012	$7.25	$8.17	$9.86	$12.50	$15.75	$19.42	$24.04	$30.77	$38.46	$48.08	$60.10
2013	$7.25	$8.17	$10.00	$12.02	$15.63	$19.23	$24.04	$30.77	$38.46	$48.08	$60.10
2014	$7.25	$8.17	$9.86	$12.26	$15.38	$19.23	$24.04	$30.77	$38.46	$48.08	$60.10
2015	$7.25	$8.17	$9.62	$12.26	$15.38	$19.23	$24.04	$30.77	$38.46	$48.08	$60.10

development of new theories of wage setting, which extend beyond the standard neoclassical model of competitive markets. What it might suggest is a similarity to some of the literature on the impact of unionized firms on nonunionized firms.

Union wages can influence nonunion wages in the following ways: nonunion firms may raise their workers' pay in order to reduce the probability of union organizing. Nonunionized firms may raise their wages to deter their workers from unionizing or leaving for unionized jobs. If union wage gains lead to a cutback in union employment, then unions may cause a large supply of labor to the nonunion sector, which is the "crowding effect," in which case nonunion workers' wages would go down, and high union wages may attract some currently nonunion workers who may be willing to be unemployed while waiting for a union job opening, in which case the effect would be to raise the nonunion wage. Because unions raise lower-paid workers' wages the most, lower-paid nonunion workers might in the absence of any reaction by their employers anticipate the greatest gains from unionizing. If unions are able to negotiate greater wage increases for those with less human capital, nonunion firms might then be able to more effectively deter unionizing activity by flattening their pay structure than would otherwise be the case. Since the unions reduce dispersion among their members, union spillovers affect the wage dispersion of nonunion workers (Kahn and Curme 1987). Nonunion firms may raise wages so as not to lose workers to higher-paying firms. In other words, union wages effectively create efficiency wages in the nonunion sector. It would similarly have to follow that firms paying above the minimum wage would also feel compelled to raise their wages following a minimum wage increase in order to prevent them from leaving for firms paying the new minimum.

The critic will naturally assert that the data from the CPS does not really prove wage contour effects because it is individual-level data. All it is telling us is that individual workers' median wages rose in each contour as minimum wages increased. In other words, it does not tell us anything about how firms behave in response to increases in the minimum wage. At the same time, studies claiming disemployment effects using CPS data also do not really tell us anything about how firms behave. Also overall national trends may be masking what is happening in individual states. A look at individual states that have raised their own respective minimum wages above the federal minimum wage in recent years may actually be quite instructive. Table 3.2 shows these trends in several states that have higher minimum wages than the federal and have taken steps in recent years to keep increasing their minimum wages. All the states in Table 3.2, with the

Table 3.2 Wage contours by states

	MW	*1st*	*2nd*	*3rd*	*4th*	*5th*	*6th*	*7th*	*8th*	*9th*	*10th*
California											
2002	$6.75	$7.35	$9.62	$12.02	$14.42	$18.27	$23.56	$28.85	$36.06	$45.03	$56.49
2003	$6.75	$7.50	$9.62	$12.02	$14.42	$18.27	$23.08	$28.85	$36.06	$45.67	$55.77
2004	$6.75	$7.45	$9.62	$12.02	$14.42	$18.75	$23.08	$28.85	$35.58	$45.29	$57.69
2005	$6.75	$7.50	$9.62	$12.02	$14.42	$18.39	$23.08	$28.85	$36.06	$45.55	$57.69
2006	$6.75	$7.21	$9.62	$12.02	$14.42	$18.75	$23.20	$28.85	$36.06	$45.67	$57.54
2007	$7.50	$8.41	$10.10	$13.46	$16.83	$20.16	$24.04	$31.25	$38.46	$48.08	$60.10
2008	$8.00	$9.38	$11.54	$14.42	$17.44	$22.60	$27.88	$33.65	$40.87	$50.96	$67.31
2009	$8.00	$9.13	$11.54	$14.42	$17.31	$22.60	$27.88	$33.65	$40.87	$50.48	$67.31
2010	$8.00	$9.23	$11.54	$14.42	$17.79	$22.12	$27.88	$33.65	$41.35	$50.48	$69.23
2011	$8.00	$9.13	$11.54	$14.42	$17.79	$22.12	$27.88	$33.65	$40.87	$50.48	$67.31
2012	$8.00	$9.23	$11.54	$14.42	$17.79	$22.12	$27.88	$33.65	$40.87	$50.48	$69.71
2013	$8.00	$9.13	$11.54	$14.42	$17.31	$22.12	$27.88	$33.65	$41.35	$51.92	$67.31
2014	$8.00	$9.13	$11.54	$14.42	$18.03	$22.12	$28.85	$33.65	$40.87	$51.92	$67.31
2015	$9.00	$9.62	$12.02	$15.38	$19.23	$24.04	$31.24	$38.46	$48.08	$57.69	$72.12
Connecticut											
2002	$6.70	$7.21	$9.62	$12.02	$14.42	$18.27	$23.08	$28.85	$35.10	$44.71	$59.93
2003	$6.90	$7.50	$9.21	$12.02	$15.14	$19.23	$24.04	$28.85	$36.06	$47.42	$57.69
2004	$7.10	$7.69	$9.83	$12.50	$15.38	$19.23	$24.04	$29.81	$37.50	$48.08	$57.69
2005	$7.10	$7.69	$9.62	$12.50	$15.38	$19.50	$24.52	$30.29	$37.50	$47.12	$57.76
2006	$7.40	$8.46	$10.32	$13.05	$16.83	$20.24	$25.00	$31.25	$38.94	$48.08	$62.50
2007	$7.65	$8.46	$10.58	$13.46	$16.83	$20.67	$25.48	$33.65	$39.90	$48.08	$60.10
2008	$7.65	$8.49	$10.58	$13.46	$16.83	$20.67	$25.00	$33.65	$39.90	$499.04	$62.50
2009	$8.00	$9.38	$11.54	$14.42	$17.50	$22.60	$27.40	$33.65	$40.87	$50.48	$67.31
2010	$8.25	$9.61	$12.02	$14.42	$17.79	$23.08	$28.85	$34.13	$41.59	$51.56	$67.31
2011	$8.25	$9.62	$12.02	$14.42	$18.25	$23.08	$28.85	$34.62	$40.87	$50.48	$65.87

(*continued*)

Table 3.2 (continued)

	MW	*1st*	*2nd*	*3rd*	*4th*	*5th*	*6th*	*7th*	*8th*	*9th*	*10th*
2012	$8.25	$9.62	$11.94	$14.42	$18.25	$23.08	$28.85	$34.62	$40.87	$50.48	$65.87
2013	$8.25	$9.62	$11.54	$14.42	$18.17	$23.08	$28.85	$34.62	$40.87	$50.48	$67.31
2014	$8.70	$9.62	$12.02	$14.90	$19.23	$24.04	$29.69	$34.06	$47.12	$47.12	$72.12
2015	$9.15	$9.62	$12.50	$15.87	$19.23	$25.00	$31.24	$39.09	$48.08	$59.86	$72.12
Massachusetts											
2002	$6.75	$7.50	$9.62	$12.02	$14.42	$18.27	$24.04	$30.77	$38.46	$48.08	$57.69
2003	$6.75	$7.59	$9.62	$12.02	$14.42	$18.75	$24.04	$30.05	$36.49	$48.08	$58.28
2004	$6.75	$7.25	$9.62	$12.02	$14.42	$18.75	$24.04	$30.29	$38.46	$48.08	$57.93
2005	$6.75	$7.50	$9.62	$12.02	$14.42	$18.75	$24.04	$29.81	$38.46	$48.08	$57.69
2006	$6.75	$7.50	$9.62	$12.02	$14.42	$18.75	$24.04	$30.29	$38.46	$48.08	$59.33
2007	$7.50	$8.65	$10.10	$13.46	$16.83	$20.19	$24.04	$31.25	$39.90	$48.08	
2008	$8.00	$9.37	$11.54	$14.42	$18.10	$22.12	$27.40	$34.13	$47.79	$51.44	$68.51
2009	$8.00	$9.62	$12.00	$14.42	$18.27	$22.50	$27.88	$33.65	$40.87	$52.00	$67.31
2010	$8.00	$9.13	$11.54	$14.42	$18.27	$22.46	$26.92	$33.65	$40.87	$51.44	$67.31
2011	$8.00	$9.62	$11.54	$14.42	$17.79	$21.75	$27.89	$33.65	$40.87	$49.04	$67.31
2012	$8.00	$9.38	$11.54	$14.42	$18.27	$22.60	$27.40	$33.65	$40.87	$50.47	$67.79
2013	$8.00	$9.13	$11.54	$14.42	$17.79	$22.60	$27.40	$33.65	$40.87	$50.48	$67.31
2014	$8.00	$9.24	$11.54	$14.42	$17.31	$22.12	$27.88	$33.65	$40.87	$52.88	$67.31
2015	$9.00	$9.62	$12.02	$15.84	$19.81	$24.04	$31.25	$38.46	$48.08	$57.69	$72.12
New Jersey											
2002	$5.15	$5.77	$7.21	$9.13	$11.54	$14.42	$17.78	$21.83	$27.50	$33.65	$41.56
2003	$5.15	$5.77	$7.21	$9.38	$11.54	$14.42	$17.78	$22.60	$27.88	$34.13	$41.10
2004	$5.15	$5.77	$7.21	$9.23	$11.88	$14.42	$17.88	$22.07	$27.88	$33.65	$41.71
2005	$6.15	$7.00	$8.65	$10.43	$13.46	$16.83	$20.19	$26.35	$33.65	$39.90	$48.08
2006	$7.15	$7.69	$10.00	$12.02	$15.38	$19.71	$24.04	$30.29	$37.50	$48.08	$58.89
2007	$7.15	$7.69	$9.86	$12.02	$15.39	$19.23	$24.04	$30.07	$38.46	$48.08	$57.69
2008	$7.15	$7.69	$9.62	$12.02	$15.49	$20.19	$24.04	$29.81	$37.21	$48.08	$57.81
2009	$7.25	$8.17	$10.00	$12.02	$15.87	$19.71	$24.04	$30.77	$38.46	$48.08	$60.10

2010	$7.25	$8.17	$9.62	$12.02	$15.38	$19.71	$24.52	$31.25	$38.46	$48.08	$60.10
2011	$7.25	$8.17	$10.00	$12.26	$15.38	$19.23	$24.04	$30.14	$38.46	$48.08	$60.10
2012	$7.25	$8.17	$9.62	$12.50	$15.61	$19.23	$24.04	$31.25	$38.46	$48.08	$60.10
2013	$7.25	$8.17	$9.62	$12.02	$15.39	$19.71	$24.04	$30.53	$37.50	$48.08	$60.10
2014	$8.25	$9.62	$12.02	$14.42	$17.78	$22.84	$28.85	$35.58	$45.67	$55.29	$67.31
2015	$8.38	$9.62	$12.02	$14.42	$18.75	$24.04	$28.84	$36.06	$43.75	$57.69	$70.05
New York											
2002	$5.15	$5.77	$7.21	$9.13	$11.54	$14.42	$17.43	$22.12	$27.88	$33.62	$41.83
2003	$5.15	$5.77	$7.21	$9.34	$11.54	$14.42	$17.73	$21.84	$27.88	$33.62	$41.88
2004	$5.15	$5.77	$7.21	$9.13	$11.54	$14.42	$17.79	$22.12	$27.64	$33.62	$40.87
2005	$6.00	$6.90	$8.65	$10.10	$13.41	$16.83	$20.19	$24.52	$31.25	$38.46	$48.08
2006	$6.75	$7.50	$9.62	$12.02	$14.42	$18.75	$23.56	$28.85	$36.06	$45.67	$57.69
2007	$7.15	$7.69	$9.62	$12.50	$15.47	$19.23	$24.04	$29.81	$36.90	$48.08	$58.70
2008	$7.15	$7.69	$9.62	$12.02	$15.38	$19.23	$24.04	$29.81	$37.50	$48.08	$60.10
2009	$7.25	$8.17	$9.66	$12.50	$15.38	$19.77	$24.04	$30.05	$38.46	$48.08	$60.10
2010	$7.25	$8.41	$9.62	$12.50	$15.38	$19.23	$24.04	$30.84	$38.46	$48.08	$60.10
2011	$7.25	$8.21	$9.62	$12.02	$15.37	$19.22	$24.04	$30.84	$38.46	$48.08	$60.10
2012	$7.25	$8.25	$9.62	$12.02	$15.37	$19.71	$24.04	$30.77	$38.46	$48.08	$57.93
2013	$7.25	$8.22	$10.00	$12.21	$15.37	$19.30	$24.04	$31.25	$38.46	$48.08	$60.10
2014	$8.00	$9.62	$11.54	$14.42	$18.00	$22.84	$27.40	$33.65	$40.87	$50.00	$67.31
2015	$8.75	$9.62	$12.02	$15.38	$19.23	$24.04	$28.85	$36.06	$40.08	$57.69	$72.12
Ohio											
2002	$5.15	$5.77	$7.21	$9.13	$11.54	$14.42	$17.31	$22.12	$27.40	$33.65	$42.31
2003	$5.15	$5.77	$7.21	$9.13	$11.54	$14.42	$17.71	$21.84	$26.92	$33.65	$40.87
2004	$5.15	$5.77	$7.21	$9.13	$11.54	$14.42	$17.78	$22.12	$27.40	$33.65	$40.87
2005	$5.15	$5.77	$7.21	$9.13	$11.54	$14.42	$17.31	$22.47	$27.40	$33.65	$40.87
2006	$5.15	$5.77	$7.21	$9.10	$11.54	$14.42	$17.45	$20.60	$27.40	$33.65	$41.83
2007	$6.85	$7.50	$9.62	$!2.02	$14.42	$18.75	$24.04	$28.85	$36.06	$44.95	$55.29
2008	$7.00	$7.69	$9.62	$12.02	$15.17	$19.23	$24.04	$29.33	$36.54	$46.25	$58.90

(continued)

Table 3.2 (continued)

	MW	*1st*	*2nd*	*3rd*	*4th*	*5th*	*6th*	*7th*	*8th*	*9th*	*10th*
2009	$7.30	$8.17	$10.58	$13.46	$16.83	$20.46	$25.96	$33.66	$40.38	$48.08	$62.50
2010	$7.30	$8.17	$10.10	$12.50	$16.83	$20.19	$25.48	$31.25	$39.00	$45.67	$59.87
2011	$7.40	$8.48	$10.05	$13.46	$16.59	$20.10	$24.75	$31.25	$38.46	$50.24	$57.69
2012	$7.70	$9.13	$11.48	$13.94	$16.83	$21.15	$26.44	$33.65	$40.87	$48.08	$62.50
2013	$7.85	$9.00	$11.54	$13.94	$16.83	$20.67	$26.44	$33.65	$40.63	$48.20	$62.50
2014	$7.95	$9.14	$11.06	$14.42	$17.79	$22.12	$27.88	$33.65	$41.35	$52.88	$62.50
2015	$8.15	$9.62	$11.54	$14.42	$17.79	$22.12	$27.60	$34.13	$44.23	$54.33	$68.27
Oregon											
2002	$6.50	$7.22	$9.13	$11.54	$14.42	$17.79	$22.02	$26.90	$35.05	$43.25	$54.81
2003	$6.90	$7.55	$9.62	$12.02	$15.38	$19.23	$23.80	$28.85	$36.06	$47.60	$59.62
2004	$7.05	$7.93	$9.62	$12.02	$15.38	$19.23	$24.80	$28.85	$36.15	$48.08	$57.69
2005	$7.25	$8.17	$10.10	$12.02	$15.48	$19.71	$24.28	$29.80	$37.50	$47.36	$60.10
2006	$7.50	$8.41	$10.58	$12.98	$16.83	$20.19	$25.00	$30.14	$38.46	$48.08	$62.50
2007	$7.80	$9.13	$11.54	$13.94	$16.83	$21.51	$26.44	$33.65	$40.87	$48.08	$67.31
2008	$7.95	$9.13	$11.66	$14.42	$17.79	$22.12	$26.92	$33.89	$41.59	$50.24	$67.31
2009	$8.40	$9.62	$11.71	$14.42	$18.27	$23.08	$28.85	$36.54	$44.20	$57.69	$68.85
2010	$8.40	$9.62	$11.71	$14.42	$18.27	$23.08	$28.70	$36.06	$43.27	$55.90	$67.31
2011	$8.80	$9.62	$12.02	$14.42	$18.27	$23.65	$28.85	$36.06	$44.23	$57.69	$71.63
2012	$8.80	$9.62	$12.02	$15.38	$19.23	$24.04	$28.85	$38.08	$45.67	$57.69	$72.12
2013	$8.95	$9.80	$12.50	$15.38	$19.23	$24.04	$30.66	$36.54	$48.08	$57.87	$72.12
2014	$9.10	$10.00	$12.50	$15.38	$20.19	$24.04	$31.25	$39.21	$48.08	$60.10	$72.12
2015	$9.25	$10.44	$13.46	$16.35	$19.23	$24.52	$31.25	$38.46	$48.08	$57.69	$72.12

Pennsylvania											
2002	$5.15	$5.77		$9.13	$11.54	$14.24	$17.31	$22.12	$27.76	$33.65	$41.35
2003	$5.15	$5.77	$7.21	$9.13	$11.54	$14.42	$17.31	$22.12	$27.16	$33.65	$41.08
2004	$5.15	$5.77	$7.21	$9.13	$11.54	$14.42	$17.45	$22.12	$26.92	$33.65	$40.97
2005	$5.15	$5.77	$7.21	$9.13	$11.54	$14.42	$17.79	$22.60	$27.40	$33.65	$41.35
2006	$5.15	$5.77	$7.21	$9.57	$11.54	$14.42	$17.48	$22.12	$27.40	$33.60	$40.87
2007	$6.75	$6.69	$9.62	$12.02	$14.42	$18.27	$23.08	$28.85	$35.10	$45.68	$57.69
2008	$7.15	$8.08	$10.10	$12.15	$15.38	$19.23	$24.04	$30.77	$38.46	$48.08	$60.10
2009	$7.25	$8.17	$10.10	$12.50	$15.48	$19.71	$24.04	$30.49	$37.50	$48.08	$62.50
2010	$7.25	$8.17	$10.10	$12.02	$15.63	$19.71	$24.04	$30.29	$38.46	$48.08	$61.78
2011	$7.25	$8.17	$9.64	$12.50	$15.38	$19.95	$24.04	$30.29	$37.98	$48.08	$58.17
2012	$7.25	$8.36	$9.62	$12.50	$15.77	$12.23	$24.04	$30.29	$37.98	$47.55	$57.69
2013	$7.25	$8.41	$10.00	$12.26	$15.38	$19.2	$24.04	$30.58	$38.46	$48.08	$60.10
2014	$7.25	$8.17	$10.00	$12.88	$15.38	$19.71	$24.80	$31.25	$38.36	$48.08	$57.69
2015	$7.25	$8.17	$10.10	$12.50	$15.58	$19.23	$24.52	$30.77	$38.46	$48.08	$59.62
Rhode Island											
2002	$6.15	$7.21	$8.65	$10.34	$13.46	$16.83	$20.67	$25.96	$32.50	$40.87	$48.08
2003	$6.15	$7.06	$8.65	$10.19	$13.46	$16.83	$20.27	$25.96	$33.03	$38.94	$48.08
2004	$6.75	$7.45	$9.62	$12.00	$14.42	$18.27	$23.08	$28.85	$36.06	$47.12	$54.84
2005	$6.75	$7.40	$9.62	$12.02	$14.42	$18.75	$23.08	$28.85	$36.06	$43.27	$54.33
2006	$7.10	$7.69	$9.71	$12.02	$15.38	$19.23	$24.04	$30.77	$38.46	$47.12	$57.69
2007	$7.40	$8.41	$10.10	$13.46	$16.83	$19.71	$25.00	$31.25	$38.46	$48.08	$58.65
2008	$7.40	$8.22	$10.10	$13.46	$16.83	$20.00	$24.52	$30.77	$38.46	$48.08	$58.65
2009	$7.40	$8.45	$10.58	$12.98	$16.35	$19.71	$25.00	$31.25	$38.46	$48.08	61.54
2010	$7.40	$8.17	$10.58	$12.98	$16.83	$19.59	$25.00	$31.25	$38.46	$48.08	$60.10
2011	$7.40	$8.65	$10.10	$12.98	$16.83	$19.23	$24.42	$31.73	$38.46	$48.08	$57.59
2012	$7.40	$8.20	$10.10	$13.46	$16.83	$19.23	$24.42	$31.73	$38.46	$48.08	$60.10
2013	$7.75	$9.13	$11.54	$14.19	$16.83	$20.67	$26.44	$33.65	$40.87	$49.22	$71.15
2014	$8.00	$9.13	$11.54	$14.42	$17.31	$22.12	$27.88	$33.65	$40.93	$57.88	$65.87
2015	$9.00	$9.62	$12.02	$15.78	$19.23	$24.04	$31.25	$37.50	$48.08	$60.10	$72.12

(*continued*)

Table 3.2 (continued)

	MW	*1st*	*2nd*	*3rd*	*4th*	*5th*	*6th*	*7th*	*8th*	*9th*	*10th*
Vermont											
2002	$6.25	$7.21	$9.13	$11.54	$13.94	$16.83	$21.08	$26.44	$33.17	$40.87	$58.48
2003	$6.25	$7.21	$9.13	$11.54	$13.94	$16.83	$20.19	$26.44	$33.17	$40.87	$52.88
2004	$6.75	$7.69	$9.62	$12.02	$14.42	$18.75	$23.08	$28.85	$35.10	$44.23	$57.04
2005	$7.00	$7.79	$9.62	$12.14	$15.38	$19.23	$24.04	$29.57	$37.20	$46.15	$57.69
2006	$7.25	$8.17	$10.10	$12.50	$15.86	$19.23	$24.04	$30.29	$37.50	$48.08	$60.10
2007	$7.53	$8.65	$10.23	$13.05	$16.83	$20.19	$25.00	$30.77	$39.90	$49.08	$59.66
2008	$7.68	$8.65	$10.50	$13.46	$16.83	$20.91	$25.48	$32.69	$40.87	$48.08	$60.10
2009	$8.06	$9.23	$11.54	$14.42	$17.79	$22.12	$26.92	$33.65	$42.07	$52.02	$67.31
2010	$8.06	$8.89	$11.80	$14.42	$17.79	$22.50	$27.40	$33.65	$40.87	$50.85	$67.31
2011	$8.15	$9.32	$12.02	$14.42	$18.04	$22.60	$27.40	$33.65	$43.37	$52.88	$67.31
2012	$8.46	$9.62	$12.02	$14.42	$18.27	$22.88	$28.85	$36.06	$45.67	$57.69	$72.12
2013	$8.60	$9.62	$12.02	$14.42	$18.70	$23.75	$28.85	$36.06	$47.12	$54.33	$72.12
2014	$8.73	$9.62	$12.02	$15.38	$19.23	$24.04	$28.85	$36.54	$48.08	$60.10	$72.12
2015	$9.15	$10.04	$12.21	$15.68	$19.95	$24.04	$31.25	$38.46	$48.08	$60.10	$73.08

MW Minimum wage

exception of Pennsylvania, have minimum wages higher than the federal minimum wage. In this regard, Pennsylvania serves as the control.

What Table 3.2 shows is that, similar to the national averages, the trends in these states are also similar. This is important because several states in response to the stagnation of the federal minimum wage passed or raised their own minimum wages in public referenda beginning in 2008 and especially after 2012. California has a higher minimum wage than the federal minimum and has since 2002. After it raised its minimum wage to $8.00 an hour in 2008 it did not raise it again until 2015. But this data only shows the minimum wage in California remaining the same from 2008 to 2014. When the minimum wage rose in 2015, median wages in all ten contours also rose. While median wages across the board rose in 2007 and 2008 when there were increases in the state's minimum wage, they remained unchanged, barring a few exceptions from 2008 to 2014. Connecticut, on the other hand, tells a slightly different story, although the overall trends do remain the same. From 2002 to 2015 there has been a consistent increase in the state's minimum wage. Generally the median wage in each of the ten contours does increase in those years when the state's minimum wage increases and not in those years when it does not. The only outlier in Connecticut is in the first contour in 2014 when the minimum wage increased to $8.70 an hour from $8.25 in 2013, where the median wage remains the same. Similarly, in 2015 when the minimum wage rose again to $9.00 an hour there were increases in all contours except the first, fourth, and tenth. Massachusetts is similar to California for the most part, but there is some variation whereby the median wages in some contours actually decrease in years when there has been no increase. Even when they do decrease, they appear to bounce back in the next year. And yet, in those years when there were increases in the state's minimum wage, 2007 and 2008, the median wages in most of the contours did increase. And when the state's minimum wage increased to $9.00 an hour the median wages in all contours also increased.

New Jersey is in part interesting because of the legislature's decision to raise the state's minimum wage over the initial veto of Governor Chris Christie. There had been a couple of state increases along the way in 2005 and 2006, and then in 2009 to the federal level, but there was not another increase in the state's minimum wage until 2014. With the increase in the state's minimum wage to $8.25 an hour from the federal minimum wage of $7.25 an hour in 2013, the increase in the median wages in each of the ten contours has appeared to be dramatic. The same trends appear to be the case in New York. There the state's minimum wage was higher than the federal from 2005 through 2008, and median wages did increase in the ten contours following increases in the state's minimum wage. From 2009 until 2013, we do see some slight increases in median wages in the first contour, even when there has been no increase in the federal minimum wage. In New York when the minimum wage increased again in 2015 to $8.75, the median wages in all contours, except for the first, increased. But as is the case with New Jersey, there appear to be significant increases in the median wage in all ten contours following the state's increase in the minimum wage to $8.00 an hour in 2014. But when the minimum wage increased an additional 13 cents in 2015 because the law pegged the state's new minimum wage to the Consumer Price Index, there was no real change in median wages in the first three contours and sixth contours. In the rest of the contours, with the exception of the eighth where there was actually a decline, there were increases.

In Ohio where there were more regular increases in the minimum wage, we see similar trends that appear to be consistent; although where the increase in the minimum wage was only slight (1.9 percent in 2013, 1.3 percent in 2014, and 2.5 percent in 2015), there was some fluctuation. From 2014 to 2015 there were increases in the first two and the last four contours. There was a slight decrease in the sixth contour. This, of course, raises an interesting question with regard to how much of a percentage increase in the minimum wage there would have to be in order for there to be increases in median wages throughout. It would appear that the increases would have to be at least 2 percent. Consider 2007 when Ohio first established a minimum wage of $6.85 which was 33 percent higher than the federal minimum wage of $5.15 an hour. The median wages in all ten contours rose significantly. In 2007, the minimum wage increased by another 2.2 percent to $7.00 an hour, and again there were increases in median wages in all contours except the second and third. Then in 2009 when the minimum wage increased by 4.3 percent to $7.30 an hour, median wages across the board increased again. In 2010 when there was no increase in the minimum wage, median wages throughout either remained the same or decreased. In 2011 when the minimum wage only increased by 1.4 percent, median wages increased in the first, third, sixth, and ninth contours, but either remained the same or decreased in the others. It is in 2012 when the minimum wage increases by 4.1 percent that we again see increases in the median wages throughout the ten contours.

In Oregon, where the minimum wage has always been higher than the federal minimum wage during this period, we have seen similar trends. There weren't always increases throughout the distribution, although from 2014 to

2015 when the minimum wage increased to $9.25, median wages in all contours, except for the fourth, sixth, seventh, eighth, and tenth contours, increased. Median wages in the fourth, seventh, and ninth contours actually decreased. In Rhode Island where during this period both states have had minimum wages higher than the federal minimum wage, the trends are similar to New York, Massachusetts, and Connecticut. There had been periodic increases in the state's minimum wage over this period. Between 2007 and 2012 when the minimum wage remained at $7.40, there were fluctuations in median wages. When the state's minimum increased to $7.75 an hour in 2013, median wages in all contours, except for the fourth, increased. When the minimum wage increased slightly in 2014 to $8.00 an hour, the only increases occurred in the fourth, fifth, sixth, seventh, eighth, and ninth contours. But when the minimum wage increased again to $9.00 an hour in 2015, an increase of 12.5 percent, median wages in all contours increased. In Vermont, however, where the increases were slight, the trends were similar to Ohio and Oregon; although in 2015 when the state's minimum wage increased by 4.7 percent to $9.15 an hour, the median wages in all contours, except for the fifth, eighth, and ninth, increased. It is only in Pennsylvania where the only time the minimum wage increased was when the federal minimum wage increased from 2007 to 2009, that median wages appeared to parallel what was happening nationally.

All of these state tables would again appear to be implying that there are positive welfare effects associated with minimum wage increases when viewed through the prism of wage contours. That median wages are rising above the third contour suggests that minimum wage increases are having an impact on the wages of the middle class. To the extent that this is true, it then is too narrow to simply view the minimum wage through the lenses of the competitive market model.

The Effective Minimum Wage Population

To the extent that there are contour effects, it becomes clear that the minimum wage has a broader impact than merely those who only earn the statutory minimum. If we follow the logic of the contours, the statutory minimum wage is merely a reference point for the wages in the larger low-wage sector of the economy. In this section, I take a closer look at just who makes up what we can classify as the "effective" minimum wage population. Critics of the minimum wage typically allege that the minimum wage is really insignificant because only 2 percent of the labor market earns the minimum wage, and of that 2 percent the majority are either teenagers or other secondary earners. A broader view of the minimum wage—the effective minimum wage population—suggests that this really is not true.

The effective minimum wage population could be defined in a couple of different ways: one is to define this group as those earning between the statutory minimum wage and 50 percent of average annual earnings. This definition would make some sense because of the historical tendency to set the minimum wage at about 50 percent of average annual hourly earnings. But the effective minimum wage population could also be defined as those earning in the first three contours, which would roughly coincide with the range between the statutory minimum and 50 percent of average annual hourly earnings. Using this range as a guide, it makes sense to look at the demographics of the first three contours. Nevertheless, Table 3.3 shows labor force figures assuming both definitions. Although the primary focus here are the years 2002–2015, it makes sense to place them in some historical context. Therefore, it is useful to also look at the years 1982 and 1992 as a historical backdrop, because they illustrate just how much the size of the effective minimum wage population has grown. To the degree that it has grown, it also becomes rather apparent how out of date the claims are that the minimum wage population is so small that it is effectively a non-policy issue.

The percentage of workers in the bottom contours is larger than those who are earning between the statutory minimum and 50 percent of average annual hourly earnings. This is because the bottom contours encompass more workers. Generally the bottom contours are the first three contours, but in 1982 it is only the first, and the wage at the top of the first contour exceeds the 50 percent of average annual hourly wage. In 1992, the bottom contours are the first two because the wage at the top of the first contour does not exceed the 50 percent of average annual hourly wage in 1992. This, of course, speaks to the declining value of the minimum wage. But by 2002 it takes three contours to get a wage that slightly exceeds the 50 percent of average annual hourly wage. Whereas in 1982, the effective minimum wage population as defined by 50 percent of average annual hourly wages was only 3.3 percent of the full-time working labor market, by 2015 it was 17 percent, an increase of 415 percent. Just between 1982 and 2002 the effective minimum wage labor market increased by 352 percent. But when the effective minimum wage population is defined by the bottom contours, the effective minimum wage population increases 162 percent from 7.4 percent in 1982 to 19.4 percent in 2015. A 150 percent of that increase is also from 1982 to 2002.

Much of the criticism of minimum wage increases centers around the claim that only a very small segment of the labor market earns it. But as Table 3.4 makes clear, when the minimum wage labor market is redefined

Table 3.3 Labor force figures

Year	*Minimum wage*[a]	*50 percent of average annual hourly wage*	*Average annual hourly wage*	*Number employed*	*Number of workers in bottom contours*	*Percentage of workers earning between minimum and 50 percent of average annual wage*	*Percentage of effective minimum wage earners in bottom contours*
1982	$3.35	$3.73	$7.46	54,936	4068	3.3	7.4
1992	$4.25	$5.91	$11.82	56,284	7363	9.8	13.1
2002	$5.15	$9.52	$19.04	81,486	15,073	14.9	18.5
2003	$5.15	$9.72	$19.44	80,034	14,325	17.2	17.9
2004	$5.15	$9.94	$19.88	78,569	13,411	16.6	17.1
2005	$5.15	$10.15	$20.30	78,062	12,907	17.4	16.5
2006	$5.15	$10.50	$21.00	78,362	12,653	17.3	16.1
2007	$5.85	$10.95	$21.90	78,846	13,476	15.8	17.1
2008	$6.55	$11.19	$22.38	78,515	16,436	14.7	20.1
2009	$7.25	$11.25	$22.50	74,988	15,799	11.3	21.1
2010	$7.25	$11.86	$23.72	73,296	15,330	12.9	20.1
2011	$7.25	$11.95	$23.90	71,486	14,629	12.9	20.5
2012	$7.25	$12.39	$24.78	71,053	14,034	15.1	19.8
2013	$7.25	$12.70	$25.40	71,646	14,030	16.4	19.6
2014	$7.25	$12.71	$25.41	50,057	9996	16.7	20.0
2015	$7.25	$13.07	$26.13	72,144	13,987	17.0	19.4

Source: Miriam King, Steven Ruggles, J. Trent Alexander, Sarah Flood, Katie Genadek, Matthew B. Schroeder, Brandon Trampe, and Rebecca Vick. Integrated Public Use Microdata Series, Current Population Survey: Version 3.0 [Machine-readable database]. Minneapolis: University of Minnesota, 2010. Files 1982. 1992, 2002–2015

[a]These wages are based on the average annual hourly wage of those in full-time work in the CPS data set

Table 3.4 Demographics

	1982	*1992*	*2002*	*2003*	*2004*	*2005*	*2006*	*2007*	*2008*	*2009*	*2010*	*2011*	*2012*	*2013*	*2014*	*2015*
Age																
15–17	.1	.1	.3	.2	.3	.3	.3	.3	.2	.2	.1	.2	.1	.2	.2	.2
18–24	26.7	21.2	17.4	17.2	17.8	17.9	19.2	16.7	15.7	12.8	12.2	11.6	11.9	12.9	13.0	12.9
23–34	28.1	31.7	26.6	25.7	25.9	25.6	25.4	26.4	25.8	26.2	27.0	27.0	26.5	27.0	27.5	27.6
35–44	18.0	22.5	26.1	26.5	24.8	24.6	23.6	23.6	23.3	23.5	22.7	22.8	22.7	22.3	22.4	22.5
45–54	15.2	14.7	19.2	19.8	20.1	19.7	19.8	20.2	20.8	22.6	22.6	22.8	22.1	21.2	20.6	20.2
55–64	10.5	8.1	8.6	8.8	9.0	9.7	9.4	10.2	11.4	12.1	12.6	12.8	13.3	13.2	12.9	13.3
65–74	1.0	1.4	1.4	1.3	1.6	1.7	1.8	1.9	2.1	2.1	2.1	2.2	2.5	2.4	2.8	2.8
75+	.3	.3	.4	.5	.5	.5	.5	.6	.6	.6	.6	.7	.9	.7	.6	.6
Education																
Up to 12 years	73.3	22.4	21.5	21.5	22.1	21.8	22.5	21.1	17.3	15.2	15.4	14.8	15.0	15.7	15.9	15.4
HS diploma	3.2	45.1	42.0	41.6	40.5	41.2	40.6	40.9	40.8	39.6	39.8	40.2	39.0	37.8	38.5	37.8
Some college, no diploma	23.5	17.4	18.4	18.6	18.6	18.1	18.3	18.2	20.0	21.0	19.9	20.0	19.9	20.1	19.3	20.8
Associate degree		5.2	7.6	7.2	7.6	7.7	7.5	8.5	9.1	10.0	10.1	10.5	10.7	11.0	10.6	10.8
BA degree		7.7	8.4	8.9	8.9	8.8	8.8	9.1	10.4	11.6	12.1	11.7	12.5	12.5	12.5	11.9
Professional degree		2.2	2.2	2.3	2.3	2.3	2.2	2.3	2.5	2.7	2.5	2.9	2.9	2.9	3.3	3.3
Sex																
Male	36.4	43.3	43.6	43.7	45.2	45.9	45.0	45.5	45.1	43.5	44.2	45.6	45.2	46.9	46.2	45.6
Female	63.6	56.7	56.4	56.3	54.8	54.1	55.0	54.5	54.9	56.5	55.8	54.4	54.8	53.1	53.8	54.4
Race																
White	84.4	84.7	79.5	78.4	77.6	78.5	78.0	78.5	77.1	77.6	76.9	76.7	76.5	77.1	77.6	75.6
Black	11.9	11.1	13.7	13.7	13.9	12.7	12.0	12.8	13.7	13.6	13.7	13.9	13.4	13.4	12.9	14.3
Industry																
Agriculture, forestry, fishing	2.7	3.0	3.0	3.0	3.5	3.5	3.9	3.5	3.4	2.6	2.8	3.0	3.4	3.2	3.6	3.6
Mining	.5	.4	.3	.3	.3	.3	.3	.3	.4	.4	.3	.3	.3	.3	.5	.4
Construction	4.2	5.1	7.5	7.1	7.6	8.1	8.7	8.5	7.7	6.6	5.8	5.9	5.5	6.4	6.5	7.1
Manufacturing	21.4	17.8	14.6	13.8	13.2	12.9	12.3	13.0	12.4	11.9	11.9	12.4	11.8	11.9	11.4	11.2

Transportation, communications, and other																
Utilities	3.8	3.4	4.2	3.9	3.6	3.5	3.5	4.0	4.0	4.7	4.5	4.4	4.4	4.6	4.5	3.4
Wholesale trade	4.2	3.3	3.1	2.7	2.8	2.5	2.6	2.4	2.7	2.7	2.9	3.1	2.1	2.4	2.3	2.4
Retail trade	19.4	23.0	21.8	23.0	23.8	23.9	24.7	22.6	22.7	21.7	21.7	21.2	22.4	22.5	22.5	22.3
Finance, insurance, and real estate	8.3	6.7	5.7	5.3	5.0	5.0	4.4	4.8	5.4	6.0	5.8	5.4	5.3	5.6	5.6	9.9
Business and repair services	4.5	5.8	7.1	7.4	7.8	7.0	6.8	7.3	7.4	7.2	7.3	7.8	8.0	7.9	8.1	1.7
Personal services	4.4	5.3	5.0	5.4	4.8	4.6	4.7	4.8	4.3	3.8	4.1	4.2	4.6	4.4	4.7	4.6
Entertainment and recreation	1.1	1.9	2.3	2.4	2.1	2.3	2.5	2.1	2.4	2.4	2.5	2.3	2.3	2.2	2.3	2.3
Professional and related	21.9	21.2	22.8	23.2	23.0	23.9	23.3	23.8	24.2	26.5	26.7	26.5	26.7	25.4	25.3	27.6
Public administration	3.7	2.5	2.7	2.6	2.5	2.4	2.2	2.9	3.1	3.7	3.7	3.4	3.2	3.1	2.9	3.4
Occupation																
Professional, technical	9.0	9.2	10.9	11.5	11.3	11.5	10.8	11.4	12.0	13.2	13.2	13.2	13.5	13.6	13.8	13.8
Farmers	.2	.4	.4	.3	.2	.2	.3	.2	.3	.3	.3	.3	.2	.3	.3	.3
Managers, officials, proprietors	5.0	8.0	8.2	6.9	6.2	5.8	6.3	6.0	6.5	8.0	7.7	7.7	7.6	8.0	7.5	8.0
Clerical and kindred	26.5	23.7	20.8	22.0	20.7	20.6	20.8	21.6	22.9	24.4	23.9	22.8	22.2	21.7	21.7	20.7
Sales workers	5.4	4.9	4.9	4.9	5.3	5.0	5.1	4.9	4.9	4.9	4.6	4.5	4.1	4.5	4.5	4.6
Craftsmen	8.2	8.4	9.0	9.2	9.3	9.5	9.3	9.0	9.4	8.7	7.7	8.7	7.7	8.3	8.1	8.0
Operatives	20.3	17.5	15.2	15.7	15.4	15.2	14.9	15.4	14.1	13.7	14.5	14.1	14.2	14.3	13.7	14.0
Service workers (private household)	.6	.5	.6	2.7	2.3	2.3	2.7	2.2	1.9	1.6	1.8	2.2	2.4	1.7	2.3	2.2
Service workers (non-private household)	18.1	19.6	20.9	20.4	21.4	22.1	21.7	21.1	20.2	19.1	20.4	20.2	21.6	20.9	20.9	20.9
Farm laborers	1.8	1.5	1.3	1.2	1.4	1.6	1.5	1.5	1.3	1.1	1.0	1.2	1.4	1.3	1.1	1.3
Laborers	5.0	6.3	7.7	5.2	6.5	6.3	6.6	6.7	6.5	5.0	4.9	5.1	5.2	5.6	5.9	6.3

as the "effective" minimum wage labor market, that segment is not that small or inconsequential. Moreover, as the demographics in Table 4 show, most of these workers are not necessarily teenagers or secondary earners.

During this 32-year period, there was among the effective minimum wage labor market a 51.7 percent decrease in the 18 to 24-year-old cohort, a 25 percent increase in the 35–44 age cohort, and a 32.9 percent increase in the 45–54 age cohort. In other words, effective minimum wage earners are older in 2015 than they were in 1982. In 1982, the vast majority of effective minimum wage earners (73.3 percent) had not even completed a high school education. By 2015 only 15.4 percent of the effective minimum wage population had less than a high school education, a decrease of 79 percent. Meanwhile, the percentage of effective minimum wage earners with a high school diploma increased 1081 percent from 3.2 percent to 37.8 percent in 2015.

On the surface, these changes alone may tell us quite a bit about the changing nature of the US economy. That only 3.3 percent of the labor market in 1982 were effective minimum wage earners and of that 3.3 percent the vast majority had not completed high school suggests that the effective minimum wage labor market—what can be referred to as the low-wage labor market—comprised predominantly low-skilled workers. To a certain extent, prior to the decline of manufacturing, a high school graduate could count on securing a decent middle-class job in a factory. These demographics actually make clear that not only has the low-wage labor market grown, it now appears to include those who previously might have been considered to possess some more skill, or at least to the extent that educational attainment can in any way be said to serve as a proxy for worker skill levels. Over this same period, there was also a decrease in the percentage of women who were effective minimum wage earners and an increase in the percentage of men who were minimum wage earners.

Over this period there were significant changes in industrial and occupational composition that speak to the changing nature of the economy. Manufacturing declined 47.7 percent from 21.4 percent in 1982 to 11.2 percent in 2015. From 2002 to 2015 the decline in manufacturing was actually 23.3 percent. At the same time, construction increased 70.7 percent from 4.2 percent in 1982 to 7.1 in 2015. And yet between 2002 and 2015 construction dropped 5.3 percent from 7.5 to 7.1 percent. Meanwhile, there was a 60 percent increase in managers, officials, and proprietors from 5.0 percent in 1982 to 8.0 percent in 2015, but between 2002 and 2015, this occupational category actually decreased by 2.4 percent. There was a 266.7 percent increase in service workers in private households from

0.6 percent in both 1982 and 2002 to 2.2 percent in 2015. Overall, between 1982 and 2015 laborers increased 26 percent from 5 percent to 6.3 percent. The greatest increase in laborers occurred between 1982 and 2002 with an increase of 54 percent. Between 2002 and 2015, however, laborers decreased 18.2 percent from 7.7 percent to 6.3 percent. At the same time, craftsmen decreased by 12.5 percent from 9.0 percent in 2002 to 8.0 percent in 2015, while operatives declined by 31 percent from 20.3 percent in 1982 to 14.0 percent in 2015; 7.9 percent of that decline occurred between 2002 and 2015.

On the surface, at least, it becomes clear that higher-paying middle-class jobs have decreased further and what has replaced them are the lower-paying and lower-skilled jobs at the bottom end of the market and higher-paying and higher-skilled jobs at the top of the market. To a certain extent, these trends only support the claims of those who argue that there is a mismatch between the skills of workers and the skills needs of employers (Katz and Murphy 1992; Katz and Krueger 1992; Juhn et al. 1993; Sandler and Wapler 2004; Balleer and van Rens 2013; Vivarelli 2014). A logistical regression analysis on the dependent variable of who is more likely to be an effective minimum wage worker may bear this out. In the following logistical regression, I test for the effects of being female, having less than a 12th grade education, being black, being between the ages of 18 and 24, 35 and 44, and 45–54, being in manufacturing, having a high school diploma, being in retail trade, being in business and repair services, being an operative, being a laborer, and being a service worker in non-private household on being an effective minimum wage earner. Regression coefficients and their statistical significance can be seen in Table 3.5. All variables are set to a value of 1.

The regression coefficients suggest that over time, skills do become an issue. In 1982, women had the highest probability of being effective minimum wage earners. The size of the female coefficient declines by 2015, but the size of the less than 12th grade education coefficient increases dramatically; although it does decrease between 2002 and 2015. Nevertheless, it does indeed appear to be the most important factor in accounting for one's likelihood of being an effective minimum wage earner. At the same time, it is worth noting that the size of the high school graduate coefficient also increases dramatically by 2015, suggesting that just high school graduates also have an increased likelihood of being effective minimum wage earners. But it too drops slightly between 2002 and 2015. And yet, most of that increase appears to be between 1982 and 2002. We also see an increase in the size of the coefficients for retail trade

Table 3.5 Regression coefficients

	1982	*1992*	*2002*	*2003*	*2004*	*2005*	*2006*	*2007*	*2008*	*2009*	*2010*	*2011*	*2012*	*2013*	*2014*	*2015*
Female	1.150	.838	.863	.863	.785	.768	.830	.801	.809	.828	.795	.729	.751	.706	.745	.767
	.000	.000	.000	.000	.000	.000	.000	.000	.000	.000	.000	.000	.000	.000	.000	.000
Less than 12th grade	.618	1.056	1.307	1.406	1.371	1.416	1.454	1.344	1.202	1.071	1.106	1.116	1.129	1.248	1.031	1.150
	.000	.000	.000	.000	.000	.000	.000	.000	.000	.000	.000	.000	.000	.000	.000	.000
Black	.318	.215	.141	.231	.259	.161	.160	.122	.239	.243	.241	.284	.226	.281	.252	.248
	.000	.000	.000	.000	.000	.000	.000	.000	.000	.000	.000	.000	.000	.000	.000	.000
18–24 Years old	.622	.857	.813	.897	.907	.917	.984	.769	.773	.626	.622	.614	.650	.786	.619	.620
	.000	.000	.000	.000	.000	.000	.000	.000	.000	.000	.000	.000	.000	.000	.000	.000
Manufacturing	−.212	−.194	−.064	−.043	−.076	−.074	−.135	−.023	−.012	.000	.043	.047	.004	.026	.012	−.050
	.000	.000	.000	.182	.023	.030	.000	.490	.706	.000	.191	.154	.917	.439	.204	.148
High school diploma	.244	.579	.724	.745	.678	.755	.745	.734	.748	.734	.746	.792	.742	.732	.720	.697
	.014	.000	.000	.000	.000	.000	.000	.000	.000	.000	.000	.000	.000	.000	.000	.000
Retail trade	.345	.588	.492	.538	.661	.547	.608	.541	.598	.546	.571	.558	.574	.595	.468	.584
	.000	.000	.000	.000	.000	.000	.000	.000	.000	.000	.000	.000	.000	.000	.000	.000
Business and repair services	.164	.111	.077	.129	.225	.111	.043	.042	.074	−.008	.033	.094	.099	.057	−.005	.354
	.045	.049	.042	.001	.000	.007	.000	.274	.000	.834	.375	.010	.007	.122	.641	.000
Operatives	.613	.626	.650	.625	.668	.603	.608	.656	.605	.612	.725	.634	.655	.644	.594	.648
	.000	.000	.000	.000	.000	.000	.000	.000	.000	.000	.000	.000	.000	.000	.000	.000
Laborers	.642	.720	1.008	.742	.923	.815	.835	.889	.926	.679	.762	.703	.738	.789	.703	.924
	.000	.000	.000	.000	.000	.000	.000	.000	.000	.000	.000	.000	.000	.000	.000	.000

Service workers (non-private household)	.614	.679	.735	.642	.771	.778	.712	.724	.686	.516	.648	.643	.747	.658	.528	.741
	.000	.000	.000	.000	.000	.000	.000	.000	.000	.000	.000	.000	.000	.000	.000	.000
35–44 years old	–.132	–.263	–.242	–.164	–.218	–.225	–.234	–.252	–.265	–.237	–.256	–.215	–.225	–.212	–.254	–.197
	.004	.000	.000	.000	.000	.000	.000	.000	.000	.000	.000	.000	.000	.000	.000	.000
45–54 years old	–.124	–.361	–.314	–.265	–.284	–.339	–.314	–.359	–.354	–.295	–.285	–.248	–.288	–.290	–.230	–.309
	.013	.000	.000	.000	.000	.000	.000	.000	.000	.000	.000	.000	.000	.000	.000	.000
Constant	3.839	2.959	2.618	2.707	2.741	2.742	2.820	2.675	2.369	2.277	2.321	2.332	2.382	2.381	2.192	2.404
	.000	.000	.000	.000	.000	.000	.000	.000	.000	.000	.000	.000	.000	.000	.000	.000

and laborers. That the size of the coefficient decreases for women does suggest that more and more men are finding themselves among the ranks of the effective minimum wage labor market. Again, all of this would appear to speak to the changing structure of the overall labor market and the low-wage labor market.

What this analysis suggests is that a segment of the labor market that once was insignificant is no longer insignificant. When the size of the effective minimum wage labor market was similar in size to the statutory minimum wage labor market, it may have been feasible to focus much of the research on the effects of teenagers. Perhaps it made policy sense to negate the wider benefits of minimum wage increases on the grounds of potential adverse employment consequences. These two data sets together suggest an entirely different reality. First, because of the changing nature of the economy, we find that the ranks of those who earn an effective minimum wage have grown and therefore cannot easily be ignored. And second, because through wage contour effects an increase in the statutory minimum wage will have a positive welfare effect for a much larger segment of the labor market than those earning the statutory minimum wage. Moreover, the wage contour effects suggest that the benefit will accrue beyond the effective minimum wage population into the broader middle class.

Conclusion

This chapter demonstrates two principal things. The first is that through wage contour effects there are indeed positive welfare effects associated with increases in the minimum wage. To the extent those in contours above the low-wage labor market were also receiving pay increases, it becomes clear that the benefits of minimum wage increases do extend to the middle class. It is through these effects that we can see how the CBO concluded that despite the fact that at most only 3.1 million people actually earn the statutory minimum wage, more than 16 million people would see their incomes increase. It may also be the case that when the CBO report is viewed within the context of wage contours, the CBO actually underestimated the potential benefits to a minimum wage increase. And yet, the implications are enormous because if more workers are getting raises, it would also suggest that their increased purchasing power will enable them to demand more goods and services in the aggregate, which in turn could be a basis for job creation, which is the subject of the next chapter.

The second is that when we view the minimum wage as a reference point for the larger low-wage labor market, it becomes clear that the issue is no longer an insignificant issue. When we look at the effective minimum wage labor market instead of the statutory minimum wage labor market, the effect is to socialize the conflict consistent with Schattschneider's (1960) theory. For Schattschneider there were two sides to a conflict: the actors who were actively engaged in the conflict and the spectators sitting on the sidelines and looking in. Critics of the minimum wage, Schattschneiderian terms have long sought to localize the conflict—make it smaller—by focusing only on the small sub-labor market that earns it. If only a relatively small percentage of workers actually earn the minimum wage, then it cannot be an issue that affects most of us who are earning above it. But if we are able to define this labor market in terms of the effective minimum wage population, then many of those spectators have been absorbed into the ranks of the actors actively engaged in the conflict, in which case the conflict has been socialized.

When we put these two things together we should be able to say the following: A minimum wage that affects more than simply the small number who actually earn the statutory minimum wage is really an issue that can be socialized even further. It is through the wage contour model that we can see the benefits extending up the wage distribution. It is through the wage contour model that we are able to seriously talk about the minimum wage being a reference point for the larger low-wage labor market whereby we are talking about effective minimum wage workers. And it is through the wage contour model that we can see how the issue can be socialized further to include the larger middle class. Obviously if the minimum wage is a political issue as well as an economic one, there will be opposition to it precisely because the benefits are larger than commonly supposed. Those with a vested interest in keeping wages low will continue to attempt to localize the issue by stressing two things: first that only a small percentage of workers actually earn the statutory minimum wage, which makes the issue a non-issue. And second that of those who earn it are primarily teenagers and other secondary earners, meaning their income is superfluous because they are not heads of households. By socializing the issue, we can broaden support for it while also pursuing a policy that benefits the middle class. By couching it as a middle-class issue, we are also following Gilens' (2012) model of targeting within universalism. And yet, we can also broaden support for it if we can demonstrate some larger macroeconomic benefits like job creation, which will be discussed in the next chapter.

Bibliography

Balleer, Almut, and Thija van Rens. 2013. Skill-Biased Technological Change and the Business Cycle. *The Review of Economics and Statistics* 95 (4): 1222–1237.

Card, David, and Alan B. Krueger. 1995. *Myth and Measurement: The New Economics of the Minimum Wage*. Princeton: Princeton University Press.

Dunlop, John T. 1957. The Task of Contemporary Wage Theory. In *New Concepts in Wage Determination*, ed. George W. Taylor and Frank C. Pierson. New York: McGraw-Hill Book Co.

Figart, Deborah M., and June Lapidus. 1995. A Gender Analysis of U.S. Labor Markets for the Working Poor. *Feminist Economics* 1 (3): 60–81.

Freeman, Alida Castillo, and Richard B. Freeman. 1991. Minimum Wages in Puerto Rico: Textbook Case of a Wage Floor? NBER Working Paper No. 3759, June.

Gilens, Martin. 2012. *Affluence & Influence: Economic Inequality and Political Power in America*. New York/Princeton/Oxford: Russell Sage Foundation and Princeton University Press.

Gordon, Robert J. 1995. *Is There a Tradeoff Between Unemployment and Productivity Growth?* NBER Working Paper 5081, April.

Gordon, David M. 1996. *Fat and Mean: The Corporate Squeeze of Working Americans and the Myth of Managerial "Downsizing"*. New York: The Free Press.

Haarlander, Lisa, and Sandra Tan. 2004. Minimum Wage Outlook: Opponents Say the Wage Will Force Price Hikes and Cuts in Staff and Their Hours, While Supporters Say It Reflects the Reality of Businesses Today. *The Buffalo News*, December 11, p. A1.

Juhn, Chinhui, Kevin Murphy, and Brooks Pierce. 1993. Wage Inequality and the Rise in Returns to Skills. *Journal of Political Economy* 101 (3): 410–442.

Kahn, Lawrence M., and Michael Curme. 1987. Unions and Nonunion Wage Dispersion. *The Review of Economics and Statistics* 69 (4): 600–607.

Katz, Lawrence, and Alan B. Krueger. 1992. The Effect of the Minimum Wage on the Fast-Food Industry. *Industrial and Labor Relations Review* 46 (1): 6–21.

Katz, Lawrence, and Kevin M. Murphy. 1992. Changes in Relative Wages, 1963–1987: Supply and Demand Factors. *Quarterly Journal of Economics* 107: 35–79.

Neumark, David, Mark Schweitzer, and William Wascher. 2004. Minimum Wage Effects Throughout the Distribution. *The Journal of Human Resources* 39 (2): 425–450.

Sandler, Manfred, and Rudiger Wapler. 2004. Endogenous Skill-Biased Technological Change and Matching Unemployment. *Journal of Economics* 81 (1): 1–24.

Schattschneider, E.E. 1960. *The Semisovereign People: A Realist's View of America*. New York: Holt, Rinehart.

Solow, Robert. 2008. Introduction: The United Kingdom Story. In *Low-Wage Work in the United Kingdom*, ed. Candice Lloyd, Geoff Mason, and Ken Mayhew. New York: Russell Sage Foundation.

Spriggs, William E., and Bruce E. Klein. 1994. *Raising the Floor: The Effects of the Minimum Wage on Low-Wage Workers.* Washington, DC: Economic Policy Institute.

Vivarelli, Marco. 2014. Innovation, Employment and Skills in Advanced and Developing Countries: A Survey of Economic Literature. *Journal of Economic Issues* 48 (1): 123–154.

Volscho, Thomas W., Jr. 2005. Minimum Wages and Income Inequality in the American States, 1960–2000. *Research in Social Stratification and Mobility* 23: 347–373.

CHAPTER 4

The Minimum Wage and Job Creation

This chapter will argue that, based on the positive welfare effects of the minimum wage for the middle class that were observed in the last chapter, the minimum wage can serve as a foundation for jobs creation. In the language of the neoclassical model, this is counterintuitive. The minimum wage, it is argued, generally costs jobs. Amid the debate over a $15 an hour minimum wage, it is often argued that a wage that high would lead many employers to substitute technology for labor. If the cost of labor goes too high that it exceeds the cost of machines that can perform the same tasks, employers will obviously substitute the latter for the former. If, however, labor costs remain low, there is no benefit for employers to make the substitution. But this focus on the microeconomic effectively negates the larger macroeconomic argument that more people with purchasing power can create more demand in the aggregate, which in turn will lead to more jobs. And yet, this argument, which in many respects represents a grassroots bottom-up approach, is often neglected in favor of the more top-down approaches of fiscal stimuli and/or monetarism—what have over the last several decades come to be referred to as the more standard approaches to job creation.

When public officials talk about creating jobs, they still mostly focus on a specific set of policy tools that will either give consumers incentive to spend more because they have more in their pockets or give employers incentive to create jobs because the cost of investment has been reduced

O. M. Levin-Waldman, *Restoring the Middle Class through Wage Policy*, Binzagr Institute for Sustainable Prosperity,
https://doi.org/10.1007/978-3-319-74448-3_4

because of a reduction in interest rates. The former falls under the purview of fiscal policy while the latter falls under the purview of monetary policy. Often policymakers focus on a combination of the two. When they talk about fiscal stimulus packages, they generally talk about one-time tax rebates so that the additional money that consumers have will be spent in the economy or investment in large-scale infrastructure projects that will potentially create more construction type jobs. What often is not included are public sector jobs created by government to employ the unemployed. Not since the Work Progress Administration (WPA) during the 1930s has government created jobs through massive programs, effectively becoming the employer of last resort. There are those who believe that job creation requires a mix of investment in infrastructure, lowering of interest rates, tax cuts at times, and worker flexibility in terms of wages. Neglected, however, has been the role that could have been played by a wage policy in creating greater demand for goods and services in the aggregate. Much of this relies heavily on political actors demonstrating the courage to fund stimulus programs. Because fiscal policy, for example, requires acts of Congress, policymakers have found it more politically expedient to rely on monetary policy because it is administered by the Federal Reserve Board (Fed), which for the most part functions as an independent regulatory agency.

The problem with this approach, however, is that it assumes that simply pumping money into the economy will create jobs. But if there is no demand for goods and services because the question of wages has been left out of the equation, then there are limits to what monetary policy can do. Monetary policy is essentially a top-down approach that assumes that investors will simply create jobs when the cost of borrowing decreases. Job creation, however, requires a more grassroots approach. Consumers, after all, have to make purchases, which means that the economy is fueled by aggregate demand for goods and services. If people lack the purchasing power because their wages are too low or because they have long been stagnant, there will not be sufficient aggregate demand to drive the economy. This means that it really won't matter how low interest rates are because if nobody is demanding goods and services because they cannot afford them, there really is no reason for firms to take advantage of lower interest rates and expand their operations.

Of course the problem with fiscal policy is that it relies on a robust political process. If Congress lowers taxes in order to put more money into people's pockets, then consumers are better positioned to demand goods and services in the aggregate. In this vein, fiscal policy may be better than monetary policy because it assumes a more grassroots approach. Although it is politically easier to reduce taxes during a recession, fiscal policy nonetheless rests in the assumption that they should rise again once the recession is over in order to prevent inflation, which is not so easy. In other words, fiscal and monetary policy rest on the same assumptions that during recessions money and purchasing power need to be expanded while during inflation they need to be contracted. It is the implementation that differs. Fiscal policy, however, is limited for yet another reason, which is there is a tendency not to cut taxes even during a recession unless those cuts can be paid for. This accords with a Senate rule that tax cuts should not add to the deficit, but must always be paid for through savings elsewhere. Keynes argued that during a time of recession, government should spend more to make up the lack of private investment, and if necessary run a deficit. An increase in public spending, it was thought, would create jobs. Today, however, there is this view that tax cuts should be neutral and ultimately pay for themselves. To offer tax cuts in the interest of stimulating the economy would require cutting spending elsewhere, which might also entail cutting other programs.

As I have alluded to in the previous chapter, there is yet a third approach, which is a wage policy. Almost four decades ago, Sidney Weintraub (1972) alluded to a wage policy when he argued that both fiscal and monetary policy needed to be complemented by an income policy. Echoing both Keynes and Commons, he argued the obvious, which was lowering interest rates and reducing taxes really are not going to generate jobs if people, because their incomes fail to keep up with inflation, don't have the purchasing power that would enable them to demand goods and services in the aggregate. Even if jobs would be created through both fiscal and monetary policy alone, a wage policy would still need to be in place in the hopes of preventing the next recession. It will be recalled that market theory assumes that if workers are flexible in their wage demands, they will be hired because they will lower their wage demand to the point where their labor is demanded by employers. But it would not matter how much workers reduce their wage demands because a reduction in wages would only result in a contraction in purchasing power thereby leading to a reduction in aggregate demand. In other words, jobs are created when there is effective demand for goods and services, and this effective demand is derived from rising incomes. That is ultimately what drives the need for new investment in plants and equipment.

On one level, the notion that wage rigidity is a key determinant of unemployment would imply that in the absence of this rigidity there really would be no need for a jobs policy because wage rigidity derived from competitive market theory assumes full employment. But on another level, the depth of the 2007 recession along with its accompanying deep long-term employment and the little effect that various Fed policies had would suggest that a jobs policy is critical. Neoclassical economists will no doubt respond that were all interventions removed, the economy would come to life, but that too is an untested theory. Although different ends of the ideological spectrum will advance different proposals, short of the government becoming the employer of last resort there is perhaps a consensus that job creation requires creating circumstances conducive to it. Over what those circumstances are, however, there is disagreement. Toward the end of job creation, policymakers have employed three models for job creation: stimulus policy, fiscal policy, and monetary policy.

Stimulus Policy

Economic stimulus policies have meant different things to different people at different times. During the Great Depression the government, based on Keynesian economics, sought to stimulate the economy through increased spending, including massive works projects that amounted to government serving as an employer of last resort. Because prices were depressed, New Deal programs, such as the Agricultural Adjustment Act, sought to inflate prices by paying farmers to take acreage out of production. Farmers could either plant less or take excess produce and store it. The idea was to contract the supply of farm produce on the market, thereby driving up the price. The other problem in the Great Depression was limited purchasing power, thereby limiting demand for goods and services in the aggregate and deep unemployment, neither of which were mutually exclusive. Aggregate demand for goods and services could be stimulated through policies that would enable consumers to demand more by increasing their purchasing power.

New Deal policy aimed at increasing purchasing power sought to put money into the hands of retirees, poor people, and the unemployed. Programs like Social Security and public assistance would provide the elderly and the poor with the ability to demand more goods and services in the aggregate. The Wagner Industrialization Act which legitimized collective bargaining and the Fair Labor Standards Act which created the federal minimum wage were both intended to increase the otherwise depressed wage rates. But they were also intended to stimulate greater aggregate demand through increased purchasing power.

Increasing purchasing power through cash transfer and wage boosting programs, however, were not enough. Workers needed to be put back to work, and the only way this could happen was if government would take the first steps and hire them. This occurred through works projects like the Work Progress Administration and the Civilian Conservation Corps. Many of these government jobs focused on building infrastructure. All these efforts reflected the inextricable links between wages, employment, and aggregate demand for goods and services, and that unless all three were addressed it would be very difficult to stimulate job creation. Jobs, after all, are created when there is demand for the goods and services that those jobs would produce. But there can't be demand for goods and services if people have insufficient purchasing power either because their wages are too low or they are unemployed due to either layoff or retirement. Although government works programs put many back to work, they did not bring the country out of the Depression, and indeed the country would not come out of the Depression until the country began ramping up for World War II.

On one level, these programs did reflect a view that government should indeed be an employer of last resort. It reflected the Keynesian position that when private investment is low, the difference should be made up through public sector investment, and if necessary the government should be prepared to run a deficit in order to get the economy moving again. The idea that government should be the employer of last resort is really a moral argument that holds that the state has a responsibility to ensure that all those who want to work are able to do so. If the private sector is unable to provide sufficient opportunities to work, then government has a responsibility to directly create jobs for the purposes of relieving unemployment (Wray 2007). And yet, this approach poses some problems. First of all, it is expensive and requires huge deficit spending.

On another level, however, these programs reflected a view that positive steps need to be taken to stimulate the economy without necessarily creating a right to a job. One of the reasons why the Employment Act of 1946 was not called the Full Employment Act, as it was originally introduced, was because the term "full" implied a positive obligation on the part of government to create jobs for those who did not have. It implied that workers would have a positive right to jobs and that government in turn would have to be the employer of last resort. In terms of stimulus spending, this may be the most extreme. The idea that the government would be a permanent employer of last resort challenges the traditional American distinction between the public and private sectors. It is one thing for government to regulate the economy but quite another for government to encroach upon the private sector by actually creating public sector jobs, which may also appear to be in competition with private sector jobs.

Although the nation has not had a stimulus package consisting of massive public works programs since the Great Depression, Congress has passed smaller stimulus packages over the years. During the Great Recession in 2009, Congress passed the American Recovery and Reinvestment Act, which included direct spending on infrastructure, education, health, and energy; federal tax incentives; and expansion of unemployment benefits and other social welfare provisions. The Act also included spending on studies of medical treatments and their effectiveness, as well as money to state and local governments on the verge of bankruptcy. The stimulus may not have actually created too many new jobs, rather its success may have been that by going to state and local governments it may have prevented others from losing their jobs. In this vein, Congress sought to stimulate the economy through bailouts of banks and auto manufacturers, which if they absolutely failed would have led to greater unemployment. Congress was offering stimulus with programs that would increase the purchasing power of people. It was also stimulating the economy with various corporate bailouts that would maintain the purchasing power of people. But Congress has also tried other stimulus packages.

Congress also attempted to put more money in the hands of workers through reductions in Social Security payroll taxes. Similarly, in 2003 Congress sought to stimulate the economy through one-time tax rebates of $300 to individuals and $600 to couples. Both types of stimulus packages raise questions about efficiency and effectiveness. These types of stimuli are well targeted to the poor who will spend the money, and right away. They are not as well targeted to the more affluent who are more likely to throw the money into the bank without spending. In this vein, they may not be the most effective way to stimulate the economy, and if they aren't that effective then they might not be that efficient. Moreover, they are short-term approaches aimed more at jump-starting the economy, rather than sustaining long-term job creation. To the extent that these represent active steps toward job creation, a stimulus could be said to fall under the purview of fiscal policy because it is attempting to stimulate job creation through budgeting adjustments.

Fiscal Policy

Fiscal policy is also a form of stimulus and centers around the raising of taxes during inflation as a means of contracting individuals' purchasing power and reducing taxes during recessions as a means of putting more money into people's pockets so that they will demand more goods and services. By effectively allowing more money to be spent in the economy, there can be greater demand for goods and services in the aggregate. Tax cuts, however, are no guarantee that the money will be spent. In this vein, they aren't always well targeted. Well-targeted tax cuts would be given to a specific socioeconomic group that it is known will spend the savings right away. Tax cuts to the poor, for instance, would be better targeted than tax cuts to the wealthy because they are more likely to spend whereas wealthier individuals may opt to throw the additional money into savings. Nevertheless, the idea is that more money in the economy chasing goods and services during a recession will generate growth, thereby leading to job creation while less money during inflation will result in a lowering of prices because less money contracts demand. This, then, leads to another problem with fiscal policy, which is that it relies on the political branches of government to act.

Both raising and lowering of taxes require an act of Congress. Although lowering of taxes will always be politically popular, the issue of paying the taxes is still present. Even lowering taxes can be difficult due to the principle that tax cuts need to be paid for so as not to add to the deficit. Unless tax cuts can ensure sufficient growth in the economy to offset the initial revenue loss, which they often cannot, or enough cuts in other programs can be found to offset them so as not to blow up the deficit, elected officials are often loathe to vote for them. During the Great Recession, Congress passed a temporary reduction in the Social Security payroll tax. It was proposed that they be paid for with higher taxes on the wealthy, but this proposal did not garner much support. Critics often view higher taxes on the wealthy to pay for even temporary payroll tax reductions as nothing other than redistribution, which can hardly be a basis for job creation, especially when the wealthy are considered to be the job creators. This is not simply an ideological statement; rather it reflects a view prevalent in welfare economics that tax cuts should preferably go to the wealthy because they can be counted upon to responsibly invest their money into new enterprises which will create jobs. The poor, by contrast, cannot always be relied upon to behave responsibly largely because they are not perceived as rational (Wagner 1996). They would argue that more tax cuts should go to the wealthy on the assumption that they will invest more and these investments will trickle down to others in the form of jobs.

The reality is that these tax holidays were granted, but never really paid for, which means that the shortfall in revenue only added to the deficit. Again, for Keynesian economists this is not a problem. On the contrary, during a recession deficits should be higher if the effect of greater government spending is to create jobs. With the reduction in Social Security payroll taxes from 6.2 percent to 4.2 percent, the Social Security Trust Fund was left short. Even if we concede that there really is no Social Security Trust Fund anymore, this temporary reduction in the payroll tax only added to the deficit. There may be an ethical problem with this approach as well. By temporarily reducing the payroll taxes for a couple of years, there is no question that consumers have more money in their pockets. But they might also get used to it and then when the rates revert back to what they were, the effect is to have had their taxes increased during a period of stagnant wages. Wouldn't raising their wages instead be a better way to put money into their pockets?

Monetary Policy

Like fiscal policy, monetary policy also rests on the premise that more money needs to be pumped into the economy during a recession while during a period of inflation there needs to be less. With monetary policy, the Fed controls the money supply through adjustments in interest rates. By controlling the money supply, the Fed attempts to maintain a stable economy. Interest rates can be driven up simply by raising the reserve requirement—the amount of money a member bank must pay to borrow from the Fed—or by raising the prime interest rate—the rate charged to its best customers. The Fed has also found money aggregates to be an effective tool because the amount of money and capital in the economy can just as effectively be reduced by raising money aggregates (Brimmer 1983). In either case, the Fed contracts the money supply, thereby inducing a recession to control inflation. Conversely, by reducing money aggregates or lowering rediscount rates, the Fed pumps more money into the economy for the express purpose of stimulating production.

Monetarism is based on the same assumptions underpinning fiscal policy. During a recession when investment is down and workers are out of work, the Fed will attempt to pump money into the economy by making it easier (cheaper) to attain. When the cost of money declines, the firms will discover that it is cheaper to borrow and will do so at lower interest rates for the purpose of expanding their operations and creating jobs. By allowing greater amounts of money to flow during times of recession, the government hopes to stimulate new investment which will yield greater growth and prosperity. It increases the supply of capital for economic expansion by devaluing the dollar, printing up more money, or lowering the interest rates. If successful, the economy expands guaranteeing lucrative returns to investors and new jobs for the otherwise unemployed. During a period of inflation, however, the Fed often seeks to contract the money supply by making it more expensive to obtain money. If the cost of borrowing increases, the demand for goods will decrease, in which case prices will fall. Consequently, the Fed seeks to balance maintaining higher employment with lower inflation. It is a trade-off because lowering interest rates in order to stimulate the economy and create jobs may lead to inflation while efforts to control inflation may lead to lower investment thereby creating unemployment. The advantage to monetarism over fiscal policy is that it doesn't require an act of Congress. Rather it is implemented by a neutral body that is essentially an independent regulatory authority. The Fed is composed of governors and a chair who are appointed to fixed terms by the president. Once confirmed by the Senate, they cannot be removed from their positions. Hence the Fed is truly independent.

Monetary policy is largely based on the work of Milton Friedman and the Chicago School of Economics but draws institutional authority from the Federal Reserve System. It is largely inferred from the language of the Employment Act of 1946, which established that it would be "the continuing policy and responsibility of the Federal Government to use all practicable means ... to promote maximum employment, production, and purchasing power" (Statutes at Large 1946, p. 23). Through monetary policy the government has been able to use "practicable means" to fulfill a general maintenance function. Its principal maintenance function has been to control for both recession and inflation. Not only is a role for the overall management of the economy implied but so too is the use of monetary policy. Maintaining high levels of employment through all practical means would imply a responsibility by government to pursue policies that will lead to greater employment. Since the cumbersome legislative process makes it extremely difficult to achieve through direct policies, those same goals can in part be achieved by deferring to the Federal

Reserve Board to stimulate the economy by increasing the money supply. The Federal Reserve Act itself never really established a mandate for policy stabilization (Reagan 1961).

Both Congress and presidents have relied heavily on the Fed to stimulate the economy precisely because it is politically independent of both the legislative and executive branches of government. And yet the Fed cannot always be relied upon to lower interest rates in order to create jobs because its principal constituency by statute is the banking industry. For this reason, the Fed has been hesitant to lower interest rates for fear that it would spark inflation. But monetarism is problematic because it assumes that pumping money into the economy will result in job creation. It fails to address whether individuals will have the financial ability to demand more goods and services. Although during the Great Recession and its aftermath the Fed continuously lowered interest rates and engaged in quantitative easing, it was too little to avail. That fiscal and monetary policy failed to lead to job creation might suggest the absence of a key ingredient in the policy mix.

The Wage Policy Model

Both the fiscal and monetary policy models might assume too much, as both assume that if money is pumped into the economy, through whatever means, it will lead to new investment and hence job creation. In other words, if interests rates are low, firms will borrow to expand which will create jobs. If through fiscal policy taxes are cut, there will be new investment and then jobs will be created. And if through monetary policy there will be new investment and job creation following decreases in interest. What these models don't consider is the issue of aggregate demand for goods and services. That is, if workers' wages are so low that they cannot afford to demand anything, does it really matter how low an interest rate is? If there is no demand, there is really no reason to create jobs. Sidney Weintraub (1972) argued that the long-neglected piece of the puzzle was a wage policy, or what he called an incomes policy. If we return to the concept of the stimulus discussed a bit earlier, it rests on macroeconomic arguments that the purchasing power of individuals needs to be boosted. In other words, monetary policy is premised on the top-down notion that adjustments at the top will lead to investment decisions and fiscal policy is premised on a grassroots model that more money in consumers' hands will drive the economy, but that boost needs to come through top-down tax cuts. Wage policy, however, assumes the solution to lie completely in a grassroots purchases and that a policy that keeps wages rising will at a minimum maintain aggregate demand for goods and services. At issue in wage policy is the maintenance of purchasing power.

Part of the problem is that macroeconomic approaches such as stimulus packages and even wage boosting programs rely on Keynesian economics which has fallen into disfavor since the stagflation of the 1970s. But as Franco Modigliani (2003) suggests, Keynes has been greatly misunderstood. The classical model is really a special case of the *General Theory*, which assumes an economy in which wages are highly flexible. This means that wages will decline quickly in the face of unemployment. So when there is excess supply, workers' wage prices will decline toward the equilibrium level, thereby reducing the excess supply. And yet, the classical model is manifestly counterfactual. It really does not provide a systematic explanation for unemployment nor does it provide any guidance on how to control it. Rather it assumes that workers through their wage demands control whether they are employed or not. The *General Theory*, however, rejects the premise of the classical postulate that wages and prices are sufficiently flexible in both directions, in which case the demand for money will quickly adjust to any given supply. Rather wages are "downward rigid" and will not fall in the presence of excess supply of labor, and if they do fall it will be very slowly. When prices do not fall in spite of the presence of an excess supply, the market will only achieve equilibrium at the point where the quantity and price stop adjusting.

At the heart of Keynes' contribution is the proposition that savings equals investment. But Keynes distinguishes between demand in the form of consumption, which is responsive to current income, and demand in the form of investment which is responsive to interest rates. Aggregate output and employment were largely determined by investment, but a return to full employment could only be achieved through those policies that would specifically increase the money supply, thereby creating an excess supply of money lowering interest rates toward full employment. And yet, if savings equals investment, an increase in money flowing through the economy could also be achieved by increasing wages. In other words, real wages, and increasing wages, increases demand. This then increases spending, thereby leading to more growth and profits, which then become savings that can be reinvested. This might then represent more concrete investment than investment based on lower interest rates, which is still borrowed rather than saved.

A wage policy would consist of positive measures intended to boost wages. Broadly defined, it would consist of a set of institutions designed to bolster the wages of the middle class. Unions are one such institution while wage floors are another. The National Labor Relations Act of 1935, otherwise known as the Wagner Industrial Relations Act, legitimized unions and collective bargaining. It rested on the premise that collective bargaining aimed at raising wages would be beneficial to all, especially as it would eliminate strife. Whereas collective-bargaining agreements would cover union members, and might even spillover to nonunion members, federal and state minimum wages would extend a degree of coverage to nonunion members. In addition to federal, state, and in some cases local minimum wages, many localities have also passed living wage ordinances, which are requirements to pay specific minimum wages to those working for firms that have contracts with municipalities to provide public services. And as we will discuss in Chap. 6, there are now broader proposals for basic and/or minimum incomes. All of these could be said to fall under the rubric of wage policy.

Weintraub (1972) considered an "incomes policy" to be an essential complement to both monetary and fiscal policy. Incomes policy would be the third point on a triangle with both monetary and fiscal policy. Milton Friedman had argued for wage restraint on the assumption that there would be steady growth in the money supply by roughly 3 percent. Therefore, wages would need to be constrained in order to maintain balance. It was simply assumed that wages would increase to match productivity (which was roughly rising at 3 percent per year overall), but faster wage growth would be harder to achieve. And yet, Weintraub believed the traditional tools of economic growth to be insufficient by themselves. Fiscal policy was poorly targeted and could not be assured its desired effects. Moreover, more public spending might require new taxes, which only leads workers to seek higher wages to pay the increased tax, thereby exacerbating inflation. But monetary policy also carried a cost. The problem with relying on the Fed to implement monetary policy was that the Fed's primary constituency, as put forth in the Federal Reserve Act of 1913 which created the Federal Reserve System. This meant that the Fed would be more likely in the face of rising inflation to apply the brakes with higher interest rates and reserve requirements, thereby causing unemployment.

Weintraub essentially accused economists of being quick to apply the brakes to control inflation, but they weren't the ones who would lose their jobs as a result. Rather "The unemployed are thus the innocent lambs led to slaughter through conventional tactics" (pp. 117–118). On the contrary, a central bank detached from the real world was really in no position to understand how the consequences of its decisions would impact real people. For those in the central bank, these consequences were merely an abstraction. If wages could be stabilized, then price stability would avert economic damage resulting from convenient stabilization tools. An incomes policy, in other words, would be a necessary complement to these traditional tools. Of course Weintraub saw an incomes policy as part and parcel of stabilization in an era of rising wages and high inflation. Wages needed to be restrained so that they could grow with productivity gains. Arguably Weintraub was writing during a time of rising wages; so stabilization was necessary. Today the main problem is stagnant wages. And yet, the application of his incomes policy would still appear to be relevant. It is just as important to have an incomes policy in tandem with the other two precisely because wages have not been rising. Neither fiscal nor monetary policy addresses the issue of stagnant wages—a wage policy does.

At a minimum, a wage policy could help prevent long-term unemployment simply by enabling people to maintain aggregate demand for goods and services. But through wage contour effects, it should form the basis for a jobs policy in its own right. To the extent that wage contour effects will be experienced through much of the income distribution, a wage policy can effectively bolster the middle class. A wage policy, then, becomes an essential ingredient in the policy mix already comprised of fiscal and monetary policy. At the bottom of the distribution, it offers low-wage workers in particular additional security. It will also reduce income inequality because it will effectively raise the wages of those at the bottom of the distribution by a higher percentage rate relative to the top. This should then lead to less social strife. In many European countries where there are centralized wage setting institutions, income inequality is less than in the USA where there are none. But a wage policy is essential because it is part and parcel of economic development.

Individuals earning higher wages will have increased purchasing power, which will enable them to demand more goods and services. This should over time fuel investment and economic expansion. Economic development is essential to the maintenance of a broad middle class. The broader the middle class, the less the extremes are at both the top and bottom of the distribution. Wage policy is about maintaining the middle class because through contour effects the wages of many within the ranks of the middle class will rise following a minimum wage increase, as we showed in Chap. 3. By raising the wages of those at the bottom, workers can achieve greater independence and power as they are placed on a more equal footing with managers.

At the heart of the neoclassical view of wage determination, which has also underpinned much of American economic policy, has been the idea that wages are determined through a natural process of supply and demand. More workers than jobs available will drive down wages while fewer workers than jobs available will drive them up. If there are fewer jobs available, workers have it in their power to lower their wage demands until their labor is consumed, that is, they are hired. Therefore, it is wage rigidity that is ultimately the source of unemployment. The idea of a wage policy does represent a direct challenge to that view. It effectively calls into question that flexible labor markets will result in full employment. Wage policy assumes that wage determination is influenced by institutions that empower workers in an environment where they don't enjoy the same power as employers. If institutions are necessary to bolster wages, there can be nothing natural about how wages are set. Wage policy effectively gives workers a measure of power to counteract the power of employers. Active wage policy categorically rejects the premise that individuals are free to negotiate over wage rates. On the contrary, through their market power, employers set rates, and the only negotiation open is to either accept or reject. Wage policy, by contrast, recognizes the asymmetrical power balance between employers and workers. By boosting wages, especially at the low end of the distribution, a wage policy can effectively give workers a share of monopoly power they otherwise would not have had (Galbraith 1998).

Job Creation

A wage policy makes the following assumption: if aggregate demand can be maintained, and even be increased over time, we then might be able to prevent a recession or at least blunt its effects. If implemented in conjunction with other policies, a wage policy can hopefully prevent long-term unemployment in the future. The objective is the maintenance of consumer purchasing power. It is conceivable, then, albeit conjecture, that had a viable wage policy been in place that the financial meltdown following the sub-prime crisis in 2008 might not have occurred because people would have been in a better position to pay off their mortgages. At a minimum, a wage policy might have arrested the wage stagnation that has plagued the country over the last four decades.

A wage policy could be a foundation for job creation by allowing individuals to effectively demand more goods and services. It will be recalled that according to the neoclassical model there really is no such thing as unemployment because workers can always drop their wage demands to the point that their labor power is demanded and then consumed. That wage rates do not drop is due to wage rigidity. Nevertheless, a drop in wages should lead to a corresponding drop in prices for goods and services. Prices, after all, will have to drop because of workers' reduced ability to demand goods and services. And yet, there is a limit to how low prices can drop because there are other costs, mainly fixed costs, associated with the production process. The only way to get around this problem is through a wage policy that would enable workers to at a minimum continue demanding goods and services in the aggregate, and perhaps more. As workers are able to purchase more goods and services because of their greater purchasing power, other firms might then be able to expand, thereby creating new jobs. This can be seen in the Wage Policy Model Diagram.

Wage Policy Model of Job Creation

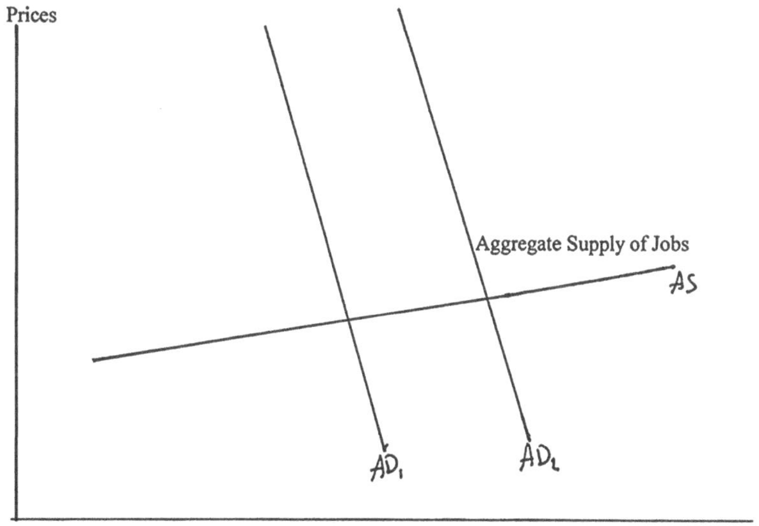

Aggregate Demand for Goods and Services

In a flexible labor market workers would reduce their wage demands during a recession with the consequence being reduced demand for goods and services in AD1, because in most likelihood aggregate prices will not drop. A wage policy should enable workers to maintain their purchasing power, if not increase it, thereby resulting in a shift in the Aggregate Demand curve from AD1 to AD 2. The macro benefits of this can be seen in Aggregate Supply (AS) curve.

According to neoclassical model, or the "orthodox view," lower wages will reduce labor costs, which should result in the Aggregate Supply curve shifting down. In this model, labor costs are assumed to be a significant element in the typical firm's cost structure, and the Aggregate Demand curve is implicitly assumed to more or less remain constant. It will remain constant because of the further assumption that aggregate prices will also drop. But if prices do not drop, reduced wages will then shift the Aggregate Demand curve to the left of AD1, thereby resulting in unemployment because of a contraction in aggregate demand. Lower wages mean that individuals have less ability to consume. Because there is in most likelihood a limit to how much wages can be reduced, prices cannot be relied upon to drop. A wage policy, then, should have the effect of shifting the Aggregate Demand curve to AD2, as depicted in the diagram. A wage policy should certainly have an effect because lower-wage workers have a relatively high marginal propensity to consume. Whatever higher wages they receive will be spent almost immediately. Of course, the orthodox view will maintain that the Aggregate Demand curve could shift to the left which would result in unemployment if wages rise and profits decline on each unit that is produced. But as we saw in Chap. 3, in years when the minimum wage increased so too did the median wages throughout the ten constructed contours, thereby resulting in welfare benefits for the middle class. A wage policy, then, especially when coupled with wage contour effects, effectively shifts the Aggregate Demand curve out from AD1 to AD2, thereby creating a need for more jobs, as reflected in the direction of the Aggregate Supply curve.

Conclusion

As it should be clear that there are positive welfare effects from minimum wage increases, it also becomes clear that wage policy is a necessary ingredient in the policy arsenal for the creation of jobs. This will strike some as counterintuitive because of the neoclassical assumption that a wage policy that artificially raises wages will have adverse employment consequences. And yet, it is really illogical to assume that merely lowering interest rates that provide incentives for firms to expand and hire new workers can really result in the long-term creation of jobs if workers, because of their stagnant wages, cannot afford to demand goods and services. It stands to reason that a policy that enables individuals to demand goods and services is more likely to be successful at job creation, in large measure, because it is grassroots and bottom-up rather than top-down.

Both the Wagner Industrial Relations Act and the Fair Labor Standards Act were predicated on these underlying assumptions. By giving workers purchasing power even through a minimum wage, aggregate demand for goods and services could be stimulated, thereby leading to the creation of new jobs. Because the minimum wage has been relegated to an anti-poverty measure, we have lost sight of its larger macroeconomic effects, with the result being that minimum wage earners have been stigmatized. It was ironically intended to be a labor-management or human resources issue (Levin-Waldman 2009). Because an oversupply of low-skilled workers meant that they lacked equal bargaining power relative to their employers, they would indeed need a boost from public policy. But there is another implication here that needs to be addressed, especially in a complex economy. That is, no single policy approach by itself will suffice to create jobs. Rather a multitude of approaches need to be pursued, but these approaches need to be coordinated. One of the challenges is that because different institutions are responsible for different functions, we are often lacking a coordinated response. And yet, it is too easy to rely on the Fed because it is immune from political pressures. Both fiscal and wage policy are difficult because they would require acts of Congress, meaning they enjoy no such immunity. At the end of the day creating jobs may require bold thinking and courage. At a minimum, it requires readjusting our assumptions. It certainly involves rethinking some of the fundamental assumptions about the minimum wage and the role it can play in job creation.

Bibliography

Brimmer, Arthur F. 1983. Monetary Policy and Economic Activity: Benefits and Costs of Monetarism. *American Economic Review* 73 (2): 1–12.

Employment Act of 1946. 1946. *Statutes at Large*. ch. 33, section 2, 60 Stat. 23, codified as 15 U.S.C. § 1021.

Galbraith, James K. 1998. *Created Unequal: The Crisis in American Pay*. New York: The Free Press.

Levin-Waldman, Oren M. 2009. The Minimum Wage and Competing Ethical Conceptions. *Advances in Industrial and Labor Relations* 16: 181–210.

Modigliani, Franco. 2003. The Keynesian Gospel According to Modigliani. *American Economist* 47 (1): 3–24.

Reagan, Michael D. 1961. The Political Structure of the Federal Reserve System. *American Political Science Review* 55: 64–76.

Wagner, Richard E. 1996. *Economic Policy in a Liberal Democracy.* Cheltenham/ Brookfield: Edward Elgar Publishing.

Weintraub, Sidney. 1972. Incomes Policy: Competing the Stabilization Triangle. *Journal of Economic Issues* 6 (4): 105–122.

Wray, L. Randall. 2007. *The Employer of Last Resort Programme: Could It Work for Developing Countries?* Economic and Labor Market Papers, International Labour Ofice, Geneva Employment Analysis and Research Unit, Economic and Labour Market Analysis Department, International Labour Organization, August.

CHAPTER 5

Minimum Wage and Income Distribution

In Chap. 3 we discovered that in years when the minimum wage increased inequality declined to some extent. In this chapter we take a closer look at the impact of the minimum wage on income distribution and how it impacts inequality. As a solution to growing inequality the minimum wage does not figure prominently in contemporary policy discussions; rather the discussion focuses on redistribution, which is also assumed by the median voter theorem. Most policy approaches to income inequality center on rates of taxation, on the assumption that income inequality can easily be addressed by overtaxing the wealthy in order to pay for programs that will benefit those at the bottom. Ideology aside, this approach follows the assumptions of the median voter theorem based on the public choice theory put forth by Anthony Downs (1957). Downs essentially postulated that political actors, including public officials, governments, and political parties behave rationally. So too do voters. Each pursues his or her self-interests. Voters vote for the candidate and/or party that will satisfy their interests.

Because the goal of each political party is to win elections and not programs and/or policies, those running for election will effectively purchase the votes of voters through public programs and/or other policies that effectively increase their money utility. According to this model of political competition, the median voter theorem, based on the work of others using the same public choice assumptions as Downs, holds that as income

O. M. Levin-Waldman, *Restoring the Middle Class through Wage Policy*, Binzagr Institute for Sustainable Prosperity,
https://doi.org/10.1007/978-3-319-74448-3_5

distributions are skewed to the right, the preferred amount of redistribution is a function of the relative position of the median voter on the income scale. The greater the distance between the median voter's income and society's average income, the greater is the society's preferred amount of redistribution. In other words, the more inequality there is, the greater preference the median voter has for redistribution. The fundamental assumption being that redistribution will take place through taxation.

In this chapter, I argue that to the extent that the minimum wage can reduce income inequality (and not to be confused with making society equal) through its wage contour effects and it has positive effects for the middle class, it may challenge some of the fundamental assumptions of the median voter theorem. I argue that the minimum wage's welfare effects potentially mitigate the need for society to redistribute because the distance between the median voter's income and the average income of society is effectively narrowed, which is to say, if the money utility of those at the bottom can be increased through an increase in the minimum wage than simply overtaxing the wealthy.

Impact on Inequality

The rise in income inequality over the last 40 years speaks less to the growing gap between those at the top and those at the bottom and more to the disappearance of the middle class. Certainly raising the minimum wage isn't going to restore the middle class, but an increase and its subsequent maintenance will work to arrest the decline in the labor market institutions that have long served to bolster the middle class. Between 1947 and 1973, the incomes of families in the bottom fifth of the income distribution in the USA grew more rapidly than the incomes of families in any of the other countries. Meanwhile, the incomes of families in the top fifth of the distribution grew more slowly than the incomes of families in other quintiles. After 1973, however, that changed. Low-income families in the USA experienced a steady decline in real income from the late 1970s through the middle of the 1990s. And it was only because of economic growth that accelerated during the course of the 1990s that the decline in their incomes came to an end. From the late 1960s into the 1970s, the average household income of the top 5 percent was 16 times the average income of the bottom 20 percent of households. During the 1980s, this ratio rose to 18 and continued into the 1990s where it averaged 20 percent. During the 2000s it rose again to an average of 26, and by 2011 it peaked at 28 percent. This rise in inequality was principally due to the rapid growth in income of the highest earning families. Between 1979 and 2007, the top 1 percent of families had 60 percent of the income gains while the bottom 90 percent only had about 9 percent of those income gains (Belman and Wolfson 2014).

As to whether a minimum wage may be an effective tool for addressing growing inequality, that is in part a function of whether inequality is the result of natural forces or deliberate public policy. If, for example, growing inequality is the result of deteriorating labor market institutions, a minimum wage as but one labor market institution could potentially be an effective tool. The standard model of competitive markets holds that a growing number of low-wage workers or a widening "effective" minimum wage market will be the result of market forces that are suppressing their wages. As a result of technological change that has been biased toward those with higher levels of education and skills, the presence of a sizeable labor market lacking skills has served to drive down wages. As the economy has evolved from industrial-based manufacturing to post-industrial service, there has been a growing mismatch between good-paying jobs and the skills available to workers.

According to this school of thought, the labor market is divided into a primary market where high premiums are placed on skilled workers and a secondary market with unskilled workers trapped in the lowest wage service sector of the economy. Increasing skills differentials between the two labor markets have only led to the growth in wage inequality (Katz and Murphy 1992; Katz and Krueger 1992). The main culprit is technological change biased toward those with higher levels of education and skills (Juhn et al. 1993; Sandler and Wapler 2004; Autor et al. 2008; Balleer and van Rens 2013; Vivarelli 2014). Claudia Goldin and Lawrence Katz (2008) note that inequality decreased during the first half of the twentieth century when more students were completing high school. There was what they refer to as the high school premium. But after 1950, and especially after 1980, increasingly greater numbers were no longer completing high school and inequality grew.

In a competitive market where the new and technologically advanced is always replacing the old and obsolete, it is a foregone conclusion that the wages of unskilled workers will be forced down while the wages of the skilled workers are driven up, thereby increasing the gap between the two. If there is an oversupply of low-skilled or uneducated workers, the wages of those jobs for which they qualify will be pushed down. Nevertheless, this view has formed the basis for what Frank Levy and Peter Temin (2010) refer to as the "Washington Consensus" that maintains that market forces favoring higher levels of education and skill to be the source of inequality, stagnating wages for the average worker, and potentially long-term unemployment. And yet, as much as this might be true, it misses the role that policy plays either in exacerbating or hindering the so-called natural process, especially policy that may have aided in the decline in labor market institutions.

Institutionalists—institutional economists and increasingly political scientists—hold rising wage inequality to be due to a shift in public policy and a corresponding decline in labor market institutions like unions and the minimum wage in the USA and wage councils in Britain (Piore 1995; Gordon, 1996; DiNardo and Lemieux, 1997; Fortin and Lemieux 1997; Lee 1997; Machin 1997; Galbraith 1998; Palley 1998; Lemieux 1998; Howell 1999; Wallerstein 1999, 2008; Craypo and Cormier 2000; Card and DiNardo 2002; Howell and Huebler 2001; Pontusson 2005). From the mid-1990s, decreasing union density was accompanied by a falling union wage premium because of the declining demand for union labor. This was due to increasing competitiveness throughout the US economy and union companies faced nonunion competition (Blanchflower and Bryson 2008). Within the union sector wage inequality was low (Freeman 2004), but declining unionism contributed to a steep increase in wage inequality in both the USA and the UK during the 1980s. And in Canada the rise in the real minimum wage may have actually offset the pressure toward increased inequality associated with the decline in union strength during the 1980s and late 1990s while in the USA it was approximately constant over the same period (Card et al. 2008).

Even those that hold that inequality increased due to market forces of supply and demand concede that a decline in the minimum wage may have contributed to rising wage inequality, at least in the lower tail of the wage distribution. Although on the basis of the 90/10 ratio there has been no impact, there has been on the basis of the 50/10 ratio (Belman and Wolfson 2014; Autor et al. 2008). Goldin and Katz (2008) maintain that the policy failure lies in the nation's school system and that education has not kept abreast of greater technological demands, with market forces pushing wages down and exacerbating inequality. While they emphasize the need for more education, casting it as a race between education and technology, they too acknowledge that the very market forces that made education more critical have been exacerbated by the decline of institutions, as well as policies that have made the tax code less progressive. As they put it, the effect of the minimum wage's decline in real value, along with the continued decline in union membership, was for the college wage premium to be increased beyond what market forces alone might have predicted (p. 302).

Joseph Stiglitz (2012), for instance, argues that the collapse of good jobs during the last quarter century was due to public policy decisions. With this collapse, wages also fell with a resultant increase in disparity between the top and the bottom. As a result of labor market polarization, more money has gone to the top while more and more people have been going to the bottom. Gordon Lafer (2002) observes that while the skills mismatch thesis has become a convenient explanation for falling wages and rising inequality, it is the decline in unionism rather than less education or training that has played a greater role in determining wages of most workers. Institutions that protected the wages of production workers have been eliminated while professional earnings have remained protected by an elaborate system of immigration control, business, educational credentials, and legal mandates. The earnings of professionals have not been propped up by the rarity of their skills but by their ability to exert institutional barriers to competition. The biggest blow to those at the bottom of the distribution has been the deterioration of unions. With this decline came a corresponding decline in wages because union wages were generally 28.4 percent higher than those of unorganized workers. Or as Freeman and Medoff (1985) most famously observed, a 10 percent increase in organizing in manufacturing generates a 1.5 percent increase in the union wage. Wage rates for workers were maintained by the union premium; not that workers receive wages equal to their marginal productivity according to traditional human capital theory. It is institutions that set rates and determine worth (Lafer 2002). It is no coincidence, then, that the value of the minimum wage declined as union membership declined. Among the functions performed by unions is that they got their members out to vote (Hacker and Pierson 2010). With the decline of unions there has been no constituency for the minimum wage (Levin-Waldman 2001), and income inequality has increased partly due to the minimum wage's deterioration (Volscho 2005).

Thomas Piketty (2014) observes that the minimum wage in France did play a role in reducing wage inequality in the post-World War II years while wage inequality in the USA rose as the minimum wage was in decline. In France a national minimum wage was created in 1950 but was seldom increased thereafter and only fell farther behind the average wage. But in 1970, the minimum wage was officially indexed to the mean wage. Moreover, governments from 1968 to 1983 felt obligated to increase the minimum wage significantly almost every year in a seething social and political climate. Between 1968 and 1983 the purchasing power of the minimum wage also increased by more than 130 percent, while the mean wage only increased by 50 percent. The result was a significant compression of wage inequality. In the USA, however, a subclass of "supermanagers" emerged. Inequality had reached its lowest ebb between 1950 and 1980, whereby the top decile of the income distribution claimed 30–35 percent of the nation's income.

After 1980, however, income inequality exploded with the top decile share of the national income rising to between 45 and 50 percent in the 2000s. The causes of rising income inequality in the USA are largely due to the unprecedented increase in wage inequality, and especially the extremely high compensation of managers at the top of the distribution. The idea that market forces are forcing down the wages of those with little skill does not offer a satisfactory explanation of the rise of the supermanager or of wage inequality in the USA after 1980. The implications would appear to be clear. Wage inequality in the USA during this period may have been less if, at a minimum, the minimum wage had kept up just as the minimum wage had kept up in France. The failure to maintain the minimum wage in the USA has to be viewed as a public policy choice.

The fact that the growth in inequality has been due to primarily the top pulling away from the rest might call into question the impact of institutions like unions and the minimum wage on inequality. Autor et al. (2008) reject what they call the revisionist alternative to the skills-biased toward technical change hypothesis, arguing that it does not really explain the main problem of the top pulling away from the rest. Using data from the Current Population Survey (CPS), they only find partial support for the revisionist literature. They did agree that the declining minimum wage contributed to a rise in wage inequality in the lower tail—the 50/10 ratio—during the 1980s, but they found little support for the strong focus of major revisionist claims. Inequality in the lower half of the distribution did increase rapidly during the 1980s, but reversed course thereafter. And yet the persistent rise in inequality in the upper tail of the distribution belies the claim that the minimum wage, in and of itself, can provide a coherent explanation in the bulk of the increase in earnings inequality. Rather changes in US earnings distribution "polarized" with a strong and persistent rise in inequality in the upper half of the distribution and a slowing of inequality trends in the lower half of the distribution. Therefore, the revisionist arguments focusing on nonmarket factors, especially the minimum wage, are unable to provide a compelling explanation for the strong steady increase in upper tail inequality over the last 25 years and the polarization of employment growth since 1990. Rather skill demand shifts have played a central role in shaping the wage structure both during the 1980s and afterward, when polarization of wage growth followed. Still, there is a difference between not being able to explain the pulling away and that institutions on the whole can at least play a role in reducing the increase in inequality. The minimum wage is but one institution, and unionization or union density may speak to another, as well as right-to-work laws speak to other institutions that actually suppress wages.

Using the same data from the CPS, we can see just what the impact of the decline of institutions, most notably the minimum wage, has been on inequality. When it comes to labor market institutions there are a couple of different issues. The major labor market institutions that have served to bolster wages have been minimum wage laws, both at the federal and state levels, and union membership. In the CPS data, there is no significant reading on the union coverage variable, but unionism can be measured nonetheless by looking at the level of union density in each state, which has declined considerably over the last three decades, with a precipitous decline occurring since 2002. But there is also the issue of right-to-work laws that could be classified as an anti-labor market institution because insofar as they were designed to make union organizing more difficult, they could potentially be seen as having the potential to suppress wages. More states in recent years have been passing right-to-work laws, especially in response to the growth of public sector unionism. In this vein, right-to-work laws can be seen as a deliberate policy choice at the state level with the potential to exacerbate wage inequality. Again the data is from the IPUMS-CPS and is based on those specifically working full-time for wages. Therefore, the third through sixth columns are the various ratios measuring specifically wage inequality. The last column, then, is the ratio of the average family income of full-time wage earners in the top quintile to the average family income of full-time wage earners in the bottom quintile. General trends in wage inequality can be seen in Table 5.1.

Overall wage inequality appears to have declined between 1982 and 2015, but at least by the measure of the ratio between the top quintile and the bottom quintile, it did increase between 1992 and 2002. By the other

Table 5.1 Relationship between minimum wage and inequality in the USA

Year	*Minimum wage*	*90/10 wage ratio*	*90/50 wage ratio*	*50/10 wage ratio*	*Top-to-bottom quintile wage ratio*	*Top-to-bottom family income ratio*
1982	$3.35	20.0	2.2	8.9	15.6	
1992	$4.25	12.3	2.3	5.4	12.4	
2000	$5.15	9.9	2.4	4.1	13.1	8.3
2001	$5.15	8.9	2.3	3.8	12.4	8.1
2002	$5.15	8.5	2.4	3.5	13.1	8.2
2003	$5.15	9.0	2.5	3.6	13.3	8.1
2004	$5.15	8.5	2.4	3.6	13.0	8.4
2005	$5.15	8.8	2.5	3.6	13.6	8.4
2006	$5.15	8.9	2.4	3.7	12.9	8.7
2007	$5.85	8.5	2.4	3.5	12.2	8.7
2008	$6.55	8.7	2.4	3.6	12.2	8.3
2009	$7.25	8.3	2.4	3.5	11.3	8.4
2010	$7.25	8.4	2.4	3.5	11.5	8.7
2011	$7.25	8.3	2.4	3.4	11.2	8.4
2012	$7.25	8.6	2.5	3.5	11.9	8.8
2013	$7.25	8.3	2.5	3.3	12.5	8.9
2014	$7.25	8.3	2.5	3.3	12.3	9.0
2015	$7.25	8.3	2.5	3.3	12.4	9.3

measures, however, it decreased. Despite variations in the rates of inequality, there was a decline in wage inequality between 2006 and 2009. Then, beginning in 2010 inequality, according to the Quintile ratio measure, ticks up again. What is important about this period is that in 2007, the first phase of a three-phase increase in the minimum wage took effect, with the last phase occurring in 2009. Between 2009 and 2015, inequality increased because the mean income of the top quintile increased by 12.2 percent while it only increased by 2.2 percent among the bottom quintile. But between 2006 and 2009, the mean income of the bottom quintile increased by 28 percent while it only increased by 11.9 percent among the top quintile. For inequality to be less, the rate of percentage increase in the mean wage among the bottom has to be greater than the rate of percentage increase in the mean among the top (Gottschalk 1997). It would also follow that if reduced inequality was due to a drop in mean wages it was because the decrease was greater among the top than among the bottom. Also on the basis of the quintile ratio, inequality increased by 9.7 percent between 2009 and 2015, which is significant because there was no further increase in the federal minimum wage.

It would appear that between 2002 and 2015, wage inequality on the basis of the quintile ratio decreased by 5.3 percent while family income inequality on the same basis increased by 14.5 percent. On the basis of the 90/10 and 50/10 ratios wage inequality decreased by 16.7 percent and 19.5 percent, respectively, but on the 90/50 ratio, it did increase by 4.2 percent. And yet, there are some interesting occurrences following the increases in the federal minimum wage, which was increased first in 2007, again in 2008, and then in 2009. If we look at the change in family income, in 2006 the ratio was 2.7 percent and remained 2.7 percent in 2007. In 2008, it dropped by 4.6 percent to 2.8 percent in 2009 with the last increase in the minimum wage. But between 2009 and 2015, the top-to-bottom family income ratio increased 10.7 percent and the top-to-bottom ratio in wage income increased by 9.7 percent. It would appear that there was a slight reduction in income inequality, especially wage inequality, by most measures following the last increase in the minimum wage in 2009. But between 2009 and 2015 when there were no increases in the minimum wage, both wage and family income inequality on the basis of the quintile measure increased. On the basis of the 90/10 measure there was no change in wage inequality, a slight increase on the basis of the 90/50 measure, and a slight decrease on the basis of the 50/10 measure.

The question, however, is how this inequality is affected by anti-labor market and labor market institutions alike. Many states following passage of the Taft-Hartley Act in 1947 passed right-to-work laws which prohibited closed union shops. Workers could no longer be forced to join a union as a condition of employment, which effectively made union organizing more difficult. Decline in union membership is in part attributable to these laws, but also to the mobility of capital from high union density states to right-to-work states. Differences between right-to-work and non-right-to-work states can be seen in Table 5.2.

In 1982 and 1992 wage inequality is lower by most measures in non-right-to-work states than in right-to-work states. In the 2000s, save for a few exceptions, this does not appear to be the case. In 2004, 2005, and 2011 wage inequality on the 90/10 measure is higher in the right-to-work states than in the non-right-to-work states. Also in 2004 and 2011 wage inequality on the 50/10 measure is higher in the right-to-work states than in the non-right-to-work states, which suggests that the absence of labor market institutions did have an effect in the lower tail of the distribution. Still the overall comparisons beg the question of why wage inequality would be higher in non-right-to-work states. Intuitively, we would expect inequality to be higher in right-to-work states because the

Table 5.2 Wage inequality in right-to-work states and non-right-to-work states (percent)

	RTW				*Non-RTW*			
	90/10	*90/50*	*50/10*	*Ratio of top quintile to bottom quintile*	*90/10*	*90/50*	*50/10*	*Ratio of top quintile to bottom quintile*
1982	70.0	2.3	30.0	20.5	13.4	2.1	6.4	12.4
1992	14.5	2.3	6.4	13.7	11.1	2.2	5.1	11.7
2002	8.3	2.3	3.6	12.6	8.3	2.3	3.5	13.1
2003	8.9	2.4	3.7	12.2	8.9	2.4	3.6	13.3
2004	8.8	2.3	3.8	12.1	8.3	2.4	3.5	12.8
2005	9.0	2.4	3.8	13.3	8.7	2.3	3.8	13.0
2006	8.3	2.5	3.3	12.2	8.9	2.4	3.6	13.0
2007	8.2	2.4	3.5	12.6	9.0	2.5	3.6	13.8
2008	8.0	2.4	2.8	11.4	8.7	2.4	3.6	11.3
2009	8.2	2.3	3.5	11.3	8.9	2.5	3.6	11.9
2010	8.3	2.4	3.5	11.8	10.7	2.5	3.5	12.4
2011	8.5	2.4	3.5	12.2	8.3	2.5	3.3	12.9
2012	8.2	2.5	3.3	10.8	8.3	2.5	3.3	12.9
2013	7.6	2.4	3.1	10.5	8.6	2.5	3.5	13.1
2014	8.0	2.4	3.4	11.5	9.5	2.5	3.8	11.9
2015	7.9	2.4	3.3	11.2	8.6	2.5	3.4	12.9

effect, if not the purpose, of such laws is to suppress wages, especially wages at the bottom of the distribution. One reason for why inequality might be less in right-to-work states is because these laws are suppressing the overall wage structure in these states, thereby resulting in less of a gap between the top and the bottom. Right-to-work laws might have the effect of compressing wages. Another reason may have something do with the overall impact of right-to-work laws on unionism. We would expect unionism, as measured by union density, to be even less in those states. In other words, it may not even be so much that right-to-work laws are suppressing wages than it is union density is raising wages. But if unionism is in decline, union density will have less of an impact on wages and the degree to which there is wage inequality.

The next question is just what the impact of union density is on wage structure and the degree to which there is wage inequality. Comparisons between high union density states and low union density states can be seen in Table 5.3.

In most years, on the basis of the 90/10 ratio, wage inequality is lower in high union density states than in low union density states. On the basis of the

Table 5.3 Wage inequality in high union density states and low union density states (percent)

	High union density states				*Low union density states*			
	90/10	*90/50*	*50/10*	*Ratio of top quintile to bottom quintile*	*90/10*	*90/50*	*50/10*	*Ratio of top quintile to bottom quintile*
1982	12.5	2.1	6.0	12.3	53.1	2.3	22.6	20.1
1992	10.4	2.2	4.8	11.8	14.3	2.3	6.3	8.2
2002	8.3	2.3	3.6	13.1	8.5	2.3	3.6	11.9
2003	8.7	2.4	3.6	13.1	8.8	2.3	3.8	12.6
2004	8.3	2.4	3.4	12.8	8.8	2.3	3.8	12.6
2005	8.5	2.3	3.6	13.0	9.4	2.5	3.8	13.4
2006	8.6	2.4	3.5	13.0	8.7	2.4	3.6	13.1
2007	9.0	2.5	3.6	13.7	8.4	2.4	3.5	13.2
2008	8.2	2.4	3.5	11.2	8.3	2.4	3.5	11.8
2009	8.7	2.4	3.6	11.8	8.7	2.4	3.6	12.2
2010	8.8	2.5	3.6	12.0	8.9	2.5	3.6	12.4
2011	8.3	2.5	3.3	12.0	8.2	2.4	3.4	10.5
2012	8.3	2.5	3.3	12.7	8.5	2.4	3.4	11.6
2013	8.3	2.5	3.3	13.1	7.9	2.4	3.3	11.4
2014	9.1	2.5	3.7	13.3	8.4	2.4	3.5	11.9
2015	8.5	2.5	3.4	12.7	8.7	2.5	3.3	11.5

quintile ratio, wage inequality is lower in high union density states than in low union density states in 1982, 1992, from 2004 to 2006, and from 2008 to 2010. It is also interesting to note that from 1982 through 2006, for the exception of 2002, and then again from 2011 to 2012, that wage inequality is lower on the 50/10 ratio in high union density states than in low union density states. But on the quintile ratio, wage inequality is higher in high union density states than in low union density states. This raises the question of what the effect of declining union density is on relative wage inequality.

As much as union density may be a factor in explaining why some states are more likely to have greater inequality than others, another institution that would be important to consider would be state minimum wage laws. Several states have their own minimum wage laws that are higher than the federal minimum wage. Comparisons between states with higher state minimum wages with those that do not have higher minimum wages or minimum wages at all can be seen in Table 5.4.

Table 5.4 Inequality by states with higher minimum wages versus those without (percent)

	States with higher minimum wages				*States without higher minimum wages*			
	90/10	*90/50*	*50/10*	*Ratio of top quintile to bottom quintile*	*90/10*	*90/50*	*50/10*	*Ratio of top quintile to bottom quintile*
1982	19.4	2.2	9.0	13.5	2000	2.3	8.7	15.3
1992	10.4	2.2	4.8	11.8	12.9	2.3	5.7	12.2
2002	9.4	2.4	4.0	13.6	8.2	2.3	3.5	12.8
2003	9.4	2.3	4.0	14.2	8.8	2.5	3.5	13.1
2004	10.0	2.4	4.1	14.1	8.3	2.4	3.4	12.4
2005	10.0	2.4	4.3	14.0	8.5	2.4	3.6	13.2
2006	8.9	2.4	3.6	13.9	8.6	2.4	3.6	13.2
2007	8.9	2.5	3.5	13.4	8.8	2.3	3.7	13.0
2008	8.3	2.4	3.4	10.6	8.3	2.4	3.5	12.7
2009	8.6	2.4	3.5	11.6	8.3	2.4	3.5	11.6
2010	8.6	2.4	3.6	11.8	8.4	2.4	3.5	11.8
2011	8.2	2.5	3.3	11.4	8.5	2.4	3.5	12.4
2012	8.7	2.5	3.5	12.7	8.2	2.4	3.4	11.5
2013	8.5	2.5	3.4	13.2	7.9	2.4	3.3	11.5
2014	9.1	2.5	3.7	13.1	8.3	2.4	3.5	11.9
2015	8.4	2.5	3.3	12.6	8.3	2.5	3.3	11.4

On the face of it, it would appear that states that have their own minimum wages that are higher than the federal minimum wage do not necessarily have less wage inequality than those states that do not. And this could very well be because there really are not that many states that have minimum wages, let alone ones that are higher than the federal minimum wage. The question, then, is how do the states we looked at in Chap. 3 where there have been increases compare to the nation as a whole. A closer look at some of the states that have their own minimum wages higher than the federal minimum can be seen in Table 5.5.

Already on the basis of this table we see some interesting things. In California, which had raised its own minimum wage over the years, the critical period is 2008–2015, with 2015 itself being a very critical year. In 2008 the minimum wage was raised to $8.00 an hour from $7.50 in 2007. From 2007 to 2008 inequality decreases on the basis of most measures.

Table 5.5 Inequality measures on state-by-state basis

Year	*Minimum wage*	*90/10 wage ratio*	*90/50 wage ratio*	*50/10 wage ratio*	*Top-to-bottom quintile wage ratio*	*Top-to-bottom family income ratio*
California						
2000	$6.25	13.4	2.6	5.1	14.4	9.0
2001	$6.25	12.5	2.5	5.0	16.5	8.9
2002	$6.75	11.1	2.6	4.3	16.4	8.8
2003	$6.75	11.4	2.7	4.3	16.4	8.9
2004	$6.75	12.1	2.7	4.5	14.8	9.7
2005	$6.75	10.9	2.7	4.1	14.7	9.3
2006	$6.75	13.2	2.3	5.8	17.0	9.3
2007	$7.50	13.3	2.7	4.9	17.4	9.7
2008	$8.00	12.3	2.8	4.4	17.1	9.5
2009	$8.00	11.3	2.6	4.3	15.9	10.1
2010	$8.00	12.5	2.6	4.8	16.3	9.6
2011	$8.00	10.0	2.6	3.9	15.2	9.4
2012	$8.00	10.5	2.7	3.9	16.5	10.1
2013	$8.00	11.0	2.8	5.0	17.1	9.9
2014	$8.00	12.2	2.8	4.4	17.3	10.4
2015	$9.00	10.9	2.8	4.0	14.1	10.5
Connecticut						
2000	$6.15	10.2	2.3	4.5	14.0	7.6
2001	$6.40	7.4	2.2	3.3	11.1	7.8
2002	$6.70	8.7	2.4	3.7	13.8	8.6
2003	$6.90	10.6	2.4	4.3	15.4	8.2
2004	$7.10	8.3	2.5	3.3	12.2	7.4
2005	$7.10	9.0	2.2	4.0	13.9	7.5
2006	$7.40	8.3	2.4	3.5	14.0	8.9
2007	$7.65	9.6	2.6	3.7	16.2	9.8
2008	$7.65	8.8	2.4	3.8	13.1	9.1
2009	$8.00	10.5	2.5	4.2	13.9	8.3
2010	$8.25	9.2	2.4	3.8	14.5	9.3
2011	$8.25	11.0	2.4	4.6	15.3	9.6
2012	$8.25	10.8	2.6	4.2	16.0	9.1
2013	$8.25	10.0	2.6	3.8	16.3	9.6
2014	$8.70	10.4	2.5	4.2	14.0	8.8
2015	$9.15	8.1	2.4	3.3	11.8	8.2
Massachusetts						
2000	$6.00	8.3	2.3	3.7	11.8	8.8
2001	$6.75	10.3	2.4	4.4	15.7	8.7
2002	$6.75	8.5	2.2	3.8	12.8	7.8
2003	$6.75	8.6	2.3	3.8	11.5	8.2

(*continued*)

Table 5.5 (continued)

Year	*Minimum wage*	*90/10 wage ratio*	*90/50 wage ratio*	*50/10 wage ratio*	*Top-to-bottom quintile wage ratio*	*Top-to-bottom family income ratio*
2004	$6.75	9.6	2.5	3.8	13.5	8.2
2005	$6.75	9.1	2.5	3.6	13.7	8.9
2006	$6.75	10.1	2.5	4.1	14.8	8.9
2007	$7.50	20.0	2.7	7.5	19.0	11.2
2008	$8.00	11.5	2.6	4.5	15.5	9.0
2009	$8.00	8.4	2.4	3.5	11.6	8.5
2010	$8.00	8.0	2.4	3.3	13.3	9.2
2011	$8.00	9.0	2.5	3.6	13.7	7.8
2012	$8.00	8.7	3.3	2.7	12.2	8.7
2013	$8.00	7.6	2.4	3.2	10.4	7.9
2014	$8.00	8.3	2.5	3.3	14.1	10.5
2015	$9.00	8.1	2.4	3.3	12.1	9.6
New Jersey						
2000	$5.15	7.7	2.4	3.2	10.9	8.3
2001	$5.15	8.2	2.4	3.4	12.7	8.7
2002	$5.15	8.6	2.6	3.3	12.8	9.4
2003	$5.15	7.8	2.3	3.3	11.4	8.1
2004	$5.15	7.7	2.5	3.1	11.3	8.5
2005	$6.15	8.3	2.5	3.3	12.4	9.4
2006	$7.15	7.8	2.6	3.1	12.3	9.4
2007	$7.15	7.6	2.4	3.1	12.5	8.9
2008	$7.15	8.7	2.7	3.2	12.7	8.4
2009	$7.25	8.0	2.7	3.0	12.8	9.1
2010	$7.25	7.6	2.5	3.0	12.0	9.3
2011	$7.25	8.0	2.6	3.1	11.6	10.4
2012	$7.25	8.8	2.7	3.2	13.7	10.2
2013	$7.25	8.3	2.6	3.2	13.0	9.9
2014	$8.25	7.4	2.6	2.8	10.3	9.1
2015	$8.38	8.0	2.4	3.3	11.8	9.0
New York						
2000	$5.15	10.9	2.5	4.4	14.0	9.4
2001	$5.15	8.4	2.5	3.3	13.0	8.9
2002	$5.15	9.1	2.6	3.5	13.9	9.3
2003	$5.15	8.0	2.5	3.2	12.6	9.0
2004	$5.15	10.6	2.5	4.3	14.9	8.9
2005	$6.00	8.8	2.5	3.5	13.2	9.8
2006	$6.75	8.8	2.5	3.5	13.4	9.7
2007	$7.15	9.3	2.5	3.8	14.0	10.3
2008	$7.15	7.8	2.5	3.2	10.5	9.2

(*continued*)

Table 5.5 (continued)

Year	*Minimum wage*	*90/10 wage ratio*	*90/50 wage ratio*	*50/10 wage ratio*	*Top-to-bottom quintile wage ratio*	*Top-to-bottom family income ratio*
2009	$7.25	8.3	2.5	3.3	11.6	9.0
2010	$7.25	7.7	2.5	3.1	12.1	9.7
2011	$7.25	7.7	2.5	3.1	12.0	9.6
2012	$7.25	7.6	2.4	3.1	11.6	9.4
2013	$7.25	9.1	2.6	3.5	14.0	10.2
2014	$8.00	7.4	2.6	2.9	13.0	10.1
2015	$8.75	8.9	2.7	3.3	13.8	10.5
Ohio						
2000	$5.15	7.2	2.2	3.3	9.8	7.6
2001	$5.15	7.0	2.2	3.2	10.7	7.0
2002	$5.15	7.2	2.2	3.3	9.8	7.6
2003	$5.15	7.5	2.3	3.3	10.9	7.9
2004	$5.15	7.2	2.2	3.3	11.1	7.6
2005	$5.15	7.1	2.1	3.3	10.0	6.7
2006	$5.15	7.2	2.1	3.4	10.2	7.3
2007	$6.85	7.2	2.3	3.2	9.4	11.0
2008	$7.00	6.7	2.2	3.0	9.5	7.4
2009	$7.30	6.4	2.2	3.0	8.8	6.9
2010	$7.30	7.0	2.2	3.1	9.8	7.0
2011	$7.40	7.4	2.3	3.2	9.8	6.8
2012	$7.70	7.5	2.4	3.1	11.1	8.6
2013	$7.85	6.9	2.4	2.9	10.6	8.3
2014	$7.95	6.3	2.3	2.8	10.3	8.4
2015	$8.15	7.8	2.4	3.3	11.3	8.7
Oregon						
2000	$6.50	33.2	2.4	13.7	18.8	9.2
2001	$6.50	10.0	2.3	4.3	13.4	8.5
2002	$6.50	11.7	2.3	5.0	15.4	8.7
2003	$6.90	10.4	2.3	4.6	13.8	7.4
2004	$7.05	9.0	2.3	4.0	12.3	7.6
2005	$7.25	16.5	2.5	6.6	16.9	9.2
2006	$7.50	20.0	2.5	8.0	19.5	9.6
2007	$7.80	17.0	2.4	7.0	16.7	9.1
2008	$7.95	12.0	2.4	5.1	12.1	8.7
2009	$8.40	8.6	2.3	3.7	12.4	8.0
2010	$8.40	9.0	2.5	3.6	14.0	8.7
2011	$8.80	10.6	2.3	4.7	12.6	8.2
2012	$8.80	8.2	2.3	3.6	10.3	7.8
2013	$8.95	11.0	2.4	4.7	12.0	8.0

(continued)

Table 5.5 (continued)

Year	*Minimum wage*	*90/10 wage ratio*	*90/50 wage ratio*	*50/10 wage ratio*	*Top-to-bottom quintile wage ratio*	*Top-to-bottom family income ratio*
2014	$9.10	8.2	2.5	3.3	10.4	7.7
2015	$9.25	10.0	2.5	4.0	13.3	8.5
Pennsylvania						
2000	$5.15	8.1	2.2	3.6	12.4	7.7
2001	$5.15	8.3	2.4	3.5	12.5	7.5
2002	$5.15	8.0	2.5	3.2	12.7	7.8
2003	$5.15	8.3	2.4	3.4	13.1	8.0
2004	$5.15	8.5	2.4	3.5	12.0	7.9
2005	$5.15	8.0	2.4	3.3	12.2	8.2
2006	$5.15	8.0	2.3	3.5	12.0	8.3
2007	$6.75	8.3	2.4	3.5	11.9	7.7
2008	$7.15	7.2	2.3	3.2	10.3	7.3
2009	$7.25	8.2	2.3	3.6	12.1	7.5
2010	$7.25	9.2	2.4	3.8	12.7	8.0
2011	$7.25	7.9	2.4	3.3	11.3	7.4
2012	$7.25	9.2	2.4	3.8	12.8	8.4
2013	$7.25	7.7	2.5	3.1	10.8	7.9
2014	$7.25	6.9	2.4	2.5	10.3	7.9
2015	$7.25	7.4	2.4	3.0	11.0	8.7
Rhode Island						
2000	$6.15	7.0	2.2	3.2	9.3	6.9
2001	$6.15	7.2	2.2	3.2	11.1	8.0
2002	$6.15	7.2	2.3	3.2	11.1	8.1
2003	$6.15	7.5	2.3	3.3	10.5	7.0
2004	$6.75	7.9	2.3	3.4	11.7	7.8
2005	$6.75	7.8	2.5	3.2	11.1	8.0
2006	$7.10	8.4	2.4	3.5	12.5	9.2
2007	$7.40	8.5	2.4	3.6	12.7	8.3
2008	$7.40	8.8	2.4	3.6	11.9	8.0
2009	$7.40	8.0	2.4	3.3	12.1	8.0
2010	$7.40	7.0	2.4	2.9	10.3	7.8
2011	$7.40	7.7	2.4	3.2	10.1	6.8
2012	$7.40	8.3	2.3	3.6	11.2	7.8
2013	$7.75	7.5	2.4	3.2	11.5	9.1
2014	$8.00	9.0	2.4	3.8	12.1	9.6
2015	$9.00	8.6	2.4	3.6	13.3	9.2
Vermont						
2000	$5.75	11.8	2.2	5.4	12.8	5.0
2001	$6.25	14.3	2.1	6.7	13.9	7.9

(*continued*)

Table 5.5 (continued)

Year	*Minimum wage*	*90/10 wage ratio*	*90/50 wage ratio*	*50/10 wage ratio*	*Top-to-bottom quintile wage ratio*	*Top-to-bottom family income ratio*
2002	$6.25	21.7	2.2	9.7	15.9	7.2
2003	$6.25	16.3	2.3	7.2	14.7	7.0
2004	$6.75	14.9	2.1	7.5	14.5	7.4
2005	$7.00	35.0	2.3	16.0	18.6	7.7
2006	$7.25	18.7	2.2	8.7	16.1	7.0
2007	$7.53	15.1	2.3	6.7	13.9	7.0
2008	$7.68	0	2.3	0	20.7	7.1
2009	$8.06	9.4	2.1	4.5	12.6	7.0
2010	$8.06	21.1	2.1	10.0	13.9	6.6
2011	$8.15	14.1	2.2	6.5	13.4	6.2
2012	$8.46	13.7	2.2	6.2	13.9	6.8
2013	$8.60	24.1	2.3	10.6	15.3	7.3
2014	$8.73	18.3	2.3	8.1	14.8	6.9
2015	$9.15	14.9	2.5	7.5	15.4	7.4

Wage inequality decreases 8.1 percent on the 90/10 measure and by 7.0 percent on the quintile measure. It also declines 7.1 percent on the 90/50 measure and by 2.3 percent on the 50/10 measure. Family income inequality, however, does increase by 6.3 percent in the quintile measure. Thereafter until 2015 we see variation in inequality. It is the change in 2015 which is important because of the increase in the state's minimum wage from $8.00 an hour in 2014 to $9.00 an hour in 2015. For the exception of the 90/50 measure which remains the same, wage inequality on all other measures does decrease. It decreases by 10.7, 7.5, and 11.3 percent on the 90/10, 50/10, and quintile measures, respectively. Family income inequality on the quintile measure does increase by 1.0 percent.

In Connecticut we see considerably more variation which may have something to do with minimum wage increases being a regular thing and the increases not being quite as large as they were in California. But from 2014 to 2015 where there was a $.45 increase in the state's minimum wage, inequality on all measures declined. On the 90/10 measure wage inequality decreased by 22.1 percent. On the 90/50 measure it decreased by 4 percent; on the 50/10 measure it decreased by 21.4 percent; and on the quintile measure it decreased by 15.7 percent. Family income inequality decreased by 6.8 percent on the quintile measure. In Massachusetts the pattern is similar to California. Again the state had historically had higher minimum wages than the federal minimum wage, and it too had a $1.00 increase in the minimum wage from 2014 to 2015. From 2007 to 2008 when the minimum wage increased to $8.00 from $7.50, there appears to be a decrease in inequality on the basis of all measures. Wage inequality drops by 42.5 percent on the 90/10 measure, by 3.7 percent on the 90/50 measure, by 22.2 percent on the 50/10 measure, and by 25.2 percent on the quintile measure. Family income inequality on the basis of the quintile measure only dropped by 5.6 percent. As was the case in California, the minimum wage in Massachusetts was not increased again until 2015. Between 2014 and 2015, following a $1.00 increase in the state's minimum wage, wage inequality decreased by 2.4 percent on the 90/10 measure, by 4.0 percent on the 90/50 measure, 0 percent on the 50/10 measure, and by 14.2 percent on the quintile measure. Family income inequality on the quintile measure decreased by 8.6 percent.

In New Jersey, where the minimum wage generally paralleled the federal minimum wage, the critical year is 2014 when the state enacted a minimum wage of $8.25. Between 2013 and 2014 wage inequality decreased by 10.8 percent on the 90/10 measure, by 0 percent on the 90/50 measure, by 12.5 percent on the 50/10 measure, and by 20.8 percent on the quintile measure. Family income inequality on the basis of the quintile measure decreased by 8.8 percent. Then in 2015 following only a $.13 increase in the state minimum wage, wage inequality, for the exception of the 90/50 measure where it decreased by 7.7 percent, actually increases. Family income inequality decreases by 4.4 percent. In New York, however, the story is slightly different. Again, the state's minimum wage runs parallel to the federal minimum during this period. Like New Jersey the critical year is 2014 when the state enacted an $8.00 an hour minimum wage. Following this initial increase in the minimum wage from $7.25 in 2013 to $8.00 in 2014, wage inequality decreased by 18.7 percent on the 90/10 measure, by 0 percent on the 90/50 measure, by 17.1 percent on the 50/10 measure, and by 7.1 percent on the quintile measure. Family income inequality on the quintile measure only decreased by 1.0 percent. And yet, following an additional $.75 increase in the state's minimum wage in 2015, inequality on all measures increases.

In Ohio and Oregon, where there have been increases in state minimum wages over the years, inequality on most measures increased. It does not necessarily follow, however, that a minimum wage will not have an impact on inequality, rather it is the size of the increase that might. In some years there are increases and in other years there are decreases. In

Pennsylvania, however, where there has been no state minimum wage, inequality does increase especially between 2009, the year the last federal increase in the minimum wage took effect, and 2015. During this six-year period wage inequality does decrease by 10.8 percent and 16.7 percent on the 90/10 and 50/10 measures, respectively. It increases by 4.3 percent on the 90/50 measure but decreases by 9 percent on the quintile measure. Family income inequality from 2009 to 2015 increases by 16 percent on the quintile measure. In Rhode Island where there had been increases in the state's minimum wage, there are periods when inequality increases and other periods when it appears to decrease. As an example, from 2012 to 2013 when the state's minimum wage rose from $7.40 to $7.75 wage inequality decreased by 9.6 percent and 11.1 percent on the 90/10 and 50/10 measures, respectively. But it increased by 4.3 percent and 2.7 percent on the 90/50 and quintile measures, respectively. At the same time, family income inequality on the quintile measure increased by 16.7 percent. Then when the state's minimum wage increases from $8.00 an hour in 2014 to $9.00 an hour in 2015, wage inequality decreases by 4.4 percent and 5.3 percent on the 90/10 and 50/10 measures, respectively. It remains unchanged on the 90/50 measure and increases by 9.9 percent on the quintile measure. And yet, family income inequality on the quintile measure actually decreases by 4.2 percent.

The real outlier here appears to be the state of Vermont where there have been consistent increases in the minimum wage. Between 2009 and 2015 when the federal minimum wage remained constant, inequality on all measures increased. During this period wage inequality increased by 47.9 percent, 19.0 percent, 66.7 percent, and 22.2 percent on the 90/10, 90/50, 50/10, and quintile measures, respectively. Family income inequality on the quintile measure during this period increased by 5.7 percent. On the other hand, the overall change between 2002 and 2015 in a state where its minimum wage has always been higher than the federal minimum wage during this period actually tells a slightly different story. Between 2002 and 2015, wage inequality decreased by 31.3 percent, 22.7 percent, and 3.1 percent on the 90/10, 50/10, and quintile measures, respectively. Wage inequality on the 90/50 measure did increase by 13.6 percent and family income inequality in the quintile measure increased by 2.8 percent. Arguably, then, the case may be made, or at least speculated, that despite fluctuations in levels of inequality that inequality was perhaps decreasing because there was a state labor market institution in place to bolster wages (Table 5.6).

Table 5.6 Changes in inequality

Year	*90/10 wage ratio*	*90/50 wage ratio*	*50/10 wage ratio*	*Top-to-bottom quintile wage ratio*	*Top-to-bottom family income ratio*
2000–2015					
USA	−16.2	+4.2	−19.5	−5.3	+12.0
California	−17.9	+7.7	−21.6	−2.1	+16.7
Connecticut	−20.6	4.3	−26.7	−15.7	+7.9
Massachusetts	−2.4	+4.3	−10.8	+2.5	+9.0
New Jersey	+3.9	0	+3.1	+8.3	+8.4
New York	−18.3	+8.0	−25.0	−1.4	+11.7
Ohio	+8.3	+9.0	0	+15.3	+14.5
Oregon	−69.9	+4.2	−70.8	−29.3	−7.6
Pennsylvania	−8.6	−9.1	−16.7	−11.3	+13.0
Rhode Island	+22.9	+9.1	+12.5	+43.0	+33.3
Vermont	+26.3	+13.6	−38.9	+20.3	+48.0
2009–2015					
USA	0	+4.2	−6.1	+9.7	+10.7
California	−3.5	+7.7	−7.0	−11.3	+4.0
Connecticut	−22.9	0	−27.3	−15.1	−1.2
Massachusetts	0	−5.7	−5.7	+4.3	+16.5
New Jersey	0	−12.5	+10.0	−7.8	−1.1
New York	+7.2	0	0	+19.0	+16.7
Ohio	+21.2	+9.0	+.10	+28.4	+26.1
Oregon	+16.3	+8.7	+8.1	+7.3	+6.3
Pennsylvania	−9.6	+4.3	−16.7	−9.0	+16.0
Rhode Island	+7.5	0	+9.1	+9.9	+15.0
Vermont	+72.3	+19.0	+66.7	+22.2	+5.7

It certainly isn't a given that inequality will be less because of the existence of labor market institutions, and there are a variety of different reasons why inequality will be higher in some states over others. But it is interesting to note that between 2002 and 2015 in states where there were regular increases in the minimum wage inequality by most measures either decreased more than it did in the USA as a whole, or it increased by less than it did in the USA as a whole. This appears to be the case in Connecticut, Oregon, and Vermont. It also appears to be the case in New Jersey and New York, where state increases in the minimum wage were less frequent. And yet, in Ohio and Rhode Island where there were increases in state minimum wages, there were increases in inequality that were greater than the USA as a whole, and in Pennsylvania where there were no increases in the minimum wage the declines in inequality were greater than in the USA and the increases were less. In California and Massachusetts where there were periodic increases in state minimum wages, the results were more mixed. On the 90/10, 50/10, and quintile measures, wage inequality in both states dropped more than in the USA as a whole. On the 90/50 measure wage inequality rose more and on the quintile measure family inequality rose more.

The question that needs to be addressed is just what are the factors that might lead to lower levels of wage inequality. The central question is whether wage inequality is lower in those states where labor market institutions like minimum wages have been stronger. Or stated the other way, has wage inequality been higher in those states where labor market institutions have been weaker. The neoclassical school would argue that wage inequality is higher in those states where levels of educational attainment as a proxy for skills levels are lower and there are fewer higher-paying and more lower-paying jobs because of industrial and occupational changes. Institutionalists, however, will argue that where institutions are present, inequality will be less. Much of this can be sorted out through a logistical regression analysis. With having a lower level of wage inequality than the national level on the basis of the quintile ratio as the dependent variable, I test for the effects of right-to-work laws, having less than a 12th grade education, being female, being in manufacturing, being in retail, being in business and repair services, being in clerical services, being in sales, being an operative, and being a laborer. I also test for whether the state minimum wage is higher than the federal minimum wage, whether the state has high union density, and whether a state's 20th wage percentile is higher than the national 20th wage percentile. Each variable is set to a value of 1 (Table 5.7).

The neoclassical school holds growing inequality to be a function of a changing economic base, especially from manufacturing to services. As the regression coefficients suggest, manufacturing is important, but it does not follow that manufacturing jobs necessarily require greater education. They have traditionally paid better because they were often union jobs. With the decline in manufacturing has also come the decline of unionism. Services requiring great skill may result in higher wages while services requiring little skill will be at the bottom of the wage distribution. Fewer people in manufacturing would appear to reflect that trend. But we don't know that those manufacturing jobs that disappeared were necessarily skilled jobs. The regression coefficients certainly bear out the changing nature of the economy. To the extent that educational attainment may at

Table 5.7 Regression coefficients

	1982	*1992*	*2002*	*2003*	*2004*	*2005*	*2006*	*2007*	*2008*	*2009*	*2010*	*2011*	*2012*	*2013*	*2014*	*2015*
Right-to-work	−.213	38.809	.213	−.732	1.248	−.238	2.814	1.468	1.105	2.956	2.606	.393	1.534	1.310	.451	2.914
	.000	.000	.000	.000	.000	.000	.000	.000	.000	.000	.000	.000	.000	.000	.000	.000
Female	.093	.117	.048	.059	.087	.036	.032	.067	.057	.054	.110	.059	.040	.055	.044	.042
	.000	.001	.011	.004	.000	.107	.090	.000	.002	.007	.000	.001	.035	.002	.027	.069
Less < 12th grade	−.076	.146	−.197	.015	−.136	.241	.061	−.232	−.322	−.262	−.159	−.367	−.145	−.298	−.304	−.320
	.001	.003	.000	.625	.000	.000	.043	.000	.000	.000	.000	.000	.000	.000	.000	.000
Manufacturing	.348	.241	−.066	−.066	.312	−.099	.133	.132	.297	.367	.226	.190	−.022	.218	.428	−.001
	.000	.000	.013	.024	.000	.002	.000	.000	.000	.000	.000	.000	.440	.000	.000	.967
Retail	.068	.006	.039	.006	.089	.097	.095	.053	.088	.124	.077	.096	.134	.119	.149	.016
	.031	.904	.126	.815	.001	.001	.000	.021	.000	.000	.004	.000	.000	.000	.000	.614
Business and repair services	.417	.317	−.062	−.046	.049	.114	.111	.044	−.035	−.008	.140	−.059	−.142	.096	.136	−.264
	.000	.000	.359	.519	.474	.143	.109	.484	.602	.920	.056	.380	.050	.154	.070	.002
Clerical	.186	.047	.030	.055	.040	.159	.120	.056	.060	.067	.080	.100	.059	.026	.140	.018
	.000	.300	.247	.042	.120	.000	.000	.015	.015	.012	.002	.000	.024	.301	.000	.572
Sales	.088	.173	−.033	.148	.064	.054	.048	.019	−.045	−.078	−.052	.052	−.035	−.072	.098	−.011
	.050	.011	.385	.000	.100	.231	.215	.569	.227	.066	.208	.172	.385	.064	.018	.826
Craftsmen	.078	−.028	.061	.122	.073	.195	.113	.143	.137	.161	.103	.211	.117	−.056	.174	.152
	.019	.601	.041	.000	.015	.000	.000	.000	.000	.000	.002	.000	.000	.066	.000	.000
Operatives	−.031	−.083	.149	.089	.149	.170	.151	.098	.154	.250	.255	.262	.209	−.036	.314	.149
	.379	.130	.000	.008	.000	.000	.000	.001	.000	.000	.000	.000	.000	.251	.000	.000
Laborer	.135	.086	.103	.236	.219	.399	.162	.256	.056	.167	.183	.199	.115	.098	.261	.116
		.294	.024	.000	.000	.000	.001	.000	.226	.001	.001	.000	.023	.041	.000	.051

Higher state minimum wage	−1.308	−19.210	−.892	−1.785	−.966	−2.059	.138	.403	−.418	1.835	.712	.497	−.667	−.030	.190	−.067
	.000	.919	.000	.000	.000	.000	.000	.000	.000	.000	.000	.000	.000	.087	.000	.037
Higher 20th percentile		41.225	3.018	3.006	2.788	3.515	2.336	.708	2.306	2.107	2.868	1.571	2.515	2.170	2.460	2.105
			.000	.000	.000	.000	.000	.000	.000	.000	.000	.000	.000	.000	.000	.000
High union density	1.565	19.272	−2.341	−.814	.372	−1.347	.403	1.083	.158	.470	.341	−.643	.177	−.172	−.698	−.165
	.000	.919	.000	.000	.000	.000	.000	.000	.000	.000	.000	.000	.000	.000	.000	.000
Constant	−.256	39.771	−.474	−.056	1.480	−.666	2.263	2.462	.910	4.980	4.204	1.350	2.316	1.899	1.205	.474
	.000	.000	.000	.059	.000	.000	.000	.000	.000	.000	.000	.000	.000	.000	.000	.000

all serve as a proxy for skills, the coefficient for less than a 12th grade education—itself a variable signifying little, if any, skill—is what we would expect. Its effects are negative, and statistically significant, for being in a state with lower wage inequality throughout. This would support the idea that the economic base has changed whereby market forces have worked to push down the wages of low-skilled workers.

Still, the most interesting effects are the institutional ones. The strongest effect in 1982 for lower wage inequality is high union density. Its effect is not statistically significant in 1992, and throughout the 2000s its effects do vary. At the same time, the effect of right-to-work laws is negative in 1982, which might suggest that they are suppressing wages at the bottom of the distribution. And yet, it becomes strongly positive for being in a state with lower wage inequality, which might have something to do with the overall impact of right-to-work laws being that they compress the overall wage structures in those states. The gap may not be as wide because the top is not pulling away from the bottom to that degree in those states without institutions to prop up wages.

The strongest effects appear to be those states where the 20th percentile of the wage distribution is higher than the 20th percentile of the national wage distribution and where states have passed higher minimum wages between 2007 and 2011. The higher than 20th percentile variable is important because wage inequality tends to be lower when those at the bottom are earning more, and when their wages are rising at a higher rate relative to the top (Gottschalk 1997). Prior to 2007, there were not many states that had their own minimum wages, let alone higher minimum wages than the federal minimum wage. But in 2007 many states began passing their own and those that already had them raised them above the federal level. What really stand out are the very strong effects of being in a state with higher minimum wages. These effects are not quite as strong as the higher than the 20th percentile, although it would follow that one is more likely to be earning at or above the 20th percentile in a state with a higher minimum wage. Or it may be that states with higher minimum wages are, through wage contour effects (Levin-Waldman 2011), able to push up the wages of those earning in wage ranges above the minimum wage, in which case the 20th percentile would also be pushed higher. Moreover, much of the recent literature on the minimum wage effects on average wages suggests that increases in the minimum wage do lead to higher average wages (Belman and Wolfson 2014).

Barring the 20th percentile, the higher state minimum wage, at least from 2007 through 2011, has the strongest effect. That its effect shrinks afterward—it is even negative in 2012—may speak more to states not having kept up afterward. It will be recalled that Autor et al. (2008) claimed this to only be the case in the lower tail of the distribution. The data in this study, however, may be suggestive of broader effects. But even if what they observed was primarily in the lower tail of the distribution, it does not negate the fact that institutions still make a difference.

It becomes clear that had institutions been in place, inequality would have been less. This implies that institutions like the minimum wage can at best result in a lower rate of growth in inequality, if not overall levels of inequality. That is, the neglect of these institutions only resulted in so-called natural market forces being allowed to go unchecked, which only exacerbated the tendency toward greater wage inequality. That is, wage inequality would have been less had there not been a deterioration in labor market institutions. Which is to say, institutions matter. So far the data suggest that higher minimum wages do have an impact, albeit a slight one, on inequality. Policies favoring business over labor certainly have that effect. If minimum wages are not maintained with inflation, then the middle class falls behind. If policies are adopted that make union organizing more difficult, the effect is for businesses to receive more favorable treatment, albeit perhaps by default. When this happens the power balance is tilted toward business and away from labor. This certainly has an impact on wage inequality. The strong effects for state minimum wages that were higher than the federal minimum wage between 2007 and 2011, along with the strong effects for states where the 20th percentile was higher than the national 20th percentile, suggest that a simple remedy for reducing wage inequality is to focus on ways to raise workers' wages. Here the answer is simpler than the more complicated proposals that policymakers often seek.

Nevertheless, it isn't just that the minimum wage could reduce inequality, or at least slow the rate of growth in inequality. Rather the overall argument that the minimum wage would assist in the restoration of the middle class also in part hinges on the argument that the minimum wage could also be a valid response to the median voter theorem. If we take a closer look at the median voter theorem we might discover that, in light of the role that the deterioration of the minimum wage has played in the growth of inequality, the minimum wage may also be a good alternative to the traditional median voter theorem model of redistribution.

Median Voter Theorem

The median voter theorem is often credited to Anthony Downs (1957), who never really mentions the term, but lays out the fundamental assumptions of behavior of not only voters but also political parties and political actors. Downs' theory rests on the assumption that all individuals, groups, and/or organizations, which would include governments, behave rationally. Each party seeks to maximize its advantage or utility, which means that each is motivated by self-interest. If individuals seek to maximize their utility, a political party will similarly seek to maximize its utility, which will often mean whatever is necessary to gain political support and win elections. The Downsian model, then, is based on the assumption that every government seeks to maximize political support. It is further assumed that in a democratic society where periodic elections are held the primary goal is reelection. A citizen in this model is rational in regard to elections if his/her actions enable him/her to play his/her part in selecting a government efficiently. A political party in the broadest sense is a coalition of individuals seeking to control the governing apparatus by legal means. All political actors seek to maximize their utility. As elected officials seek to retain power, they are most likely to serve those interests that are most able to maximize their utility and get them reelected. Therefore, political actors seeking to retain power will support the interests of those who (1) can contribute to their campaigns and (2) are most likely to vote.

In the Downsian model, politicians are motivated by a desire for power, prestige, income, and the "thrill of the game" (p. 30). When voters make their voting decisions they are considering the utility they derive from government activity. Moreover, all citizens are constantly receiving benefits of one kind or another from government activity. Therefore, each citizen will vote for the party that he/she believes will provide him/her with the higher utility income, that is, benefit and/or advantage. In efforts to maximize political support, governmental spending is based on what will gain the most votes or which will lose the fewest votes. As citizens only vote to influence government policies, they are only interested in each party's statements, positions, and/or ideologies to the extent that they serve as guides to the policies the party will pursue once in office. Consequently, a government may pursue policies that are in the interests of certain key players and not in the interests of others because the expected loss is not presumed to be great.

This might then suggest that in the case of growing income inequality, if the interests of those who benefit from inequality are served and these interests are the prime donors to those seeking office, and every actor is pursuing his/her self-interest, then there is no reason to address the issue of income inequality. We can only presume that there is no benefit to assisting low-income citizens who are more likely to be hurt by growing income inequality. A key reason for this might be that low-income citizens don't have the resources to contribute to campaigns and they tend to be less likely to participate in the political process, even at the most nominal level of voting. Downs, however, suggests something a bit different, which ultimately forms the basis of the median voter theorem. He assumes that at some point low-income citizens will eventually tire of being discriminated against, or ignored by, government policy. To counteract the influence of high-income citizens and their domination, they may seek to form large collective bargaining units, similar to unions in the labor market. Once part of such a collective bargaining unit, or interest group, this individual voter will no longer feel that his/her vote is worthless, "since he can join a group and, by doing so, raise the probability that his vote—seen as the vote of the whole group—will be decisive."

Of course, Downs assumes that the formation of a collective can result in poor people attaining voice. In a regime that is more authoritarian and less democratic their recourse may be to violence and rebellion. The implication here is that public officials want to maintain calm and one means of doing so is through redistribution. These same public choice assumptions figure into the calculations that more authoritarian regimes might make to allow greater democracy, again on the assumption that the goal is to maintain calm. On the basis of game theory, Daron Acemoglu and James A. Robinson (2006) posit a simple theory of democratization: citizens want democracy while elites want non-democracy, and it is the balance of power between the two groups that determines whether society will be able to make the transition. Whereas in democracy citizens have de jure power, in non-democracy they do not. Nevertheless, they may still have de facto power in that they are able to create a challenge to the system. Understanding this potential, the elite in control of the regime begins to transition to democracy, but the elite might only begin this process of democratization when there is a sufficient threat of revolution coming from the citizens. And yet, the elite wouldn't begin a process of democratization unless an economic and/or political crisis with the potential for social unrest necessitated a change in political institutions.

Among those issues that could lead to unrest is inequality. Changes are more likely to occur in those societies with greater inequality between elites and citizens. The more equal the society, the less likely are the masses to demand democratization. Democratization actually requires that society be sufficiently unequal so that the threat of revolution is credible. Therefore, an elite may be willing to begin a transition by extending the right of franchise because it is in its interests to do so. The transition effectively preserves the status quo by staving off a threat of revolution, which in the end may preserve the power base of the elite. That the elite only democratizes to the degree necessary to stave off the threat of revolution, this might also explain why some societies might opt for say representative democracy over participatory or direct democracy. That is, because the former effectively limits the power of the majority by diluting popular pressure and undermining the power of the majority. Staving off the revolution can also be accomplished through the provision of goodies to low-income voters—the price for their quiescence.

To illustrate the theory of democratization based on political and distributional conflict, they rely heavily on several different models, including the median voter theorem, Downs' theory that voters base their voting decision on whichever party will implement the promised policy, and Nash's equilibrium to determine the level of redistributive taxation. While their framework represents a composite of all the models, it essentially rests on the assumption that voters are not ideological, but vote based on whatever policies are being pursued by the ruling elite. Most notably, their decisions and/or preferences are sensitive to taxation, because if it is severe enough it could lead to social unrest and the threat of revolution. In the end, however, their framework is intended to demonstrate that the public, whether its power is de jure or de facto, will register its preferences for whatever situation serves its interests, and that whoever is in control of the government needs to be responsive, because unresponsiveness, in short, leads to an opposing negative reaction.

What democratization effectively does is transform power to the majority of citizens. And it occurs when the elite decides to "extend the franchise" (p. 175) and include wider segments of society in the decision-making process. This only enables citizens to become more powerful. But this too is a matter of balance, because citizens who become too powerful relative to the elites may trigger the elites to respond by staging a coup against democratization. The origins of coups against democracies lie in their tendency to pursue redistributive policies. As an example, they cite the military coups in Latin America that were justified on the grounds that they were protecting the capitalist system. The greater the redistribution away from the elites, the more likely are they to find it in their best interests to mount a coup against it. Greater inequality, then, is more likely to destabilize democracy because the burden of democracy on the elites increases the gap between them and the citizens. But if elites have sufficient power, they don't need to undertake coups.

Downs, however, goes on to say that low-income citizens have essentially traded their vote for money utility. This would seem to imply that as long as low-income residents get benefits in the form of money income, they will happily trade away any political influence to the government to in turn pursue policies that serve the interests of more affluent interests—interests that don't need money income from the government per se, but do need policies that may enable them to become wealthier in the market place. And yet, everybody in this scenario is behaving rationally. Because the goal of elected officials is to win election and then reelection, policies will only be pushed insofar as they serve to purchase votes from the electorate. Public officials are more likely to serve the interests of higher-income groups than lower-income groups because they are more active in the political system and contribute money to campaigns. When lower-income voters tire of being ignored, they will form coalitions along the lines of market collective bargaining in order to achieve a measure of voice. Public officials can effectively purchase their quiescence with programs or through redistribution that increases their effective money utility. In exchange for more money utility, they are trading away their political voice. So by purchasing the quiescence of lower-income voters with policies that increase their money utility, they now have the leisure to pursue policies that benefit those at the higher end of the distribution because by doing so they will ensure that they continue to be reelected.

The central feature of the Downsian model, on which the median voter theorem subsequently depends, is spatial mobility of two parties competing for votes. Downs assumes that all voters vote, thereby establishing the median as the unique equilibrium for a two-party contest over single dimensional issue space (Rowley 1984). Typically the median voter theorem is presented in terms of tax rates that the median voter is willing to pay for redistribution in the face of rising income inequality. According to the Meltzer-Richard (1981) construct, the median voter, that is, the voter in the middle, determines the effective size of government by choosing the rate of taxation. The more they opt to pay in taxes, the larger the government will be because it is redistributing income. In the Meltzer-Richard model, the median voter is the decisive voter, and the size of government is dependent on the relationship between mean income and the income of this decisive voter.

Therefore, if mean income lies to the right of, or above, median income, there is added incentive to redistribute income. The greater the distance between the two, the greater is the incentive for redistribution. And yet, the higher the level of income inequality, the greater will be the distance between mean and median income. The median voter, then, chooses the tax rate that maximizes his/her utility. But in making this choice, the median voter is aware that his/her choice will affect everyone's decision to work and consume because increases in the tax rate can be expected to have two effects. While each dollar of earned income raises more revenue, each dollar also distorts because it takes away from leisure time. If everyone chooses more leisure, they will effectively be choosing to subsist on redistribution. The size of government is contingent on voter demand for redistribution.

The median voter theorem, then, would suggest that the best approach to rising income inequality is redistribution. In other words, it maximizes everybody's utility. Still, the question remains: what exactly is government purchasing through redistribution, if not the quiescence of the low-wage voter, who in a more authoritarian regime may be inclined to get what they want through violent means? In other words, why specifically redistribution, if there isn't a concern that the unrest and turmoil that might arise from a growing distance between median and mean incomes won't lead to some type of violent response—a revolution of sorts assumed in the Acemoglu-Robinson model of democracy? All of this raises an interesting question: if the American political system, as some have suggested, is not responsive to low-income and middle-class voters but only to the more affluent, then why would there be redistribution at all?

Downs would seem to be suggesting that if policymakers purchase low-income voters' quiescence through whatever means—and it could be redistribution—it is then free to pursue policies that are favorable to the more affluent. But is Downs not also assuming that if it doesn't then the masses who might be harmed through those policies may indeed resort to violence? Perhaps overtaxing the wealthy in order to pay for programs that will subsidize the low wages of those closer to the bottom of the wage scale? Although they pay a higher marginal tax rate, they still benefit from the preponderance of policy that is favorable to their interests. The money utility that lower-income groups are receiving through redistribution has effectively been purchased with their collective political influence. Lane Kenworthy and Jonus Pontusson (2005) contribute to the debate about the relationship between market inequality and redistribution, specifically about the utility of the median voter theorem proposed by Meltzer and Richard. They note that the Meltzer-Richard model predicts that as market inequality increases, so too does redistribution.

Although labor economists typically attribute the rise in inequality to the relative supply and demand for more or less skilled labor, they do concede that supply and demand alone cannot adequately explain cross-national variation. Rather differentials between countries may have something to do with the role of labor market institutions, and that more centralized forms of wage setting have generated wage compression. Nevertheless, union decline and public sector retrenchment are often associated with changes in earnings inequality on a cross-national level. What matters to most people, however, isn't market income but disposable income, and the Meltzer-Richard model does not account for the redistributive effects of public processes of services, such as education and health care. Almost all welfare states have become more redistributive during the 1980s and 1990s. There are two different paths to increased redistribution. One is a new policy initiative aimed at redistributing income, and the other is a compensatory response by existing welfare states to rising market inequality.

The Meltzer-Richard model assumes that government spending funds a certain amount of consumption for all individuals and is financed by a proportional income tax. The model rests on the assumption that low-income earners have more to gain and less to lose from increasing government spending than do high-income earners. Consequently, the level of support for government spending is a function of the distance between the income of the median voter and the average income of all voters. As market inequality rises, the distance between the median and mean income increases and support for government spending also increases as a result. The model, then, implies that countries with more unequal distributions of market income should exhibit higher levels of redistributive spending than countries with less unequal distributions.

The Meltzer-Richard hypothesis, however, assumes the median voter's interest in redistribution to be greater in more unequal societies because of self-interested politicians' desire to maximize their chance of gaining or retaining power. Therefore, they will attempt to translate the median voters' preferences into policy actions, and in democratic societies this should result in high initial inequality yielding to higher subsequent redistribution. The model draws on the standard assumptions of rational choice that individuals are rational actors who maximize their own narrowly defined interests. They conceptualize redistribution as a "Robin Hood"-type process where the rich pay more taxes than they receive from the state in the form of transfers and where the poor gain from redistribution. They also assume that all proceeds from taxation are redistributed; so the total sum of income does not change. Political conflict, then, is about determining the tax rate.

Social insurance institutions are one of the main mechanisms for welfare states to redistribute incomes and their design is of central importance for redistributive outcomes. And yet, as Malte Luebker (2004) observes it isn't entirely clear that this model is testable in the real world. After all, given that inequality in the USA tends to be higher than in the rest of the developed world, there should be more redistribution in the USA. Luebker's question, then, is whether the USA stands out for ignoring the redistributive preferences of its voters. The Meltzer-Richard assumptions imply that relative redistribution should rise in line with initial inequality. But an increase in absolute redistribution should arise from the automatic stabilization properties of the welfare state, and that finding such a relationship would not prove conclusively that the median voter theorem is true. Rather the failure of the real world to behave according to the model's predictions calls into question at least one of its underlying premises—that voters' support for redistributive structures depend on what they personally have to gain, and that the political system produces outputs that are aligned to the median voter's interests. If the system is more responsive to wealthier interests, and coupled with lower levels of civic engagement among lower-income households, it would be more reasonable to infer that redistribution would be contrary to the interests of public officials seeking reelection because it is contrary to the interests of more affluent voters, unless there is fear the masses will rebel.

Still the question remains why the median voter would necessarily opt for policies of redistribution during periods of increasing income inequality. Downs does not really address that issue; rather Meltzer and Richard infer it from Downs' assumptions. The idea that voters don't possess perfect information is almost akin to John Rawls' (1971) veil of ignorance. Rawls famously asks us to imagine ourselves under a veil of ignorance where we know nothing of our attributes, endowments, and/or resources.

Given this ignorance, what principles of justice would we choose? He claims that we would choose the priority of the right over the good—principles that protect our rights from the utilitarian impulses of the masses. Priority of the right over the good could lead to the famous organizing principle of equality of opportunity over equality of result. It does not necessarily follow that individuals would choose redistribution over policies aimed at a level playing field where individuals are afforded an opportunity to pursue their interests. And yet, there is an assumption that policies that safeguard against the irrational passions of the masses will be pursued. Of course, it should similarly follow that individuals would choose a set of arrangements whereby they are paid fair wages for their work. On one level, growing disparities between the top and the bottom suggest an unfair playing field. Redistribution might be one means of leveling the playing field in which the more fortunate members of society are called upon to assist the least fortunate members of society. Rawls himself argues that any scheme of redistribution that might interfere with the rights of others has to be such that it makes the least fortunate members of society better off.

And yet, it does not follow that such a scheme would necessarily follow from increasing marginal tax rate driven redistribution. If we follow the logic of Downs' model of increasing marginal tax rates we get the following scenario: low-income citizens have essentially traded their political influence for money utility. This would seem to imply that as long as low-income voters get benefits in the form of money income, they will happily trade away any political influence to the government to in turn pursue policies that serve the interests of more affluent interests—interests that don't need money income from the government per se, but do need policies that may enable them to become wealthier in the market place. And yet, everybody in this scenario is behaving rationally.

If we apply this to the current labor market, we get the following scenario: public officials don't raise the minimum wage because it is not in the monied interests of those who donate to their reelection to do so. But in order to obtain the quiescence of low-wage voters, these officials provide the low-wage voters with subsidies. Low-wage voters, in other words, have traded their voice—political influence—away for money utility. The monied interests have gotten the policies that serve them, and public officials have been reelected. And yet, the point is that we are all paying for this. This isn't so much redistribution as it is what Theodore Lowi (1964) famously referred to as distributive politics. Lowi distinguished between three types of politics: regulatory, redistributive, and distributive. In regulatory politics, the activities of one group are restricted for the benefit of another. Each group can be easily identified. In redistributive politics, one group is paying more in taxes so that another group can derive benefits through programs. Again, each group can be easily identified. In distributive politics, however, everybody derives some benefit and we all effectively pay.

Ken Jacobs et al. (2015) found that low-wage labor actually costs American taxpayers $152.8 billion a year for social supports. Because low-wage workers are not earning enough to support themselves, they need subsidies whether it be through the Earned Income Tax Credit (EITC) or food stamps and other social supports. Although all American consumers benefit from low prices, which necessitate the payment of low wages, all American taxpayers are effectively paying for it. Arguably, however, this might also be viewed as a form of redistribution in the direction of corporate profits. When, through social supports, taxpayers are subsidizing the low wages of low-wage workers they are really subsidizing the profits of employers. Moreover, if employers know that there are subsidies available to their low-wage workers, then what incentive do they have to pay more livable wages? Perversely this would appear to follow the logic of Downs' model. Employers oppose increases to the minimum wage because it will eat into their profits. Low-wage workers who might prefer higher wages can afford to be neutral on the minimum wage because their quiescence is effectively being bought off with these social supports. And of course everybody is paying for it. And yet, their report suggests that a $15.00 an hour minimum, which many states, and even localities, have been enacting, is the point where there may be less reliance on these social supports.

This, of course, leads to another possibility which might be redistribution through wage policy. Critics of the minimum wage will no doubt argue that it is a form of redistribution from the profits of employers to the wages of workers. If they have to pay their workers more, then they need to effectively forego profits. If they cannot raise prices too much for fear that this will result in a loss of customers, then it will have to come out of profits. If this is not a form of redistribution, it is surely a mandated reallocation of the total revenues the employer has taken in. Because the employer is going to be able to claim less of a profit, he/she will no doubt claim that his/her profits have been redistributed to the workers. Even early institutional economist John R. Commons conceded this point when he recognized that labor market institutions like labor unions—and by extension minimum wages—that force employers to pay more than they otherwise would have are effectively redistributing income from profits to workers' wages. But Commons also considered this to be a worthy type of redistribution because the workers will at least be returning something of value to the employer.

Relationship Between Minimum Wage and Median Voter Theorem?

The logic of the median voter theorem is that the greater the inequality, the greater will be the distance between the income of the median voter and the average income of society. Given that there may be some impact on inequality from minimum wages, it might stand to reason that in states where there have been increases in the minimum wage, we would expect to see less distance between the income of the median voter and the average income of society. Table 5.8 shows the possible relationship between the minimum wage and the median voter theorem.

As a point of departure it should be noted that during this 15-year period the distance between median and average wages in the USA as a whole grew 34.0 percent and the distance between median and average family income grew 25.3 percent. At the same time, the distance appears to have decreased following federal minimum wage increases in 2007, 2008, and 2009. From 2006 to 2007, the distance between median and average income declined by 32.1 percent, and between 2007 and 2008, it declined by .7 percent. Then between 2008 and 2009 following the final increase to $7.25 an hour, the distance declined another 4.3 percent. And yet, between 2009 and 2015 when there was no increase in the minimum wage the distance increased by 20.5 percent. In terms of family income the distance between the two following increases in the federal minimum wage did increase, but the distance in median family income and average family income did increase by 16.8 percent between 2009 and 2015 when there was no increase in the minimum wage. That there was a decrease in the distance between median and average wages following increases in the minimum wage is suggestive that there might be a relationship between higher minimum wages and lower levels of inequality. If true, this would then imply less of a need for redistribution in the traditional sense as formulated by the Meltzer-Richard model.

Table 5.8 Minimum wage and median voter theorem

Year	*Minimum wage*	*Individual distance*[a]	*Family distance*[b]
USA			
2000	$5.15	26.8	23.3
2001	$5.15	26.0	23.9
2002	$5.15	32.0	24.2
2003	$5.15	34.8	23.5
2004	$5.15	30.4	24.9
2005	$5.15	32.0	24.6
2006	$5.15	31.2	26.2
2007	$5.85	30.2	27.9
2008	$6.55	30.0	23.3
2009	$7.25	28.7	25.0
2010	$7.25	29.8	26.7
2011	$7.25	27.3	24.7
2012	$7.25	28.9	28.1
2013	$7.25	32.1	27.2
2014	$7.25	33.4	28.4
2015	$7.25	35.9	29.2
California			
2000	$6.25	33.1	26.1
2001	$6.25	30.1	26.0
2002	$6.75	37.3	28.2
2003	$6.75	38.9	26.7
2004	$6.75	39.2	28.5
2005	$6.75	36.2	30.6
2006	$6.75	40.5	31.1
2007	$7.50	38.5	34.6
2008	$8.00	40.3	23.2
2009	$8.00	37.0	32.5
2010	$8.00	36.6	30.7
2011	$8.00	32.1	29.4
2012	$8.00	41.4	36.1
2013	$8.00	40.1	32.3
2014	$8.00	39.1	31.0
2015	$9.00	43.7	35.4
Connecticut			
2000	$6.15	23.1	28.7
2001	$6.40	25.6	18.0
2002	$6.70	32.2	25.5
2003	$6.90	29.7	20.7
2004	$7.10	31.8	20.6
2005	$7.10	30.3	22.9
2006	$7.40	34.1	24.0

(*continued*)

Table 5.8 (continued)

Year	*Minimum wage*	*Individual distance*[a]	*Family distance*[b]
2007	$7.65	40.8	33.2
2008	$7.65	31.9	31.3
2009	$8.00	34.1	20.6
2010	$8.25	37.9	31.0
2011	$8.25	31.5	29.0
2012	$8.25	39.8	33.4
2013	$8.25	42.3	30.0
2014	$8.70	33.7	27.7
2015	$9.15	27.4	23.3
Massachusetts			
2000	$6.00	24.7	23.1
2001	$6.75	33.5	30.0
2002	$6.75	28.5	22.4
2003	$6.75	29.5	20.7
2004	$6.75	30.5	25.1
2005	$6.75	34.0	22.8
2006	$6.75	37.6	23.7
2007	$7.50	40.2	27.2
2008	$8.00	35.2	24.3
2009	$8.00	28.1	24.9
2010	$8.00	29.6	26.3
2011	$8.00	27.7	25.9
2012	$8.00	30.2	31.1
2013	$8.00	26.5	18.6
2014	$8.00	34.9	26.7
2015	$9.00	30.2	25.8
New Jersey			
2000	$5.15	31.0	28.3
2001	$5.15	33.6	24.4
2002	$5.15	40.0	27.8
2003	$5.15	30.1	25.3
2004	$5.15	30.7	21.0
2005	$6.15	37.8	23.1
2006	$7.15	42.8	23.4
2007	$7.15	35.4	22.4
2008	$7.15	35.7	19.1
2009	$7.25	37.1	23.3
2010	$7.25	38.4	26.3
2011	$7.25	35.3	21.1
2012	$7.25	47.6	28.9
2013	$7.25	38.2	24.5
2014	$8.25	35.2	25.3
2015	$8.38	28.9	23.7

(*continued*)

Table 5.8 (continued)

Year	*Minimum wage*	*Individual distance*[a]	*Family distance*[b]
New York			
2000	$5.15	27.4	29.9
2001	$5.15	36.7	29.0
2002	$5.15	40.1	30.2
2003	$5.15	35.4	25.5
2004	$5.15	33.1	25.3
2005	$6.00	36.2	33.2
2006	$6.75	38.4	32.3
2007	$7.15	33.2	34.5
2008	$7.15	31.3	27.8
2009	$7.25	28.3	26.8
2010	$7.25	34.1	30.0
2011	$7.25	36.7	31.8
2012	$7.25	33.8	30.4
2013	$7.25	40.4	32.8
2014	$8.00	40.6	34.9
2015	$8.75	40.3	35.6
Ohio			
2000	$5.15	22.4	20.9
2001	$5.15	23.8	19.3
2002	$5.15	23.7	22.1
2003	$5.15	26.8	22.6
2004	$5.15	24.6	21.9
2005	$5.15	18.6	15.1
2006	$5.15	17.9	19.8
2007	$6.85	22.4	20.6
2008	$7.00	26.6	19.7
2009	$7.30	23.6	19.2
2010	$7.30	23.8	16.8
2011	$7.40	24.9	16.6
2012	$7.70	33.9	24.7
2013	$7.85	32.7	23.9
2014	$7.95	25.5	20.6
2015	$8.15	29.1	26.8
Oregon			
2000	$6.50	23.7	23.4
2001	$6.50	27.5	26.6
2002	$6.50	23.6	22.5
2003	$6.90	22.6	22.1
2004	$7.05	25.8	20.6
2005	$7.25	28.9	23.7
2006	$7.50	32.6	22.0

(*continued*)

Table 5.8 (continued)

Year	*Minimum wage*	*Individual distance*[a]	*Family distance*[b]
2007	$7.80	27.3	32.1
2008	$7.95	22.4	34.9
2009	$8.40	27.4	21.9
2010	$8.40	32.8	22.6
2011	$8.50	21.1	18.8
2012	$8.80	20.3	21.5
2013	$8.95	22.6	25.8
2014	$9.10	27.6	26.1
2015	$9.25	31.7	21.9
Pennsylvania			
2000	$5.15	24.6	23.7
2001	$5.15	30.1	20.8
2002	$5.15	36.6	26.2
2003	$5.15	34.8	28.0
2004	$5.15	33.6	21.6
2005	$5.15	32.0	23.5
2006	$5.15	30.5	27.5
2007	$6.75	28.8	20.9
2008	$7.15	22.3	19.5
2009	$7.25	27.5	25.0
2010	$7.25	25.1	24.8
2011	$7.25	26.1	27.9
2012	$7.25	30.2	26.6
2013	$7.25	31.7	21.8
2014	$7.25	27.6	23.9
2015	$7.25	34.0	26.5
Rhode Island			
2000	$6.15	17.7	18.8
2001	$6.15	29.3	21.3
2002	$6.15	24.9	24.1
2003	$6.15	24.0	19.4
2004	$6.75	27.0	21.5
2005	$6.75	32.1	19.4
2006	$7.10	32.9	32.7
2007	$7.40	34.3	24.1
2008	$7.40	29.6	24.0
2009	$7.40	30.9	21.8
2010	$7.40	30.6	19.2
2011	$7.40	21.7	15.6
2012	$7.40	23.6	19.6
2013	$7.75	31.8	31.4
2014	$8.00	26.4	23.7
2015	$9.00	35.3	33.1

(continued)

Table 5.8 (continued)

Year	*Minimum wage*	*Individual distance*[a]	*Family distance*[b]
Vermont			
2000	$5.75	18.2	18.5
2001	$6.25	24.6	24.2
2002	$6.25	19.3	18.1
2003	$6.25	20.1	15.7
2004	$6.75	22.8	19.2
2005	$7.00	22.6	22.3
2006	$7.25	19.0	18.9
2007	$7.53	22.5	19.1
2008	$7.68	23.1	18.6
2009	$8.06	21.3	18.8
2010	$8.06	15.7	17.7
2011	$8.15	17.2	17.4
2012	$8.46	19.2	21.2
2013	$8.60	19.2	21.2
2014	$8.73	22.4	19.6
2015	$9.15	26.9	20.4

[a]Percentage difference between median and average individual income
[b]Percentage difference between median and average family income

In the states where there have been increases in the minimum wage, we see quite a bit of fluctuation. Although it isn't true in all cases, in many the distance between median and mean wages and between median and mean family incomes is less than in the USA as a whole. In Connecticut, for instance, the distance between median and mean wages was 36.5 percent less in 2015 than it was in the USA and the distance between median and family income was 25.3 percent less. Although in some years there were decreases and in some years not, between 2013 and 2014 when the state's minimum wage increased from $8.25 to $8.70, the distance in wage inequality decreased by 20.3 percent and the distance in family income inequality decreased by 7.6 percent. Then between 2014 and 2015 when the state's minimum wage increased again from $8.70 to $9.15 an hour, the distance in wage inequality decreased by another 19.0 percent and the distance in family income inequality decreased by an additional 15.9 percent. And yet, the distance between median and mean wages and family income did increase overall between 2000 and 2015. The same was also true for California. In Massachusetts the overall distance does increase between 2000 and 2015, but in 2015 the distance between median and mean wages is 18.9 percent less than in the USA, and the distance between median and mean family income is 13.2 percent less than the USA as a whole. It is also interesting to note that between 2014 and 2015 when the state's minimum wage increased from $8.00 to $9.00, the distance between median and mean wages decreased by 13.5 percent and the distance between median and mean family income decreased by 4.1 percent.

In New Jersey the distance between median and mean wages from 2000 to 2015 decreases by 4.2 percent and the distance between median and mean family income decreases by 16.3 percent. But in 2015 the distance in wage income is 24.2 percent less and the distance in family income is 23.2 percent less than in the USA as a whole. Still, between 2013 and 2014 when the state's minimum wage increases from $7.25 an hour to $8.25 an hour, the distance between median and mean wages decreases by 7.9 percent, although the distance between median and mean family income increases by 3.3 percent. But between 2014 and 2015 when the state's minimum wage increases an additional $.13 the distance between median and mean wages decreases by 17.9 percent and the distance between median and mean family income decreases by 6.3 percent. In New York, however, the distance between median and mean wages and between median and mean family income increases. Also both are higher in New York in 2015 than they are in the USA as a whole. In both Ohio and Oregon there is fluctuation, with the distance between median and mean wages being higher in 2015 than in 2000 and the distance between median family income being higher in Ohio but lower in Oregon. Still, in 2015 the distance between median and mean wages is 23.4 percent lower in Ohio than in the USA and the distance between median and mean family income is 9.0 percent less. In Oregon, the distance between median and mean wages in 2015 is 13.2 percent less than the USA as a whole and the distance between median and mean family income is 33.3 percent less.

In Pennsylvania, which has never had its own state minimum wage, there is a 39.0 percent increase in the distance between median and mean wages and an 11.8 percent increase in the distance between median and mean family income between 2000 and 2015. In Rhode Island where there have been more regular increases in the minimum wage the distance between median and mean wages increases 99.4 percent and the distance between median and mean family incomes increases by 76.1 percent from 2000 to 2015. Although the distance between median and mean wages in 2015 is 1.7 percent less than in the USA as a whole, the distance between median and mean family income is 13.4 percent more. Similarly in Vermont where wage and family inequality has been high relative to the

USA as a whole, the distances between the median and mean in both wages and family income are both lower in 2000 and 2015 than in the USA. Still, the distance between median and mean wages increases by 47.8 percent and the distance between median and family income increases by 10.3 percent from 2000 to 2015. And yet, in 2015, the distance between median and mean wages is 33.5 percent less than in the USA as a whole and the distance between median and mean family income is 42.2 percent less.

Although there are a number of factors that could explain why the distance between median and mean wages and between median and mean family income increases, the fact that in many cases these distances tend to be less in some states where there are higher minimum wages cannot be dismissed. It is suggestive that a minimum wage could accomplish the same objective of reducing inequality as traditional redistribution through higher taxes to pay for programs as suggested by the Meltzer-Richard model. Nevertheless, it would be useful to test the proposition that states with higher minimum wages than the federal are more likely to have less of a distance between median and mean wages and median and mean family incomes and thereby less inequality through a logistical regression analysis.

Analysis

There are a couple of propositions in need of testing. The first is the proposition that states with higher minimum wages would also be states with a greater distance between median and mean wages. If this is true, it might suggest that higher minimum wages were indeed a response to the greater distance, thereby suggesting an alternative to the Meltzer-Richard model of the median voter theorem that the only response is greater redistribution through higher taxation. The second proposition is that states with higher inequality will have, in line with the Meltzer-Richard model, a greater distance between median and mean wages. And the third proposition is that states with inequality will also have lower wages. States with higher inequality are more likely to pass higher minimum wages and states with higher minimum wages are likely to have less inequality. If true, then, higher minimum wages should lead to a narrowing of the distance between median and mean wages. That is, states with higher minimum wages are also states with higher inequality. States with higher inequality are also states with a greater distance between median and mean wages. States with a greater distance would appear to be a factor in having higher minimum wages than the nation as a whole.

Therefore, it would be reasonable to infer that a higher minimum wage could be a response to the Meltzer-Richard model. In the first set of regressions, the dependent variable is a higher minimum wage than the federal minimum wage. States with higher minimum wages in a given year than the federal minimum wage in that year were set to a value of 1. This first set of regressions can be seen in Table 5.9.

Table 5.9 already implies that a reasonable response to a growing distance between median and mean wages would be higher minimum wages. As to be expected, states with right-to-work laws are unlikely to support higher minimum wages, and the regression coefficients make it clear that the effects of right-to-work laws on having higher minimum wages are negative, and the size of this coefficient increases over time. Or stated more accurately, those in states with right-to-work laws are not likely to be in states with minimum wages that are higher than the federal. Meanwhile, those in states with high union density are more likely to be in states with higher minimum wages, suggesting that high union density is a factor in a state having a higher minimum wage. This only makes sense if we understand union density as a sign of union presence and union presence speaks

Table 5.9 Effects for having higher state minimum wages

	2009	*2010*	*2011*	*2012*	*2013*	*2014*	*2015*
Greater distance between median and mean family income	−.166	2.301	.854	.223	.742	1.300	.064
	.000	.000	.000	.000	.000	.000	.000
Greater distance between median and mean wages	.913	−2.073	.497	.724	.375	.893	1.785
	.000	.000	.000	.000	.000	.000	.000
Right-to-work states	−28.860	−27.998	−.348	−.247	−.571	−1.790	−2.111
			.993	.000	.000	.000	.000
High union density	1.428	2.459	18.154	1.809	1.134	.565	.998
	.000	.000		.000	.000	.000	.000
Constant	2.352	3.134	19.236	1.746	1.106	−.929	−.935
	.000	.000	.000	.000	.000	.000	.000

to a political constituency that will lobby lawmakers to pass higher minimum wages. These coefficients make it clear that those living in states with a greater distance between median and mean wages are likely to be in states with higher minimum wages. What is most interesting is the size of the coefficient, and that it is much larger in 2015 than in 2014 following even more states passing higher minimum wages. The first wave of states passing minimum wages occurred in a series of referenda in the 2008 national election. This may explain the size of the coefficient in 2009. The anomaly appears to be in 2010 when the effects are negative. But the next wave of states enacting and then implementing higher minimum wages occurs in 2014 followed by more in 2015. The increase in the size of the coefficient from 2014 to 2015 would appear to suggest a strong positive effect of a growing distance between median and mean wages for having higher minimum wages. At the same time effects of high union density appear to diminish over the same time frame. The Meltzer-Richard model posits that a greater distance between median and mean wages will lead to more redistribution through higher taxes. Although these coefficients do not discount redistribution as a response, they do suggest that to the extent that they have positive effects for higher minimum wages, that higher minimum wages can have the same effects. Let's consider what happens when we remove the median voter theorem variable and substitute in its place higher inequality, which are those states that have higher levels of inequality than the USA as a whole according to the quintile ratio.

If we substitute the variable of higher inequality for the variable of greater distance between median and mean wages, as is the case in Table 5.10, we see that it does appear to have an effect for higher minimum wages. Nevertheless, it diminishes over time. To say that those living in states with higher inequality are also likely to be in states with higher minimum wages is not the same as saying that public officials in those states necessarily enacted higher minimum wages in response to higher levels of inequality. If the median voter theorem variable is removed from the equation, then high union density becomes a more important variable for explaining why certain states are more likely to have minimum wages higher than the federal minimum wage. Although there is fluctuation in the size of this variable, it appears to be the most important variable in 2015, when again many more states enacted higher minimum wages or implemented the next phase of an increase that had been enacted in 2014. It is important to note that the greater distance between median and family

Table 5.10 Effects for having higher state minimum wages

	2009	*2010*	*2011*	*2012*	*2013*	*2014*	*2015*
Greater distance between median and mean family income	−.354	1.962	.199	.532	.769	1.570	.292
	.000	.000	.000	.000	.000	.000	.000
Higher inequality	1.598	.251	1.675	.317	.429	−.411	.718
	.000	.000	.000	.000	.000	.000	.000
Right-to-work states	−28.419	−28.581	−.189	−.091	−.508	−1.737	−1.776
			.996	.000	.000	.000	.000
High union density	1.862	2.089	18.281	1.976	1.162	.763	1.413
	.000	.000		.000	.000	.000	.000
Constant	3.370	3.650	19.764	1.776	1.172	−1.037	−.608
	.000	.000	.000	.000	.000	.000	.000

income also has strong effects for higher minimum wages in 2010, 2013, and 2014. But in those years, for the exception of 2014, the effects of high union density are even stronger.

The next question that arises is just what happens when we look at higher inequality as the dependent variable. In other words, what factors might account for some states having even higher levels of inequality over the federal level. These regression coefficients can be seen in Table 5.11.

What stands out, and which clearly confirms the Meltzer-Richard model, is the effect of greater distance between median and mean wages on having higher levels of inequality. To repeat the basic premise of the Meltzer-Richard construct of the median voter theorem, the more inequality there is, the greater the distance will be between median wages and society's average wages. Over time, we see that the size of the coefficient for greater distance between median and mean wages increases. That is, those living in states where there is a greater distance between median and mean wages are also very likely to live in states with higher levels of inequality. This would appear to confirm the Meltzer-Richard construct. And yet, what is true for the relationship between median and mean wages does not appear to be true when it comes to the relationship between median and family income. Nevertheless, there are some results in this table that lend support to the idea that higher wages, especially at the bottom of the distribution, will result in less inequality.

Table 5.11 Effects for having higher inequality

	2009	*2010*	*2011*	*2012*	*2013*	*2014*	*2015*
Greater distance between median and mean family income	1.827	1.060	2.708	.800	.737	−.296	−.851
	.000	.000	.000	.000	.000	.000	.000
Higher state minimum wage	1.431	−.151	1.015	.158	.358	−.828	−2.248
	.000	.000	.000	.000	.000	.000	.000
Right-to-work states	−2.523	−1.945	−.573	−1.145	−.846	−.775	−6.156
	.000	.000	.000	.000	.000	.000	.000
High union density	−1.344	−.070	.175	−.949	−.328	−.123	−1.887
	.000	.000	.000	.000	.000	.000	.000
Greater distance between median and mean wages	1.607	−.017	.322	1.452	2.384	2.429	6.424
	.000	.139	.000	.000	.000	.000	.000
Higher wages at the 20th percentile than the percentile of the nation	−2.989	−2.560	−1.927			−2.269	−2.769
	.000	.000	.000			.000	.000
Constant	−3.016	−2.565	3.911	.169	1.368	−1.113	−3.024
	.000	.000	.000	.000	.000	.000	.000

One might expect right-to-work states to have positive effects for higher levels of inequality because they might be suppressing wages. Although there is fluctuation in the size of the coefficients, we see that there are years when it is strongly negative. It is possible that it has a negative effect because if right-to-work laws are suppressing wages, they are suppressing wages throughout the distribution, in which case there will be lower levels in inequality because of wage compression. The variable that seems to have the strongest negative effects, for when a reading can be obtained, is the higher 20 percentile threshold variable. That is, those living in states where the 20th percentile is higher than the 20th percentile for the USA as a whole are the least likely to be in states with higher levels of inequality. Why? Because inequality tends to be higher when the rate of increase is higher among those at the top of the distribution than at the bottom (Gottschalk 1997). At the same time the effects of a higher minimum wage are strongly negative, especially in 2014, and more so in 2015 following state minimum wage enactments and increases (Table 5.12).

What, then, are the factors that might explain why some states would have a greater distance between median and mean wages than in the USA as a whole? Certainly there is a correlation between family income and wage income. It appears to be the case that those living in states where there is a greater distance between median and mean family income are also likely to be living in states where there is a greater distance between median and mean wages. Of course, as to be expected there is a strong correlation between higher inequality and a greater distance between median and mean wages. And yet, there also appears to be a strong correlation between high union density and greater distance between median and mean wages. Although the coefficients for higher state minimum wages are positive and statistically significant, they are small relative to the other variables. What does appear to stand out is that there is a strong positive correlation in most years between right-to-work states and greater distance between median and mean wages. Those living in states with right-to-work laws are also likely to be in states with a greater distance

Table 5.12 Effects for having greater distance between median and mean wages

	2009	*2010*	*2011*	*2012*	*2013*	*2014*	*2015*
Greater distance between median and mean family income	1.362	1.183	2.742	3.251	2.044	2.544	21.953
	.000	.000	.000	.000	.000	.000	.000
Higher state minimum wage	.603	−2.372	.488	.705	.225	1.160	.656
	.000	.000	.000	.000	.000	.000	.000
Right-to-work states	817	−.045	3.428	1.043	.519	1.116	42.977
	.000	.002	.000	.000	.000	.000	.000
High union density	1.436	.048	2.326	1.429	.459	2.410	23.535
	.000	.001	.000	.000	.000	.000	.000
Higher inequality	1.242	−.017	.209	1.582	2.386	2.480	23.958
	.000	.117	.000	.000	.000	.000	.000
Constant	2.881	−.150	3.911	2.997	2.678	5.752	67.515
	.000	.000	.000	.000	.000	.000	.000

Table 5.13 Effects for having a higher 20th percentile wage threshold

	2009	*2010*	*2011*	*2012*	*2013*	*2014*	*2015*
Higher state minimum wage	−2.614	−2.544	−2.873	−.093	−1.130	.622	−1.172
	.000	.000	.000	.000	.000	.000	.000
Right-to-work states	−2.181	−2.661	−2.145	−1.525	−2.560	−7.25	−2.527
	.000	.000	.000	.000	.000	.000	.000
High union density	1.696	1.520	1.507	.421	.269	.246	.666
	.000	.000	.000	.000	.000	.000	.000
Higher inequality	−2.245	−2.686	−1.409	−2.425	−2.691	−2.446	−2.142
	.000	.000	.000	.000	.000	.000	.000
Constant	−2.518	−2.790	−2.026	−2.388	−3.731	−1.735	−1.949
	.000	.000	.000	.000	.000	.000	.000

between median and mean wages, which could be explained by the tendency of right-to-work laws to suppress wages, especially at the bottom (Table 5.13).

Higher wages at the bottom would likely yield lower levels of inequality and hence less distance between median and mean wages. Can we then explain why some states are likely to have a higher 20th percentile threshold than the USA as a whole? One might think that higher state minimum wages might yield a higher 20th percentile threshold than the rest of the nation. But the coefficients in Table 5.13 appear to be an anomaly because they are negative. To the extent that right-to-work laws suppress wages, the coefficients are what we might expect, which in most years are strongly negative. And to the extent that high union density may be a factor pushing wages up, we would expect that the coefficients for high union density would be positive. And yet, they appear to weaken over time. Those living in states with high inequality are least likely to be living in states with a higher 20th percentile threshold. Again, this too is to be expected.

Conclusion

It would appear that there is a correlation between higher inequality and greater distance between median and mean wages. We saw in Chap. 3 that inequality did decrease following increases in the minimum wage and that states with higher minimum wages also had lower levels of inequality. But we also see in this chapter that in years when there were many states either adopting for the first time or increasing existing minimum wages, the size of the coefficient for greater distance between median and mean wages also increases. This suggests that the minimum wage may be a response to the median voter theorem in that the distance appears to be a factor in states adopting higher minimum wages. This, then, suggests that a higher minimum wage could be a viable response to the median voter theorem, and that the median voter theorem need not necessarily lead to redistribution. Although the case can be made that higher minimum wages are a form of redistribution, it is not the same as traditional redistribution whereby the taxes of some are raised to pay for programs that will benefit others. Rather profit is being redistributed to workers, but workers still need to work in exchange for the higher wages. As mentioned earlier, Commons did acknowledge that unions represented a form of redistribution away from profits to workers, but the workers were working for what would be their higher wages. To the extent that the minimum wage seeks to extend coverage to nonunion workers, the minimum wage redistributes in the same way that unions do. States with higher minimum wages are less likely to have higher levels of inequality. It doesn't follow, then, that traditional redistribution need be the only response to rising inequality. Rather higher minimum wages could be a valid response too. Moreover, it would be just as much in keeping with Downs' public choice theory in that a higher minimum wage will increase the money utility of those at the bottom just as much as traditional redistribution would. Of course we don't know that traditional redistribution couldn't be a response to growing inequality, assuming that a higher tax burden will result in money being redistributed to those at the bottom. Rather it isn't a given that overtaxing the wealthy will pay for programs to benefit those at the bottom; it is only an assumption. This chapter suggests that higher minimum wages might be a more effective response because states with a greater distance between median and mean wages have higher minimum wages. Therefore, when it comes to growing inequality, the minimum wage has to be viewed as yet another tool in the larger policy toolbox.

Bibliography

Acemoglu, Daron and James A. Robinson. 2006. *Economic Origins of Dictatorship and Democracy. Cambridge & New York:* Cambridge University Press

Autor, David H., Lawrence F. Katz, and Melissa S. Kearney. 2008. Trends in U.S. Wage Inequality: Revising the Revisionists. *The Review of Economics and Statistics* 90 (2): 300–323.

Balleer, Almut, and Thija van Rens. 2013. Skill-Biased Technological Change and the Business Cycle. *The Review of Economics and Statistics* 95 (4): 1222–1237.

Belman, Dale, and Paul J. Wolfson. 2014. *What Does the Minimum Wage Do?* Kalamazoo: W.E. Upjohn Institute for Employment Research.

Blanchflower, David G., and Alex Bryson. 2008. What Effect Do Unions Have on Wages Now and Would Freeman and Medoff Be Surprised? In *What Do Unions Do?: A Twenty-Year Perspective*, ed. James T. Bennett and Bruce E. Kaufman. New Brunswick: Transaction Publishers.

Card, David, and John DiNardo. 2002. Skill Based Technological Change and Rising Wage Inequality: Some Problems and Puzzles. Working Paper No. 8769. National Bureau of Economic Research, February.

Card, David, Thomas Lemieux, and W. Craig Riddell. 2008. Unions and Wage Inequality. In *What Do Unions Do?: A Twenty-Year Perspective*, ed. James T. Bennett and Bruce E. Kaufman. New Brunswick: Transaction Publishers.

Craypo, Charles, and David Cormier. 2000. Job Restructuring as a Determinant of Wage Inequality and Working-Poor Households. *Journal of Economic Issues* 34 (1): 21–42.

DiNardo, John, and Thomas Lemieux. 1997. Diverging Male Wage Inequality in the United States and Canada, 1981–1988: Do Institutions Explain the Difference? *Industrial and Labor Relations Review* 50 (4): 629–650.

Downs, Anthony. 1957. *An Economic Theory of Democracy.* Boston: Addison-Wesley.

Freeman, Richard B. 2004. What, Me Vote? In *Social Inequality*, ed. Kathryn Neckerman. New York: Russell Sage Foundation.

Freeman Richard B. and James L, Medoff. 1985. *What Do Unions Do?* New York: Basic Books

Fortin, Nicole M., and Thomas Lemieux. 1997. Institutional Changes and Rising Wage Inequality: Is There a Linkage? *Journal of Economic Perspectives* 11 (2): 75–96.

Galbraith, James K. 1998. *Created Unequal: The Crisis in American Pay.* New York: The Free Press.

Goldin, Claudia, and Lawrence F. Katz. 2008. *The Race Between Education and Technology.* Cambridge, MA/London: Belknap Press of Harvard University Press.

Gordon, David M. 1996. *Fat and Mean: The Corporate Squeeze of Working Americans and the Myth of Managerial "Downsizing".* New York: The Free Press.

Gottschalk, Peter. 1997. Inequality, Income Growth, and Mobility: The Basic Facts. *Journal of Economic Perspectives* 11 (2 (Spring)): 21–40.

Hacker, Jacob S., and Paul Pierson. 2010. *Winner-Take-All Politics: How Washington Made the Rich Richer – And Turned Its Back on the Middle Class.* New York: Simon & Schuster.

Howell, David. 1999. Theory-Driven Facts and the Growth in Earnings Inequality. *Review of Radical Political Economics* 31 (1): 54–86.

Howell, David, and Friedrich Huebler. 2001. *Trends in Earnings Inequality and Unemployment Across the OECD: Labor Market Institutions and Simple Supply and Demand Stories.* Working Paper No. 23. Center for Economic Policy Analysis, New School University, May.

Jacobs, Ken, Ian Perry, and Jennifer MacGillvary. 2015. *The High Public Cost of Low Wages.* University of California Berkeley Center for Labor Research and Education. Research Brief, April.

Juhn, Chinhui, Kevin Murphy, and Brooks Pierce. 1993. Wage Inequality and the Rise in Returns to Skills. *Journal of Political Economy* 101 (3): 410–442.

Katz, Lawrence, and Alan B. Krueger. 1992. The Effect of the Minimum Wage on the Fast-Food Industry. *Industrial and Labor Relations Review* 46 (1): 6–21.

Katz, Lawrence, and Kevin M. Murphy. 1992. Changes in Relative Wages, 1963–1987: Supply and Demand Factors. *Quarterly Journal of Economics* 107: 35–79.

Kenworthy, Lane, and Jonas Pontusson. 2005. Rising Inequality and the Politics of Redistribution in Affluent Countries. *Perspectives on Politics* 3 (03).

Lafer, Gordon. 2002. *The Job Training Charade.* Ithaca/London: Cornell University Press.

Lee, David S. 1997. Wage Inequality in the United States During the 1980ss: Rising or Falling Minimum Wage. *Quarterly Journal of Economics* 114 (3): 997–1023.

Lemieux, Thomas. 1998. Estimating the Effects of Unions on Wage Inequality in a Panel Data Model with Comparative Advantage and Nonrandom Selection. *Journal of Labor Economics* 16 (2): 261–291.

Levin-Waldman, Oren M. 2001. *The Case of the Minimum Wage: Competing Policy Models.* Albany: State University of New York Press.

———. 2011. *Wage Policy, Income Distribution, and Democratic Theory.* London/New York: Routledge.

Levy, Frank, and Peter Temin. 2010. Institutions and Wages in Post-World War II America. In *Labor in the Era of Globalization*, ed. Clair Brown, Barry Eichengreen, and Michael Reich. Cambridge: Cambridge University Press.

Lowi, Theodore J. 1964. American Business, Public Policy, Case-Studies, and Political Theory. *World Politics* 16 (4): 677–715.

Luebker, Malte. 2004. Income Inequality, Redistribution, and Poverty: Contrasting Rational Choice and Behavioral Perspectives. *Review of Income and Wealth* 60 (1): 133–154.

Machin, Stephen. 1997. The Decline of Labour Market Institutions and the Rise in Wage Inequality in Britain. *European Economic Review* 41: 647–657.

Meltzer, Allan H., and Scott F. Richard. 1981. A Rational Theory of the Size of Government. *Journal of Political Economy* 89 (5): 914–927.

Palley, Thomas. 1998. *Plenty of Nothing: The Downsizing of the American Dream and the Case for Structural Keynesianism*. Princeton: Princeton University Press.

Piketty, Thomas. 2014. *Capital in the Twenty-First Century*. Cambridge, MA/London: Belknap Press of Harvard University Press.

Piore, Michael J. 1995. *Beyond Individualism*. Cambridge, MA: Harvard University Press.

Pontusson, Jonas. 2005. *Inequality and Prosperity: Social Europe v. Liberal America*. Ithaca/New York: Cornell University Press.

Rawls, John. 1971. *A Theory of Justice*. Cambridge, MA: Harvard University Press.

Rowley, Charles K. 1984. The Relevance of the Median Voter Theorem. *Journal of Institutional and Theoretical Economics*. 140:104–126.

Sandler, Manfred, and Rudiger Wapler. 2004. Endogenous Skill-Biased Technological Change and Matching Unemployment. *Journal of Economics* 81 (1): 1–24.

Stiglitz, Joseph E. 2012. *The Price of Inequality*. New York: W.W. Norton.

Vivarelli, Marco. 2014. Innovation, Employment and Skills in Advanced and Developing Countries: A Survey of Economic Literature. *Journal of Economic Issues* 48 (1): 123–154.

Volscho, Thomas W., Jr. 2005. Minimum Wages and Income Inequality in the American States, 1960–2000. *Research in Social Stratification and Mobility* 23: 347–373.

Wallerstein, Michael. 1999. Wage-Setting Institutions and Pay Inequality in Advanced Industrial Societies. *American Journal of Political Science* 43 (3): 649–680.

———. 2008. Centralized Bargaining and Wage Restraint. In *Selected Works of Michael Wallerstein: The Political Economy of Inequality, Unions, and Social Democracy*, ed. David Austen-Smith, Jeffrey A. Frieden, Miriam A. Golden, Karl Ove Moene, and Adam Przeworski. Cambridge/New York: Cambridge University Press.

CHAPTER 6

Other Theoretical Frameworks

A wage policy approach does not merely break down traditional partisan battle lines but may also be more politically feasible than some of the other approaches that are currently circulating in academic and policy circles. If we could get beyond the conception of the minimum wage as nothing more than a wage floor that effectively redistributes income from profits to the wages of workers, we might come to realize that the minimum wage is a much more conservative approach and one that ironically comports with Milton Friedman's libertarian ethos. This is despite the fact that Friedman opposed the minimum wage because he thought it infringed individual liberty. First it would infringe the freedom of employers to contract with workers as they see fit on their property. Second, it would infringe the freedom of workers to work for a wage beneath the official wage floor. And yet, there is a conservative argument to be made in favor of the minimum wage. If we believe that liberty is essential to protecting our autonomy as individuals we have to ask whether it is possible to be truly autonomous in an economy where, in the absence of a serious wage policy, wages will be driven down with the effect being that workers are only driven further into poverty and greater dependence on the state. Although we typically refer to the minimum wage as a wage floor that will boost incomes, there may be other approaches that could ensure a minimum income that would enable workers to live free and autonomous lives. More than guaranteeing a

O. M. Levin-Waldman, *Restoring the Middle Class through Wage Policy*, Binzagr Institute for Sustainable Prosperity,
https://doi.org/10.1007/978-3-319-74448-3_6

perhaps minimum guaranteed income, we might even ask whether there are larger social benefits to be derived. Can the minimum wage, for instance, serve as a larger efficiency wage? Or is a minimum income a right that we as citizens of a democratic society have? Some thinkers have raised the possibility that a minimum wage might in fact be a legitimate civil rights issue. But the minimum wage may be more than just a wage floor. It could be the end product of a policy to ensure everybody who wants to work will have a job through a government program of employer of last resort (ELR). Or it might be the very beginning of what could be considered a larger universal basic income (UBI). Not only might the minimum wage be conceived of as a step in that direction, but it may be that the nature of the global economy only makes a UBI inevitable. As much as the critic argues that a higher minimum wage could lead to a substitution of machinery for workers, that process could ironically hasten the emergence of a UBI. Once we accept the plausibility to these arguments, it then behooves us to consider just what other forms a minimum wage could take. In this chapter we look at other theoretical frameworks for analyzing the concept of a minimum wage as a measure aimed at both achieving greater productivity and boosting income. In other words, more than simply raising some workers' incomes, the minimum wage may serve to fulfill other social purposes.

A New Efficiency Argument

Because the minimum wage has too often been couched either as an antipoverty measure that will help the poor or an intervention that will result in lower employment, not enough attention has been paid to the efficiency arguments. Even neoclassical economist George Stigler (1946) made it clear that the minimum wage would result in one of two consequences. Either it would lead to lower employment assuming the wage floor was set above the market-clearing wage or it would lead to greater efficiency because workers would be forced to become more productive. Of course, Stigler might have been assuming that employers would achieve greater efficiency because they would end up substituting more technology for labor, which could result in both lower employment and greater efficiency. Still, there was a strain of thought, particularly among institutional economists and progressives, that efficiency not only was a desirable social good but was in fact a matter of managerial responsibility. Therefore, the efficiency argument assumes two basic forms: managerial efficiency and the concept of an efficiency wage, neither of which are mutually exclusive. Early supporters of the minimum wage couched their arguments in terms of achieving greater productivity and efficiency. At the same time, some of the early management theorists like Frederick Winslow Taylor talked about how overall efficiency could be improved if management undertook to make second-class workers into first-class workers. The efficiency wage argument put forth by Sidney Webb held that a minimum wage would actually encourage managers to invest in their workers' human capital. The Webb argument assumes that many second-class workers will become first-class workers on their own simply by virtue of receiving higher wages.

Frederick Winslow Taylor has long been considered to be the founder of the school of scientific management. On the basis of time and motion studies conducted at the Bethlehem Steel Plant in Pennsylvania, Taylor sought to ascertain how firms could achieve greater efficiency in the emerging Fordist assembly line production economy. At issue was what managers would do with greater knowledge, and how this newly acquired knowledge would be used to get greater productivity from workers, thereby making firms more efficient. In *The Principles of Scientific Management* (2013) written in 1911, Taylor posits that the country suffers a great loss because of inefficiency. A peripheral reading of Taylor leads one to conclude that a simple response to unproductive workers is their replacement with more productive workers. But rather than search for some unusual or extraordinary man, the real problem is in systematic management. On the contrary, it is really management's responsibility to take unproductive workers and transform them into productive ones—to transform them from what he calls second-class workers into first-class workers. Management's principal objective should be the attainment of maximum prosperity, coupled with maximum prosperity for each worker. Achieving greater prosperity, however, can only occur when the establishment's newest machines are achieving greater productivity, that is, when each man and each machine are turning out the largest possible output. Taylor writes:

> If the above reasoning is correct, it follows that the most important object of both the workmen and the management should be the training and development of each individual in the establishment, so that he can do (at his fastest pace and with the maximum efficiency) the highest class of work for which his natural abilities fit him. (p. 11)

Taylor assumes that workers naturally tend toward laziness and therefore are by nature second-class workers. Management, then, is obligated to take these workers and transform them into first-class workers, or the highest class of workers that they can be. Taylor calls the second-class worker's laziness "soldiering" which can only be eliminated through scientific management. It is up to management, then, to provide their workers with the resources for them to become first-class workers. This would imply the following: managers surely need to provide their workers with those materials that they need to perform their tasks, but they also need to provide the necessary training so that their tasks can be performed in the most efficient manner possible.

One means by which managers might get more product from their workers, and Taylor certainly says as much, is through a carrot-and-stick approach. Offering inducements is one way to get more product from workers, thereby making the firm more efficient. But because inducements also imply punishment for failure to achieve, it has also been commonplace to view Taylor as anti-worker. But Taylor's emphasis on management responsibility calls that assumption into question. Many years after Taylor, Douglas McGregor (1960) distinguished between two different management approaches: Theory X and Theory Y. Those practicing Theory X tend to view their workers as children in need of supervision. They need to be controlled and at times treated harshly in order to ensure that the objectives of the firm are realized. But those practicing Theory Y tend to take a more behavioralist approach. Here workers are assumed to be individuals with human needs, and managers seeking productivity from them need to find positive ways to motivate them. Taylor, however, was really somewhere along the continuum between Theory X and Theory Y. As Louis Fry (1976) suggests, while Taylor's views of human nature may have been pessimistic, he was optimistic that it could be improved.

According to scientific management, management must plan and effectively prepare the way for workers to perform better. If managers want workers to show some initiative, they must give their workers some special incentive that extends beyond that which is given to the average of the trade. This would suggest that among low-wage workers, for instance, where the average wage may revolve around the statutory minimum wage, managers seeking to obtain greater productivity from their workers must in fact pay more. Taylor writes that "This incentive can be given in several different ways, as, for example, the hope of rapid promotion or advancement; higher wages, either in the form of generous piece-work prices or a premium or bonus of some kind for good and rapid work; shorter hours of labor; better surroundings and working conditions that are ordinarily given" (p. 30). Not only would the adoption of scientific management double the average worker's productivity but it will benefit society as a whole. How will it benefit society? Friction and discontent will in turn be reduced by fostering cooperation between managers and workers. As production costs decline due to the adoption of scientific management, society will prosper as output is doubled. As workers prosper and poverty among them declines, their communities in which they live will also prosper. And yet, it also becomes clear that if workers aren't transformed into first-class workers, it is really management's fault. This would seem to imply that if we are not a high-wage society that too is the fault of businesses and their management.

To a certain extent, Taylor may have been an early pioneer of institutional economics, whereby institutional structures are conceptualized as incentive structures and the goal of conflict resolution is to generate mutual advantages. Were managers to take back those rewards initially given to workers to achieve greater performance, then productivity could be expected to decrease. Taylor was actually critical of a reward and distribution system that failed to take into account the contributions of individual members of the organization, that is, workers. Rather it was incumbent upon management to view workers as having similar interests to management (Wagner-Tsukamoto 2007). If profits increased because of the application of scientific principles of management, then they should be shared among all who had contributed to generating them. At a minimum, then, gains in productivity should be shared among the workers in the form of higher wages.

To not share productivity gains with workers in the form of higher wages was simply an example of poor management. If managers did not share, how could they expect there to be the necessary cooperation between workers and management that would yield greater efficiency? As a precursor to the efficiency wage, Taylor maintained that employer prosperity in the long term was contingent on employee prosperity and vice versa. Although scientific management is intended to serve management, it is also designed to enhance the welfare of all parties in the organization. Still, scientific management meant that managers would direct workers in the "one best way," which was understood to mean cooperation between managers and workers. At the heart of Taylorism was the idea that science and reason based on data would allow management and workers to collaborate. Because this collaboration would yield greater productivity, it would also yield scientific management's ultimate goal of efficiency.

Despite the fact that Taylor is often portrayed as an authoritarian who views labor as matter that has to be tamed by the mind of management, Taylor's scientific management prefigures the idea of increased worker participation in decision-making. Hindy Schacter (1989) cites Peter Drucker's brief note in the 1970s that Taylor's motivational strategy actually provided the worker an opportunity for full personality development. Through training, workers would achieve long-term development. It wasn't only managers that could learn from scientific management, but workers were afforded the opportunity to learn time-study and job analysis. Once they understood the importance of higher motivation, then workers would be given the opportunity to make suggestions. For Taylor, esteem would serve as a tool of motivation. If employers would undertake through training to develop their unskilled laborers, these workers would actually be given a chance at self-actualization. The introduction of technological thinking into shop management spurred articulation of what was sometimes referred to as "the human factor" (Derksen 2014).

Not everybody, however, supported the introduction of scientific management. In an editorial in the *American Federationist*, Samuel Gompers called it a "machinery to perfect the living machine" (p. 151). He charged that Taylor wanted to turn workers into high-speed automatic machines. By separating planning from execution workers were only being robbed of "initiative" in a system that "preys upon the independence, the development, and the character of the worker," and "his individuality, initiative, and vitality" (p. 152). For Taylor, however, scientific management is more than mechanism and efficiency. Almost echoing Marx, Taylor maintained that the main organizing principle in industry was strife. Employers wanted low labor costs and workers wanted higher wages. Because these goals were incompatible it was all too obvious that strife would emerge with labor unions and strikes. As employers would cut wages, workers would only respond in kind by soldiering. This only became a vicious circle, thereby leading to unnecessary inefficiency. On the contrary, low labor costs and higher wages are not incompatible if the work is done according to principles of scientific management. Managers could pay higher wages to fewer workers. At the same time, the workers would be able to earn more without being driven to exhaustion. An employer who shows an interest in his/ her employees will ultimately get more product from them.

Efficiency Wage

Although Taylor does not discuss the concept of an efficiency wage, there would nonetheless appear to be some symmetry between Taylor's idea that management showing greater interest in workers and getting more product from them and efficiency wage theories, both in institutional and in neoclassical economics. Moreover, the idea of investing in workers, if for no other reason than to improve the efficiency of the firm, would appear to presage Amartya Sen's idea that such investment can help develop the capabilities of workers, which in turn will lift them out of poverty.

The early institutional view of the efficiency wage was first proposed by Sidney Webb, and has since come to be known as the "Webb effect." Webb (1912) argued that higher wages would increase productivity, which in turn would improve overall efficiency. Because better-paid workers would be able to better maintain themselves they would be more productive because they would have greater energy. Therefore, a legal minimum wage would increase the productivity of the nation's industry by ensuring that those who are left unemployed would be the least productive members of the workforce. On the one hand, employers would be forced to look for the best workers so as to increase their overall productivity. But on another level, employees would be forced to develop their skills so that they could be counted among the better class of workers. And in fact, employers might find it in their best interest to invest in the human capital of their workers so that they could indeed be counted among that better class of workers.

The neoclassical economist typically couches the efficiency argument in terms of shirking. In a competitive market, workers who are paid higher wages will take steps to avoid shirking. Because they are paid higher wages workers have an incentive to hold onto their jobs because the costs of losing their jobs are also now higher. Here the efficiency wage is an anti-shirking wage which also benefits employers who now save on monitoring costs. The higher-wage costs are offset by these savings, which at the same time offer a positive inducement to work. The result is that workers work harder and become more productive (Shapiro and Stiglitz 1984).

Although not necessarily couched as an anti-shirking wage, this is not anything new. A similar argument was made by John Bates Clark (1913) who said that in the absence of a minimum wage, employers would pick from the ranks of the most necessitous men and women.

Edward Filene (1923) too maintained that higher wages would produce higher quality workers. Employers simply would not be able to get effective organization out of those who weren't intelligent, and they couldn't be intelligent if they did not have enough to live on properly. A higher minimum wage will attract better workers into the labor market. Most efficiency wage theories predict that a higher wage will produce better performance. Omer Gokcekus and Edward Tower (2003), for instance, found that higher wages in Chile attracted more people, especially those with higher reservation wages into the minimum wage sector of the labor market.

An efficiency wage also yields costs savings to employers from higher wages, who now experience lower turnover and therefore save on recruitment and training costs as a result (Howes 2002; Fairris 2003; Reich et al. 2003). Edward Leamer (1999), for instance, argues that most economists assume the labor contract to be one-dimensional, in that it covers wages but overlooks working conditions. Moreover, the typical labor contract fails to account for varying degrees of effort on the part of workers. On the contrary, in a competitive labor market there will be several different contracts offered based on work effort. Consequently, the higher wages being paid by the employer are offset by a higher work effort on the part of the workers. An efficiency wage, then, becomes a wage for greater effort. Instead of causing unemployment as predicted by the standard model, a minimum wage forces effort in low wage and low effort contracts up enough to support the higher wage. This is essentially the Webb effect: employers forced to pay higher wages will now find it worth their while to invest in the human capital of their workers in order to increase their productivity, thereby making them worth the higher wage.

As a result of greater effort in both the high-wage and low-wage sectors, output levels rise in both. But by forcing effort levels to more closely conform, the minimum wage creates comparative advantage in the labor-intensive sector, which is the opposite of what might be expected. In exchange for the higher wage, employers are getting greater effort. If capital is then interpreted as human capital, and if workers themselves invest in their own education, the message of the model is that those who choose education are also choosing higher effort. And yet, it is also true that when employers invest in their workers' human capital, they too are choosing higher effort. The point is that if work effort is variable, a minimum wage could then generate enough extra work effort to compensate for the increased wage level, thus ensuring a degree of Pareto optimality.

Allan Drazen (1986) illustrates this with a simple model that assumes entry into the labor market to be contingent on maximizing income. There are two markets—a primary one with higher wages and a secondary one with lower wages. Those individuals entering the primary labor market expect their income to be higher than the foregone (and lower) income in the alternative or secondary market. The model also assumes a worker's productivity in the primary market to be an increasing function of his foregone income. In other words, based on these two assumptions, there is a positive relation between an individual's acceptance wage and his/her productivity. The minimum wage, then, becomes important because employers would prefer to pay higher wages if they could be assured higher labor quality. But in the absence of a mandated minimum, they will not raise wages on their own for fear that their competitors may still opt to pay lower wages. That is, in the uncertainty that others will do the same, they are forced to lower their wages in order to remain competitive. Employers, in other words, need a little push in the form of mandatory wage floors. It is here that there would appear to be some symmetry with Taylor in that he assumes the transformation of workers into first-class workers requires a managerial top-down approach. Here the efficiency argument appears to assume the same top-down approach in the anti-shirking wage—that employers can push their workers into anti-shirking behavior simply by offering them an efficiency wage. And yet, the anti-shirking wage is no different from Webb's minimum wage whereby the worker himself may become a first-class worker on his own.

At a minimum, Taylor's management approach would appear to be consistent with the neoclassical anti-shirking wage. Although Taylor says nothing about an efficiency wage, his call to reward more productive workers with higher wages nonetheless implies an efficiency wage. Because Taylor assumes it is management's responsibility to take so-called second-class workers, who are otherwise lazy and tend toward shirking, and turn them into first-class workers he is effectively acknowledging a managerial responsibility to prevent shirking. The neoclassical anti-shirking wage assumes a high opportunity cost to be associated with losing a job because of shirking. As the worker becomes more productive to avoid losing the job, the employer willingly pays the higher wage, not only for the greater productivity but to also save money on monitoring costs.

If the end result is that the worker becomes a first-class worker, then at least the anti-shirking version of the efficiency wage would appear to be in line with Taylor's exhortation to turn the second-class worker into a first-class worker. It then bears repeating that Taylor used the term "soldiering" to describe the laziness of these workers. It is not inconceivable that he would have viewed a worker's tendency to shirk no differently than the worker who soldiers. They are one and the same. That there is a responsibility on the part of managers to ensure that low-wage/low-skilled workers will be productive is akin to suggesting that an efficient economy relies on more than simply individual responsibility. It might suggest that the state has a responsibility to ensure that efficient wages are paid, even through a wage floor. But the efficiency wage argument is also saying something else. By talking about the benefits of higher pay, it is effectively dismissing the standard criticism of the minimum wage that it simply results in lower employment. Whether it does or does not is really beside the point. Rather in the standard calculus of costs and benefits, it is important to weigh society's overall benefits against the overall costs. The efficiency wage argument is saying that there are clearly economic and social benefits that outweigh the narrow costs of the possibility of employment consequences.

Personal Development

Economist and philosopher Amartya Sen (1999) has defined poverty as not only the deprivation of income but the deprivation of capabilities. These capabilities enable individuals to be autonomous beings. These two types of deprivation are nonetheless inextricably linked. A worker at the bottom of the wage distribution who needs support in order to subsist is also poor because that worker below subsistence wages is also effectively being deprived of his/her capabilities. For Sen, a capability is the alternative combination of functionings that are feasible for a person. A capability is a kind of freedom. It is in fact "the substantive freedoms he or she enjoys to lead the kind of life he or she has reason to value" (p. 87). Sen would appear to imply that a society that pays its workers low wages, which as a result forces them to live in poverty, effectively deprives them of their capabilities. Therefore, a society that fails to maintain a reasonable minimum wage, or allows the size of the effective minimum wage population to grow, not only aids and abets the deprivation of capabilities but also aids and abets the diminution of their capabilities. Higher incomes, then, would enable workers to develop their capabilities.

It might be objected that principles of scientific management cannot easily be applied to the low-skilled service economy where most of the effective minimum wage population is to be found. Taylor was specifically applying scientific management to the nation's factory system at the heyday of the Industrial Revolution. At the time, factories were the largest employers of what we would today refer to as unskilled labor. Factory workers only achieved dignity because through collective bargaining over wages and working conditions organized labor was able over time to effectively transform the way society viewed these workers (Glickman 1997). Over time those in manufacturing came to be viewed as possessing skill while those in low-paying service did not. In the post-industrial service economy, we think of low-skilled workers as the prototypical hamburger flippers in the fast-food industry. Although it is commonplace, especially among minimum wage critics, to assume that low-skilled workers simply aren't worth higher wages, similar arguments appear to have been made in Taylor's time. In talking about low-skilled shovelers, Taylor (2013) addresses that very question:

> the average man would question whether there is much of any science in the work of shoveling. Yet there is little doubt, if any intelligent reader of this paper were deliberately to set out to find what may be called the foundation of the science of shoveling, that with perhaps 15 to 20 hours of thought and analysis he would be almost sure to have answered as the essence of this science. On the other hand, so compellingly are the rule-of-thumb ideas still dominant that the writer has never met a single shovel contractor to whom it had ever occurred that there was such a thing as the science of shoveling. This science is so elementary as to be almost self-evident. (p. 56)

In the Bethlehem Steel Company, Taylor tells us that there were 600 shovelers and laborers of this general class. The low-skilled work of the shoveler is no different from the low-skilled work of those in the low-wage service sector, but through scientific management, this low-skilled worker can be made more productive. Even though Taylor's specific focus on scientific management doesn't mention the efficiency wage, there are clearly implications for it in his assumptions about management's responsibility.

As the data in Chap. 3 on the "effective" minimum wage population shows, their ranks have certainly increased and they are doing the work today that unskilled factory workers did at the beginning of the twentieth century. On the surface, at least, it becomes clear that higher-paying middle-class jobs have decreased further and what has replaced them are the lower-paying and lower-skilled jobs at the bottom end of the market and higher-paying and higher-skilled jobs at the top of the market. Although these trends clearly support the idea that the economic changes that have occurred favor those with advanced technical skills, it may also suggest that Taylor's formula still has application in the changing economy. A much larger proportion of the workers clearly fall into the effective minimum wage labor market, and it may no longer be credible to write them off as simply lacking the skills and therefore they should retrain.

Taylorism might suggest that good management would have implemented the Webb effect as a component part of scientific management. After all, the offer of higher wages as a reward for greater output does imply an efficiency wage as a basis of motivation. Therefore, when the efficiency argument as formulated by both Taylor and Webb is considered within the context of data on the growing "effective" minimum wage labor market, we need to conclude that this growth and the failure to ensure higher wages for this segment of the labor market ultimately is a failure of management. It is perhaps suggestive of this failure to make first-class workers out of second-class workers that low-skilled workers, as exemplified by the growing significance of the less than a 12th grade education variable, comprise the bulk of this labor market.

A more radical approach would suggest that apart from the argument that higher wages in the form of a wage floor will lead to greater efficiency, capitalist economies will only need greater regulation if they are to survive. The Marxist position has always been that capitalism will implode under its own weight. Ironically, the greater efficiency that Taylor's scientific management is intended to bring about will only hasten that implosion. Therefore, in order to preserve capitalism, class struggle needs to institutionalize in a system of regulation. Regulation that protects the interests of workers while simultaneously encroaching upon the rights of managers, especially their property rights, also protects the manager's interests and overall system in the long term. Michael Aglietta (1979) argues that the general conditions of capitalist resolution of the crisis assembly line production can only be understood in the context of laws of capitalist regulation. Aglietta explains: "The scope of changes in the condition of existence of the wage-earning class that are necessary for creating a new coherence in the regime of accumulation implies a new development of state influence within the structural forms" (p. 386). This would clearly imply a role for government to ensure higher wages in order to ensure the survival of capitalist markets.

For Aglietta, Taylorism only makes these policies a foregone conclusion. It becomes an interesting catch-22. On the one hand, efficiency requires that firms produce greater output for lower costs. But on the other hand, to get workers to produce more, workers' wages have to rise. On their own, employers will not raise wages because they cannot be sure that their competition will follow suit. Therefore, they need to be prodded through wage floors. A minimum wage does fall under the rubric of Aglietta's "a new development of state influence within the structural forms." The neoclassical, then, retorts that the manager is now compelled to find ways to become more efficient. But for the radical, this is just another example of the capitalist class finding a way to institutionalize class struggle—to exert control over their workers—in order to maintain their position in the wage relation. Ironically, however, both the radicals and neoclassicals appear to be on the same page.

Arguably, managers that pay higher wages to their workers, even if their goal is greater productivity rather than meeting their human needs, will have greater legitimacy in the eyes of their workers. In this vein too, it would fit Taylor's exhortation for managers to find means by which they can take second-class workers and turn them into first-class workers. If management has a responsibility, then management writ large—society—shoulders a similar responsibility. Individuals cannot be first-class citizens if they aren't sufficiently economically independent that they can be fully autonomous. If they are unable to be economically independent because employers enjoy the power to pay low wages, then they are relegated to second-class citizenship, if not even lower. But that management would pay efficiency wages because it is a social good and that workers are entitled to them are two different matters entirely.

Is the Minimum Wage a Civil Right?

All too often we think of the minimum wage in terms of a wage floor which I have argued has macroeconomic benefits. Overlooked, however, are the moral and possibly civil rights arguments. The minimum wage debate for too long has revolved around those arguing the adverse economic consequences, especially to those with little skill on the one hand, and those arguing the benefits to the poor on the other. But as suggested in Chap. 2, there was an argument to be made that the minimum wage was necessary because of the asymmetrical power balance between workers and their employers. Institutionalists specifically took aim at the neoclassical model because it did not account for power. Conceived differently, employers have power because they are property owners whereas the workers are not. Already the question arises as to whether the minimum wage might not be viewed as a means of effectively giving their workers property rights in their jobs. James Galbraith (1998), for instance, argued that a minimum wage was essential to giving workers a degree of monopoly power they otherwise lacked in its absence. A mere wage floor, however, is not the same as conferring property rights in labor. It merely says that workers cannot be forced to work for less than the floor because their lack of monopoly power would compel them to accept whatever lower wages are being offered. A wage floor, however, does not change this reality. It merely raises the threshold for the low wages that they will be compelled to accept.

If workers' labor then could be defined in terms of property rights, could the effective deprivation of those rights by not paying their workers livable wages be seen as tantamount to a civil rights violation? Noah Zatz (2009), for instance, raises the question of whether the minimum wage perhaps ought not to be considered a larger civil right. To a certain extent, the language of procedural democracy assumes that individuals as equals in standing before the law do enjoy certain basic civil rights. The implication being that without respect for the basic civil rights of voting, free speech, due process, and the right to pursue one's interests based on one's human agency, democracy is non-existent, even if nominal elections are being held. Zatz asks the question of whether a minimum wage law serves to protect the civil rights of workers. In other words, is it necessary to have a wage floor to protect their civil rights, and if so would a more general wage policy be a necessary and sufficient condition?

Zatz would also like to move the minimum wage debate away from the standard debate between those arguing the disemployment effects on the one hand and those arguing the anti-poverty benefits on the other. Rather the minimum wage should be seen as a policy that aims to remedy an injury to workers' civil rights, and to the extent that this may be true, the current debate over the minimum wage is misinformed. While "civil rights" is most often identified with anti-discrimination law, it is more broadly associated with legal responses to inequality and subordination along lines of socially significant group differences. Many may see disparities as being inconsistent with a commitment to human equality, which is as good a watchword for anti-discrimination law as any. As the lowest paid workers tend to hail from groups central to anti-discrimination projects, it would appear that their status as low-paid workers means that they are not being treated on an equal footing with others, and certainly not with those with more resources.

One approach to justifying the minimum wage that has been obscured by a focus on anti-poverty arguments is that it offers a corrective to defects in the wage bargain between employers and employees. As Zatz puts it:

> In its most stylized form, the minimum wage remedies employer theft. If an employer refuses to pay a worker the agreed-upon wage for work performed, the employer is a thief. The same is true if the employer forces the worker at gunpoint to agree to work for no wage at all or tricks her into the same. Furthermore, it can make no fundamental difference if what the employer steals is not the entire wage but only some fraction of it (p. 7).

Nevertheless, what matters most about the minimum wage is that it is no defense to show that the employer simply paid the going rate in a complex competitive market. The "inequality of bargaining power" provides the moderate alternative to the labor theory of value. What a minimum wage does is enact a presumption that when wages fall below a certain level, they are low for morally arbitrary reasons. Therefore, mandating a higher wage brings us closer to a world of fairness. Or at a minimum, it may serve to place some on an equal footing with others, and in this vein it becomes a civil rights issue in a broader sense.

Bruce Kaufman (2003), however, points out that both Webb and his wife Beatrice were also concerned about the social costs of paying low wages. In addition to efficiency, the minimum wage also leads to fairness. The Webbs' case for the minimum wage was built on two main pillars: the doctrine of labor's *inequality of bargaining power* (IBP) and the *social cost of labor* (SCL) doctrine. IBP holds that employers individually and/or collectively enjoy a power advantage in wage determination, even in what we would consider a competitive labor market. The party benefitting from extra-low wages in labor markets is employers. But employers are not the only beneficiaries. Consumers, and especially affluent consumers who have a disproportionate share of income, also benefit from low-wage labor in the form of lower prices. One social rationale for a legal minimum wage, as Kaufman points out, is that it offsets the workers' weak bargaining power in the labor market. Therefore, IBP creates a social rationale on efficiency and fairness grounds for state abridgment of freedom of contract. Add to the SCL doctrine, the argument for a legal minimum becomes stronger and the traditional neoclassical opposition to it becomes weaker. Neoclassical economists typically treat social costs arising from production processes where product prices are low and output high as negative externalities arising from an absence of property rights for, in this case, the workers.

The innovation of the Webbs and American institutionalists was to apply the negative externality concept—missing property rights—to the employment relationship in order to develop a positive rationale for both legal minimum wages and collective bargaining. Their argument rests on the assumption that labor—human capital—as is the case with physical capital requires some minimum ongoing expenditures for upkeep, repair, and depreciation. That is, if product prices were to cover the full costs of production, then firms must pay the workers a wage sufficient to cover individual and family subsistence costs or provide in-kind compensation. But when the wage falls short of subsistence level, the social costs exceed the private labor costs borne by the firm and its customers. "In this case, either someone else bears this expense, or, socially viewed, the nation's stock of human capital starts to depreciate and wear out" (Kaufman 2003, p. 313). Each worker requires a minimum level of health care to cover physical and mental wear and tear. A minimum wage, then, is seen as contributing to a solution of the social cost problem, and with far greater efficiency and fairness than can competition and laissez-faire. The idea is to use the minimum wage in the labor market that approximates the social cost of labor. Although a minimum wage can in effect be viewed as a tax on firms, firms paying low wages are nonetheless making a profit without paying the full social costs. A minimum wage, then, serves to end the social subsidy to otherwise parasitic firms.

This would seem to suggest that the absence of a wage policy which effectively results in society bearing the social costs so that a few producers can derive benefit is inherently anti-democratic. Or that the profits of firms are the result of the diminution of workers' property rights in their jobs. Society bears the costs for the benefit of a few. Is it not effectively infringing on the collective property interests of the rest of society who are now compelled to support others through higher taxes which also diminish the value of their property? Holzner (2007) observes that in Latin America where the lower classes make up more than half of the population in many countries, participation of the poor is all that much more important. The empirical evidence suggests that while neoliberal policies, or market-based reforms, may have stabilized democratic politics in the region, it has also been at the expense of political participation, representation, and government responsiveness. Neoliberal policies particularly have a devastating effect on the ability of popular groups to mobilize against market reforms by atomizing workers and peasants, thereby weakening their ability to organize and closing off access to key allies and ministers. In Mexico, for instance, political activity and growing feelings of political engagement among the poor initially surged during the 1990s, but after 1997 participation in terms of voter turnout, petitioning activity, and feelings of political interest and efficacy declined overall. It was specifically actions by the Mexican state during this period, many of which served to deepen the free-market model of development, that actually affected the poor more severely than other groups. As a result, "the poor are less and less able to afford the increasing costs of political action, are increasingly pessimistic about their ability to influence the decisions and actions of their government, and are more and more often choosing political strategies that do not enhance their voice."

The net effect of institutional reforms, therefore, has been to stifle poor people's political activity, especially in comparison with more "affluent groups" (p. 91). Political participation in Mexico, especially the political activity of popular groups, was always heavily influenced by the actions of the state and by these groups' relationship to political parties and corporatist organizations. The severity of poverty and income inequality have only worsened in Mexico, as there has been a systematic redistribution of resources away from the lower classes to the elites since government began implementing free-market reforms since the second half of the 1980s. Free-market reforms weaken lower-class political mobilization by fragmenting and dividing organizations, eroding their membership, and denying them key material and organizational resources. The erosion of organizational power is very damaging to lower-class political participation because the poor rely more heavily than other groups on organizations to mobilize them into politics.

Neoliberal reforms have particularly hampered the poor's political participation "by decreasing their income, their access to politically relevant resources, and their overall capacity for political action" (p. 96). Wages declined sharply due to the stabilization programs of the 1980s. The real value of the minimum wage in Mexico City declined from the indexed value of 23.2 in 1982 to only 48 in 1993. Declining incomes mean that the opportunity cost of political participation is higher now than during the pre-reform eras. And interviews with the poor only suggested that the costs of attempting certain kinds of political activity were becoming prohibitive for many of the poor. Have these people not effectively lost value in their labor? If their labor could effectively be defined in terms of property, has their property not effectively been taken without just compensation? If we apply Kaufman's analysis to Holzner's study of market reforms in Mexico, it becomes clear that paying low wages not only imposes social costs on society, it effectively excludes an entire segment of the population from the democratic process because it effectively denies them voice. It also strips them of their property rights by diminishing the value of their labor. Democracy cannot survive if increasingly more workers, because of the dual nature of the economy, are denied voice and in effect their civil rights. At a minimum, each individual and/or organization must bear responsibility.

Perhaps there is also the larger context in which the emphasis on growth has been occurring, namely the stagnation of American wages and growing income inequality. Frank Levy and Peter Temin (2010) tell us that the US "Golden Age" was from 1947 to 1973 and the central feature was upward mobility. Individuals saw sharply rising incomes through much of their careers and each successive generation was living better than the previous one. But between 1980 and 2005 while productivity increased, wages stagnated. While business productivity increased 71 percent, the median weekly earnings of full-time workers rose only 14 percent from \$613 to \$705. They suggest that a useful way to describe why significant productivity growth since 1980 did not translate into growth in earnings is the declining bargaining power of the average full-time worker. That wages stagnated because of declining bargaining power, it becomes clear that workers only had bargaining power because they were members of unions, not because the right to earn a respectable living is considered a civil right. Of course, there is a problem with this. If a civil right, how do we enforce it? A minimum wage is not the same as a positive obligation to ensure that workers earn a respectable living. But if the state were to have such a positive obligation, might it not also have another obligation to ensure that all who want to work are able to do so?

The Conservative Case for the Minimum Wage

The minimum wage is often thought of as a liberal policy, if not progressive policy, intended to assist the poor. I have been attempting to argue that the issue is much larger. Sen's argument of capabilities suggests that it is ultimately about personal autonomy and independence. Ironically, then, there is a conservative argument to be made in favor of the minimum wage. Although the conservative position certainly exploits the standard model as a rationale for its ultimate objective of liberty and political freedom, it does not rely solely on the standard model. Milton Friedman, for instance, defined political freedom as the absence of coercion. The market place is free of coercive power when the economic activity is separated from political authority. Government's role, then, should be restricted to no more than the performance of what the marketplace cannot: maintaining, arbitrating, and enforcing the rules of the game. Based on the assumption that workers and employers bargain as equals, Friedman assumes that government intervention effectively limits freedom. That is, in the standard model steeped in the neoclassical ethos there is no power imbalance between workers and their employers. Moreover, workers aren't assumed to be seeking employment in order to satisfy their needs, rather they, like all actors in the market place, are assumed to be motivated by their respective preferences.

According to Friedman, government typically justifies intervention with the excuse that it is to achieve both "full employment" and "economic growth" to justify intervention. But intervention usually leads to greater unemployment, thereby justifying even more intervention. When government intervenes more, individual freedom is only limited further. The greatest achievement of capitalism is that it affords individuals opportunities to improve and develop themselves—not necessarily in the accumulation of property and wealth, although those are no small achievements either. For Friedman, the minimum wage has the opposite effect of what was intended, which is that those most likely to be displaced from their jobs are the poor and low-skilled workers. This means that the minimum wage effectively deprives these people of the opportunity to improve themselves (Friedman 2002). All government will have accomplished in the name of helping those people who will be hurt the most is the creation of precedent for further intervention and infringement of personal freedom and autonomy (Budd 2004). Moreover, because this assault on personal autonomy will have been inefficient, it is considered to be even more egregious.

The minimum wage effectively denies workers the ability to accept lower wages. If that is the difference between being employed and not being employed, their personal freedom has been interfered with. This argument actually echoes the argument against minimum wages and maximum hours offered by the Supreme Court at the dawn of the twentieth century, which was they restrict the liberty of contract. If workers are truly free, then they should be able to accept lower wages. Not only does the minimum wage restrict the liberty of workers to accept lower wages, it restricts the liberty of employers because it interferes with their business decisions. In the 1923 case of *Adkins v. Children's Hospital*, the Supreme Court ruled that a minimum wage for women in the District of Columbia was unconstitutional because it violated their liberty of contract. To a certain extent, this case was an outlier because the Court had previously maintained that women did not enjoy the same liberty of contract enjoyed by men. In *Muller v. Oregon* decided in 1908 the Court held that a 60-hour-per-week maximum hours law for women working in laundries was not a violation of liberty of contract because as mothers of the next generation they needed special protection. In *Adkins,* however, the Court decided that women did enjoy the liberty of contract because they were now considered to be the equals of men following the Nineteenth Amendment to the Constitution giving them the right to vote.

Nevertheless, the Court would continue to cling to its *Lochner*-era view of the world that unless a regulatory measure was essential to the protection of public health and welfare, one's liberty of contract could not be infringed. This idea came from the 1905 case *Lochner v. New York* where the Court held that there was nothing in what bakers in New York did that required a 60-hour maximum for protecting their health and welfare. This line of thinking well reflected the conservative position that individuals were free to bargain over the terms of their employment. It wasn't until *West Coast Hotel Co. v. Parrish* decided in 1937 that the Supreme Court turned away from this position. Citing Justice Oliver Wendell Holmes' terse dissent in *Adkins*, the Court stated: "This statute does not compel anybody to pay anything. It simply forbids employment at rates below those fixed as the minimum requirement of health and right living" (pp. 396–397). As far as the conservative position is concerned, there is no asymmetrical power relationship between employers and employees because both are presumed to be equal. The *Lochner*-era Court clearly missed the reality that the only real bargaining power that workers had was to reject the offer that was being made. And in a world where no assistance programs existed, that was tantamount to starving.

The conservative tradition as represented by Friedman, however, is actually ironic. Conservatives never really embraced free-market ideology and personal freedom, rather they embraced tradition, order, and rule of aristocrats, who by virtue of their greater wisdom had a better sense of what was good for individuals than individuals themselves. Contrary to this Friedmanite idea that conservatism is about liberty, it is really a statist political philosophy. According to Theodore Lowi (1996), there was nothing about the expansion of government during the 1930s, including the adoption of the Fair Labor Standards Act (FSLA), that would have been considered an assault on conservatism (p. 130). In this vein, Friedman's emphasis on personal freedom is really classical liberalism, not conservatism. And yet, conservatives in America appear to have adopted the classical liberal ideal enshrined in the *Declaration of Independence*. That is, the essence of "life, liberty, and the pursuit of happiness" is human agency, which means that individuals are free to choose how they will live their lives and enjoy the liberty to make choices to that end. Whether they can truly make choices if their income is so low that they are deprived of their capabilities is, of course, the critical question.

The American conservative tradition has really been about conserving a view of the world grounded in the past—one grounded in the pre-industrial era, where one's choices had little effect on others. In recent years, however, the American conservative position has focused more on personal responsibility rather than individual rights. This position finds expression in both Charles Murray's and Lawrence Mead's critiques of public assistance programs prior to the welfare reform of 1996. According to Murray (1984), public assistance fostered dependency, out-of-wedlock births, and the deterioration of the family. He therefore called for the elimination of all programs so that the poor would have no choice but to enter the labor market and take responsibility for themselves. On a philosophical level, he asks why one necessarily has a responsibility to support others simply because they are poor. Ironically, however, by maintaining that the poor indeed are rational actors because they were choosing not to work due to work paying less than their benefits, he effectively conceded that the poor really could not adequately support themselves or their families in the low-wage labor market. Mead (1986, 1992), on the other hand, argued that individuals needed to think more in terms of their obligations rather than their rights. All citizens have an obligation to participate in the common project of society, which for Mead is work. Moreover, participation in the common project of work was the very definition of equality. For Mead, this participation was to be considered the very definition of equality. This meant that for poor people—those on public assistance—to truly make their claim to equality, they should be forced to work, and even coerced if necessary. He even claimed that most shied away from their societal obligations for what he referred to as "mysterious" reasons. Of course, there was nothing that mysterious about the low-wage labor market not affording them opportunities to be self-sufficient. And if they could not be self-sufficient, it would in the words of Sen be difficult to assume personal responsibility.

Still, if one wants to maintain that the essence of what American conservatism has evolved into is indeed Friedman's position on personal freedom, then there is an argument to be made that a minimum wage actually enhances personal freedom by adding to individual capabilities. But there is another side which traces back to early republican thought, which is that people paid wages below subsistence cannot be truly free because they are effectively enslaved by virtue of their dependence on others. When Friedman views the minimum wage as an assault on personal freedom, early republican thinkers, who also believed in free labor, viewed wage labor as an assault on personal freedom. In other words, the Industrial Revolution, which created the wage labor system, pushed down wages thereby making labor market institutions like unions and the minimum wage inevitable. Later reformers would view the minimum wage as an essential ingredient in the wage worker being able to be free.

Early republicans considered free labor to be the basis of personal freedom. One who was self-employed or earned enough because one was in a craft was truly independent. To work in a factory in the employ of others was not considered to be free. Rather workers earning low wages because of the Industrial Revolution not only viewed themselves as slaves, but they were viewed as slaves by others. Although the wage contract was considered to be an essential element in the development of an industrial, manufacturing-based economy, wage labor was not considered to be the same as free labor. Free labor was the ideal to be achieved; wage labor was the reality of the new economic system and represented the unfree nature of labor. As the wage contract was becoming more commonplace during the early 1800s, it was also establishing the norm by which other social and political relationships would be defined (Montgomery 1993, pp. 12–13).

Wage labor was initially viewed as a debilitating departure from the republican idea of free labor in a commercial republic because workers would not only be dependent on others but would be so poorly paid that they could no longer be considered autonomous. And yet, because the economy was changing, workers couldn't avoid their transformation into wage labor. Wage labor was particularly problematic because of new conceptions of liberty, freedom, and independence. Politically, workers only believed that equality was possible if each member of the polity was economically independent. Despite the language of voluntary contract, workers felt they were being compelled in a way that would only make it impossible for them to exercise their citizenship. Those receiving wages could not possibly participate in the civic life as the equals of their employers. To workers, the wage system was viewed as promoting the formation of an aristocracy. On the contrary, liberty, as it was understood at the time, and very much owing to the influence of Locke, was defined as the complete ownership of one's labor, and by extension one's self.

The concept of citizenship was grounded in a system of property ownership. The republican tradition in the USA stressed the independence of individuals as the basis for citizenship (Foner 1998). Following the Civil War, all segments of the American labor reform movements used the term "wage slavery" to describe the new wage labor contracts. Moreover, workers contrasted the term "slavery" with "manliness" (Shefter 1986, pp. 203–206). Property owners, on the one hand, were both independent and free citizens of the republic, whereas slaves were not. While workers under the old feudalistic system had no formal property rights in their jobs, they could at least be assured that they would be provided for materially. Under the new system, there were no guarantees and no assurances, and the law was slow to recognize these rights. It would fall to unions to secure these rights, but under the old system unions were viewed as an encroachment upon the free labor contract (Hattam 1993). This created a challenge for organized labor to make wage labor respectable. But the challenge was also to ground the essence of citizenship within a system of wage labor where property ownership would be in the labor power that workers would sell in exchange for wages, rather than in land.

Classical republicanism assumed that citizens achieved their greatest moral fulfillment from participating in a self-governing republic. A virtuous citizen was one willing to sacrifice private interests for the sake of the general community. Only when they were virtuous did they achieve liberty. This meant that one could not be an autonomous individual if one was economically dependent on others, which included being paid wages by one's masters. Therefore, it followed that since liberty and independence were the bases for virtue, one who wasn't independent could not qualify as a citizen. Those who worked for wages were to be precluded from citizenship because they lacked independence and were absorbed in their narrow occupations. Ironically it would also preclude those engaged in the liberal professions if they too were dependent on their work for their incomes. They would be no more qualified for positions of virtuous leadership than mechanics and other manual laborers (Wood 1993, pp. 106–107). Only through economic independence could one be politically independent. The ideal worker only achieved independence through property ownership, because it was through property ownership that this worker would not be dependent on others.

An economy revolving around factories challenged many of the certainties upon which the work ethic had been based and upended the association in the minds of many between work and morality. Work in factories at the beck and call of owners no longer appeared to be what one did of one's free will. The worker no longer felt as though he owned his own labor; rather he sold it to somebody else for a pittance and was subject to the owner's control while in his employ (Rodgers 1978). The sense among workers, especially organized workers, was that by selling their labor they were losing ownership of themselves and to someone who now had a great amount of power over them. Men forced to work for wages no longer saw themselves as independent citizens, but as children, or even "wage slaves." If, however, they could earn a livable wage, they would then be able to rise above the shameful image of a prostitute. Social reformers who advocated living wages during the late part of the nineteenth century viewed a living wage as the vehicle by which workers would be able to achieve full citizenship. One could only be independent to the extent that one could control one's own labor. The early union movement, which sought to obtain "living wages," was really about removing the stigma associated with wage labor. It was about restoring the worker's dignity and independence. Similarly, a minimum wage could be viewed in the same way.

A minimum wage that would enable workers to support themselves would not only be in support of individual freedom but, given the transformations that have occurred and continue to occur, be in line with the republican tradition that has underpinned American culture and institutions. Within this context, a minimum wage is hardly radical, rather it is quite conservative. But it is conservative for yet another reason. If as we argued in the section on personal development that a capitalist economy requires regulation so that it will not implode, a minimum wage, as but one policy in that larger arsenal of regulations, not only helps it not to implode but in so doing helps to conserve a tradition of the past.

Employer of Last Resort?

Free labor, of course, presupposes that there are jobs for people to utilize their labor. A minimum wage is ultimately about achieving a minimum income, and if sufficient it may be about achieving autonomy and independence. But it might be possible to achieve both without necessarily legislating a specific wage floor. One approach would simply be to create public jobs with wages paid becoming the putative minimum wage. Randall Wray (2007) argues for government as ELR to offer employment to those who are "ready, willing, and able" to work, but have not been able to find jobs. ELR would not replace traditional welfare but would supplement private sector employment. ELR would not be workfare and would not replace existing social programs. It would not pay starvation wages, nor would it provide union-busting low-wage labor. It would, however, eliminate the need for a minimum wage, as the ELR wage would become the effective minimum wage. It could also establish the base package of benefits that private employers would have to supply. Although it could replace unemployment insurance, it could also just be added on to give workers who lost their jobs greater choices.

The object here is, through creating jobs for some of the unemployed, to increase aggregate demand through the multiplier and thereby increase private sector employment. If it succeeds in doing this, it should also result in a reduction of the number of ELR jobs required. What it does not do is concede that increasing aggregate demand by increasing the living standards of those at the bottom must necessarily cause a demand-pull wage-price spiral. Rather with fixed prices, government's ELR wage is perfectly stable and sets a benchmark price for labor. Although Wray suggests that if ELR were to be implemented, it most likely would not be inflationary in the sense of generating continuing pressure on wages and prices. Because it obligates government to make the initial investment into creating these ELR jobs, it is highly unlikely to garner much political support in today's political climate. Still, the underlying assumption is critical to addressing the issue of long-term unemployment, which is that more than investment in retraining to meet the needs of an increasing technical skills-biased economy, we need to return to the basics of macroeconomics and find ways to increase demand for goods and services in the aggregate. This begins with having the wherewithal to do so.

A more comprehensive income policy representing a greater welfare state commitment is not likely to fly in the USA given the strong anti-statist tradition. Because of the individualistic culture upon which the nation was built, a wage floor is perhaps as good as we are going to get. The ELR concept did initially find expression in the 1930s Work Progress Administration (WPA) which put many who had been displaced back to work. But the WPA never survived the end of the Depression. Even when Congress passed the Employment Act of 1946, it eliminated the concept of full employment, which had been the bill's authors' intention. Initially introduced as the Full Employment Bill, opposition quickly surfaced over the term "full" because it implied a positive right to work in which case the government would be obligated to ensure people had jobs even if it meant that it would be ELR. The USA, however, has never been a nation of positive rights—but one of negative rights. A negative right to a job merely means that government cannot interfere with one's right to take a job in the private market place. A positive right would require that government employ people. And for a nation that was just entering the Cold War, this idea that the state would be this deeply involved in the market place was too much. A wage floor, on the other hand, does assume the basic framework of the free-market place, with the added assumption that the free-market place needs some assistance in the form of labor market institutions.

Universal Minimum Income?

Another approach which could be just as costly, but perhaps less intrusive is the idea of a UBI. A UBI might flow logically from the minimum wage, but it might ironically be inevitable if the critics are correct about paying higher minimum wages. If a higher minimum wage would indeed lead to a substitution of machinery for workers in the low-skilled service economy, then there is the obvious question of how these people will live. Here a UBI may just be the next logical step. If we assume that a conservative argument for the minimum wage rests on personal autonomy, and without wages to be self-sufficient there can be no autonomy, then why simply a minimum wage in the form of a wage floor? What is clear about the history of the minimum wage in the USA is that the minimum wage has fallen short of what would be necessary for one to be autonomous.

Amy Guttman and Dennis Thompson (1996) argue for autonomy on the basis of what they call a fair opportunity. In a deliberative democracy a basic opportunity principle secures citizens an adequate level of basic opportunity goods. Such opportunity goods include an adequate income level, defined as that which enables one to live a decent life according to society's current standards. Their basic opportunity principle is within the context of welfare provision, but the same arguments could just as easily be applied to wage policies in whatever form. A wage that enables workers to live with dignity is at the root of what it means to have a fair opportunity. The call for a fair opportunity, then, might really be seen as a response to the unequal opportunities that are the product of income inequality. By calling for fair opportunity they are asserting that society has an obligation to redress the imbalance and ensure that each has the resources to participate.

Fair opportunity would actually suggest something broader than the statutory minimum wage. As a broader measure, Philipe Van Parijs (1992) calls for Basic Income Capitalism, defined as a socioeconomic regime in which the means of production are for the most part privately owned, but where each citizen is entitled to substantial unconditional income over and above what he/she might earn through normal participation in the labor market. A basic income as such is essentially a pathway toward the achievement of a just society, which Van Parijs understands to be a free society in which all members are as free as possible. To be truly free, one must possess the means to whatever one might want, and not just the "right" to do it. A basic income, then, especially if it is unconditional, and ideally if set at as high a level as possible, provides individuals with the means to be truly free. As Van Parijs (1995) explains, real freedom extends beyond formal freedom, which involves the ability to make choices among various goods that may be consumed. Rather it involves the "real freedom to choose among the various lives one might wish to lead" (p. 33), or to be free of external controls. But without a basic minimum income, one's ability to take advantage of opportunity, that is, make choices, is indeed adversely affected. Real freedom, in other words, entails being able to effectively act on one's formal freedom. To earn an income that enables one to take advantage of opportunity is to effectively enable one to be autonomous.

The other argument for a UBI is that it safeguards against domination. The notion that individuals should be free from domination comes from the republican idea that true freedom requires that one will not be subject to domination. Philip Petit (1997) argues that under an older republican way of thinking about freedom, individuals in situations where they are dominated are unfree. To be free means that one is not in any way subject to the arbitrary whims of another. Therefore, freedom involves more than being able to make decisions without others' interference. And yet, domination speaks to a relationship between masters and slaves or masters and servants, and by extension could include the relationship between employers and wage workers, particularly low-skilled wage workers. When one is not being dominated, one then enjoys the absence of interference by arbitrary power. The republican tradition is unanimous in casting freedom as the opposite of slavery. A slave, by contrast, is subject to the arbitrary will of the master. To enjoy non-domination means to be in a position where no one has the power of arbitrary interference over that person and where that person is correspondingly powerful. For the republican tradition freedom as non-domination is indeed a supreme political value. Therefore, freedom as non-domination requires reducing the capacities for arbitrary interference in which a person may be exposed. It requires that a person not be exposed to the possibility of interference on an arbitrary basis.

All of this raises a question: is the low-wage worker exposed to the possibility of interference on an arbitrary basis? To the extent that these workers are deprived of their capabilities, as Sen would put it, are they the same as wage slaves? Petit answers that question as follows:

> The image of workers as wage slaves casts them as dependents on the grace and mercy of their employers, and as required to court paths of caution and deference in dealing, individually or collectively, with their bosses. If that image is to serve as a way of showing what is objectionable in the condition of workers, then it is premised on the appeal of the idea that workers should not be exposed to the possibility of arbitrary interference, that they should enjoy freedom as non-domination. (p. 141)

Kyle Swan (2012) notes that a republican theory of distributive justice begins with an assessment of the effects of poverty on an individual's republican freedom. As poverty induces vulnerability, it also makes the domination by others more likely. This clearly has implications for low-skilled and low-wage workers who need to work because they are needs traders and cannot afford not to. Swan asks us to consider the example of the low-skilled worker who encounters sexual harassment at her job because all the alternatives are that much worse. In this sense, she is dominated. A commitment to republican equality, then, would support the idea that people should be guaranteed the social and economic conditions of their freedom as non-domination. What, then, might these conditions be? Swan suggests that they could avoid vulnerability simply by being entitled to the provision of certain types of resources or capabilities in the event that one would need to opt for unemployment as a response to domination. This would clearly imply a UBI. A UBI would enable individuals to be more choosy about the jobs they take (Jackson 1999).

Stuart White (2003) too talks about a basic minimum as a vehicle for achieving what he defines as justice as fair reciprocity. According to this conception of justice, a good society is one of mutual concern and respect—it is one in which individuals exhibit what he calls *democratic mutual regard*. A society governed by democratic mutual regard is one in which "individuals seek to justify their preferred political and economic institutions to others by appealing to shared basic interests, and to related principles that express a willingness to cooperate with their fellow citizens as equals" (pp. 25–26). Each citizen has a basic interest in having adequate opportunity to reflect and deliberate critically about those matters that are essential to each's ethical agency. Therefore, the primary commitment of justice as fair reciprocity is the upholding of basic liberties and securities. In a society built around the ethos of democratic mutual regard, citizens must accept and affirm each other as equals, and consequently design a common set of institutions that will govern their lives together in a fundamental way.

Justice as fair reciprocity, however, entails more than this give and take; it also involves a commitment to substantive economic reciprocity. Society, then, has a responsibility to ensure that all who participate, which by definition would have to include all regardless of endowments and where one falls in the wage distribution, are in no way burdened by their participation. This would imply that workers who do not earn wages sufficient to sustain themselves in dignity are indeed burdened. They may in fact be dominated. Therefore, society has to guarantee a UBI, not because one merely exists but because as a member of the community who is expected to participate in the productive enterprise of that community, that person has a right to expect that he/she will be able to live with dignity. To live with dignity is essentially to live without being exploited. In a larger sense, White is suggesting that a member of the community, who participates in the common project of society by working, has a right not only to expect that he/she will live with dignity but that government through policy will ensure conditions that enable individuals to continue being autonomous. The UBI, of course, reflects a broader wage policy than a mere minimum wage, but it nonetheless assumes that the path to freedom, and ultimate capabilities, is indeed a livable wage. But it also assumes freedom to mean not being dependent on the whim of others like employers.

All of these arguments effectively turn Friedmanite arguments of freedom on their head. On the contrary, Friedman appears to be defining freedom narrowly to include mainly the freedom of employers. A UBI could potentially lead to greater autonomy, but at considerable social cost. Still, there could be some benefits to a UBI that have been overlooked. If we assume that its effect might be similar to the ELR, it would effectively create minimum wages for those who still want to work and earn additional money in the labor market. As we have seen previously, the critic of the minimum wage maintains that because employers will substitute technology for workers, it is better for workers to accept low wages just in order to be employed, and if need be they can receive subsidies. But if they are going to receive subsidies, then why not simply have a UBI as a replacement for all social and income supports? The concept would transform the nature of work as we have understood it. Until now, work has been understood as that which is necessary because workers are needs traders who have to work in order to make a living. But if everybody were to receive a UBI, workers would be working because they want to. Workers, just like their employers, would become wants traders and could use their desire to work as a new protection against exploitation. The employer, after all, can exploit because he has the power to do so and the worker needing wages is at his mercy. With a UBI, workers who are exploited simply walk away. It is now conceivable that employers who still need actual workers will be forced to pay higher wages in order to attract workers who otherwise don't really need to work.

Therefore, it is possible that a UBI could result in supply-side effects in that more workers will be attracted into the labor market as employers are offering higher wages. We could also see more flexible scheduling, more family friendly workplaces as employers seek to make work more attractive. Workers working because they want to could be beneficial to society as a whole. Of course, high-paying employers have already been doing this, but now low-paying employers would be forced to offer similar inducements. On one level, a higher minimum wage could be viewed as a first step on the way to a UBI. It helps us figure out the level for this UBI. On another level, the UBI renders the minimum wage obsolete. Workers will get their UBIs from the state and their employers will be forced to pay them wages that make them want to work. Because they want to work, they will be more efficient, in which case the wages they are paid are efficiency wages.

Will the labor force be smaller? It is possible that fewer people will want to work. But it is also possible that more people will be working, except that they will be working part-time because they want a better balance between work and family. And it is also possible that it could lead to greater human capital investment as some might opt to go back to school and acquire the type of skills that will place them in the higher-wage economy. Still, we are left with the question of cost. And yet, when we consider the costs of the current welfare state, it may be that a UBI, which would replace all social programs, might not cost that much more. The real challenge is that by creating a greater role for government it challenges American conceptions of independence. But then again, those conceptions have been under assault from the march of technology which may be making the UBI inevitable. Ironically, a UBI, which might strike some as radical may even fall into the category of a conservative argument for a wage policy. If we consider that Friedman opposed a minimum wage because it would interfere with personal freedom, the UBI ultimately renders the minimum wage obsolete. It also ironically builds on another idea that Friedman had for preserving individual liberty while also attempting to meet the needs of the poor—the negative income tax.

The UBI is considerably more expansive than a negative income tax, but it rests on the same idea. Friedman opposed public assistance because poor people dependent on government bureaucracies for sustenance could not be free if they were subject to the rules and regulations imposed on them by those bureaucracies. A negative income tax would simply be money given to them in lieu of the various supports and they could spend it as they would see fit. This way they could function as autonomous and free individuals. If they worked and earned over a certain threshold, the negative income tax would phase out. During the Nixon administration in the early 1970s, then White House counselor Daniel Patrick Moynihan proposed the Family Assistance Plan which would be a grant of $1600 to a family. Again, it would have phased out and would have replaced traditional public assistance transfer payments. Conservatives opposed it because they claimed it would undermine the incentive to work, and they would most likely oppose the UBI for the same reasons. Indeed, because it would begin to phase out, people might have less incentive to work. Liberals, however, opposed it because it was not generous enough. The UBI goes well beyond this and would be available to all and would not phase out. Therefore, if there is a desire to work, it is because workers truly want to. Of course, this could reduce the control that employers currently have over their employees, which is perhaps why they have opposed the minimum wage all along: it gives workers a measure of monopoly power in their jobs they otherwise do not have (Galbraith 1998).

Conclusion

Although politically it is unlikely that we as a society would be thinking in terms of either ELR or a UBI, it is important to note that the minimum wage does raise a series of issues which do not get addressed when the debate is constructed narrowly between those arguing its adverse employment effects, particularly among teenagers, on the one hand and those arguing for it as an anti-poverty tool on the other hand. A minimum wage conceived as a middle-class policy can be conceived of as a matter of achieving greater efficiency and as a necessary civil rights issue essential to achieving greater democracy. But it is also a more practical approach because it is an example of what Martin Gilens (2012) refers to as "targeting within universalism" (p. 250). This rests on the assumption that universal policies like Social Security and Medicare have broader appeal precisely because they do have middle-class support. In other words, policies that don't seek to redistribute downward but which benefit the middle class are bound to appeal to a broad spectrum of voters. To the extent that declines of inclusion resulted from policy preferences that were more in response to those with more resources, there needs to be a recalibration of the political system so that it is responsive to all, in the spirit of what we would expect from democratic governance.

There may be more to this. If we can couch all of these possibilities in terms of a trajectory, it becomes clear that there really is no such thing as a natural marketplace. If the market place is to be of benefit to most people, then there is a role for public policy, whether it be in minimal form, that is, a wage floor, or a maximum form in terms of being an ELR or a UBI. It becomes clear that the continued survival of capitalist markets requires their regulation. And that without labor market institutions even the limited conception of liberty that Friedman talks about really becomes untenable. If anything, the notion of an increasing global economy only demonstrates the need for more regulation—not less. It may be leading us in a particular direction because of the march of technology. If, however, we don't believe we can reach this maximalist position because it would be politically impossible, then we should start with the basic minimum wage and recognize its potential beyond the narrow confines of the standard disemployment versus anti-poverty debate. Given the issues that it raises, increasing the minimum wage for the benefit of the middle class may still be the most conservative approach that could be taken.

Bibliography

Aglietta, Michael. 1979. *A Theory of Capitalist Regulation: The U.S. Experience*. London/New York: Verso.

Budd, John W. 2004. *Employment with a Human Face: Balancing Efficiency, Equity, and Voice*. Ithaca/London: ILR/Cornell University Press.

Clark, John Bates. 1913. The Minimum Wage. *The Atlantic Monthly* 112 (3): 289–297.

Derksen, Maarten. 2014. Turning Men into Machines? Scientific Management, Industrial Psychology, and the 'Human Factor'. *Journal of the History of the Behavioral Sciences* 50 (2): 148–165.

Drazen, Allan. 1986. Optimal Minimum Wage Legislation. *The Economic Journal* 96 (383): 774.

Fairris, David. 2003. *The Impact of Living Wages on Employers: A Control Group Analysis of the Los Angeles Ordinance*. Riverside: University of California. (April 11–12).

Filene, Edward A. 1923. The Minimum Wage and Efficiency. *American Economic Review* 13 (September): 411–415.

Foner, Eric. 1998. *The Story of American Freedom*. New York: W.W. Norton & Co.

Friedman, Milton. 2002. *Capitalism and Freedom*. Chicago/London: University of Chicago Press.

Fry, Louis W. 1976. The Maligned F.W. Taylor: A Reply to His Critics. *Academy of Management Review* 1 (July): 124–129.

Galbraith, James K. 1998. *Created Unequal: The Crisis in American Pay*. New York: The Free Press.

Gilens, Martin. 2012. *Affluence & Influence: Economic Inequality and Political Power in America*. New York/Princeton/Oxford: Russell Sage Foundation and Princeton University Press.

Glickman, Lawrence B. 1997. *A Living Wage: American Workers and the Making of Consumer Society*. Ithaca/London: Cornell University Press.

Gokcekus, Omer, and Edward Tower. 2003. An Efficiency Enhancing Minimum Wage. *Policy Reform* 6 (4): 247–259.

Guttmann, Amy, and Dennis Thompson. 1996. *Democracy and Disagreement*. Cambridge, MA: Belknap Press.

Hattam, Victoria C. 1993. *Labor Visions and State Power: The Origins of Business Unionism in the United States*. Princeton: Princeton University Press.

Holzner, Charles A. 2007. The Poverty of Democracy: Neoliberal Reforms and Political Participation of the Poor in Mexico. *Latin American Political Society* 49 (2): 87–122.

Howes, Candace. 2002. *The Impact of a Wage Increase on the Workforce Stability of IHSS Home Care Workers in San Francisco Country*. Working Paper. University of California Institute for Labor and the Economy and the University of California, Berkeley, Center for Education and Labor Research, November.

Jackson, William A. 1999. Basic Income and the Right to Work: A Keynesian Approach. *Journal of Post Keynesian Economics* 21 (4): 639–662.

Kaufman, Bruce E. 2003. John R. Commons and the Wisconsin School of Industrial Relations Strategy and Policy. *Industrial and Labor Relations Review* 57 (1): 3–30.

Leamer, Edward E. 1999. Effort, Wages, and the International Division of Labor. *Journal of Political Economy* 107 (6, Part 1): 1127–1162.

Levy, Frank, and Peter Temin. 2010. Institutions and Wages in Post-World War II America. In *Labor in the Era of Globalization*, ed. Clair Brown, Barry Eichengreen, and Michael Reich. Cambridge: Cambridge University Press.

Lowi, Theodore J. 1996. *The End of the Republican Era*. Norman/London: University of Oklahoma Press.

McGregor, Douglas. 1960. *The Human Enterprise*. New York: McGraw-Hill.

Mead, Lawrence M. 1986. *Beyond Entitlement: The Social Obligations of Citizenship*. New York: The Free Press.

———. 1992. *The New Politics of Poverty: The Nonworking Poor in America*. New York: Basic Books.

Montgomery, David. 1993. *Citizen Worker: The Experience of Workers in the United States with Democracy and the Free Market During the Nineteenth Century*. Cambridge/New York: Cambridge University Press.

Murray, Charles M. 1984. *Losing Ground: American Social Policy, 1950–1980*. New York: Basic Books.

Petit, Philip. 1997. *Republicanism: A Theory of Freedom and Government*. Oxford/New York: Oxford University Press.

Reich, Michael, Peter Hall, and Ken Jacobs. 2003. *Living Wages and Economic Performance: The San Francisco Airport Model*. Institute of Industrial Relations. University of California, Berkeley, March.

Rodgers, Daniel T. 1978. *The Work Ethic in Industrial America 1850–1920*. Chicago: University of Chicago Press.

Schacter, Hindy Lauer. 1989. Frederick Winslow Taylor and the Idea of Worker Participation. *Administration & Society* 21 (1): 20–30.

Sen, Amartya. 1999. *Development as Freedom*. New York: Anchor Books.

Shapiro, Carl, and Joseph Stiglitz. 1984. Equilibrium Unemployment as a Worker Discipline Device. *American Economic Review* 74 (3): 433–444.

Shefter, Martin. 1986. Trade Unions and Political Machines: The Organization and Disorganization of the American Working Class in the Late Nineteenth

Century. In *Working-Class Formation: Nineteenth-Century Patterns in Western Europe and the United States*, ed. Ira Katznelson and Aristide R. Zolberg. Princeton: Princeton University Press.

Stigler, George. 1946. The Economics of Minimum Wage Legislation. *American Economic Review* 36 (June): 358–365.

Swan, Kyle. 2012. Republican Equality. *Social Theory and Practice* 38 (3): 432–454.

Taylor, Frederick Winslow. 2013. 1911. *The Principles of Scientific Management.* Amazon/CreateSpace.

Van Parijs, Philippe. 1992. Basic Income Capitalism. *Ethics* 102 (3): 465–484.

Van Parijs, Philippe. 1995. *Real Freedom for All: What (If Anything) Can Justify Capitalism?* Oxford/New York: Claredon/Oxford University Press.

Wagner-Tsukamoto, Sigmund. 2007. An Institutional Economic Reconstruction of Scientific Management: On the Lost Theoretical Logic of Taylorism. *Academy of Management Review* 37 (1): 105–117.

Webb, Sidney. 1912. The Economic Theory of a Legal Minimum Wage. *The Journal of Political Economy* 20 (10): 973–998.

White, Stuart. 2003. *The Civic Minimum: On the Rights and Obligations of Economic Citizenship.* Oxford/New York: Oxford University Press.

Wood, Gordon S. 1993. *The Radicalism of the American Revolution.* New York: Vintage Books.

Wray, L. Randall. 2007. *The Employer of Last Resort Programme: Could It Work for Developing Countries?* Economic and Labor Market Papers, International Labour Ofice, Geneva Employment Analysis and Research Unit, Economic and Labour Market Analysis Department, International Labour Organization, August.

Zatz, Noah D. 2009. The Minimum Wage as a Civil Rights Protection: An Alternative to Antipoverty Arguments? *The University of Chicago Legal Forum.* Downloaded from http://www.lexisnexis.com/ex-proxy.brooklyn.cuny.edu:2048/Inacui2api/delivery/PrintDoc

CHAPTER 7

Minimum Wage and Greater Democracy

We have already seen that the minimum wage has positive welfare effects and could form the foundations for job creation. We have also seen that there may well be other theoretical frameworks for viewing the minimum wage and the larger concept of wage policy and the role it can play in restoring the middle class. In this chapter, I argue that a minimum wage, insofar as it serves to maintain the middle class, does further the ends of democracy. Democracy requires that individuals be autonomous, and to the extent that it enhances personal autonomy, it fulfills that requirement. Democracy also requires the existence of a broad middle class, and if the minimum wage through wage contour effects serves to shore up the middle class it fulfills that requirement as well. Moreover, democracy requires an element of economic development, and if the minimum wage can form the foundations of job creation, it furthers that end as well. Wage policy in an economy where global market forces can undermine democratic governance can be viewed as a prerequisite for democracy. Amartya Sen (1999) has argued that poverty is more than simply income deprivation; it involves the deprivation of capabilities. Therefore, a minimum wage that enables individuals to be autonomous does indeed enable them to develop their capabilities.

A minimum wage which increases on a regular basis may also lead to greater democracy to the extent that it may serve to develop the social capital of low-wage workers. Very little attention has been paid to the

O. M. Levin-Waldman, *Restoring the Middle Class through Wage Policy*, Binzagr Institute for Sustainable Prosperity,
https://doi.org/10.1007/978-3-319-74448-3_7

relationship between low wages and social capital, or we should say the extent to which income affects one's ability to be civically engaged. Various studies show that those with higher incomes are more likely to be engaged in the civic affairs of their communities (Verba et al. 1972, 2004; Manturuck et al. 2012; Levin-Waldman 2013a). It certainly has been a staple of institutional economics that labor market institutions are essential for addressing the asymmetrical power relationships between labor and management. We cannot be fully autonomous if we can be dominated by others. The institutionalists, in part, recognized that workers could not be fully productive if employers could exercise domination over their workers. It is one thing to work for an employer who has the authority over his/her workers by virtue of his/her property rights as employers. It is another to exercise domination because of a fundamental power imbalance. There can be no question that if skewed power not only makes for difficult labor-management relations, but makes for inefficiencies in the economy, it certainly is a threat to democracy. This chapter intends to make the argument for why a minimum wage is an essential ingredient in achieving greater democracy (Levin-Waldman 2013b). And yet, in making this argument, I am suggesting that much more is at stake than simply lifting the wages of low-wage workers.

Core Democratic Principles

Democratic theory assumes a society of free, equal, and autonomous individuals. Although democracy may have different meanings to different people, an ideal of democracy is that all individuals are supposed to have equal standing. That is, each individual is equal before the law, has the same vote as other individuals, the same right to express one's self in the political sphere, and perhaps most importantly the same potential to influence what government does, even if they opt not to exercise that potential. All citizens, then, have the same access to governing institutions. Within this theoretical construct, which may also characterize American democracy, money is supposed to be irrelevant to one's standing. Both the rich and the poor are equal before government (Hacker and Pierson 2010). It is perhaps a bedrock principle of democratic theory, at least in its procedural form, that all individuals as citizens enjoy the same consideration of their preferences and interests. Individuals enjoy the same rights of citizenship as others and must enjoy their autonomy so that they can participate as full-fledged citizens in the democratic process. The greater their autonomy, the more likely they are to participate in the democratic process.

Also core to democratic theory is a conception of equality, but equality is a difficult concept to define. It has meant different things to different people. Four common meanings are legal, political, social, and economic. Legal equality usually means that when any member of society is subject to a law all are subject to the same law. Political equality, then, may be considered an extension of legal equality in that each individual has the same vote and access to political institutions. To a certain extent, legal and political equality speak to bare minima. Social and economic equality, then, attempt to go beyond the minima. Social equality refers to a person's standing within society, which also has to do with how a person is regarded by both public institutions and other individuals. And economic equality means that individuals not only enjoy the same economic resources as one another but that they are not in a position to be exploited. Stuart White (2007) suggests that the demands for legal, political, social, and economic equality are in essence demands for certain types of social arrangements. Economic equality might be valued because it is viewed as being instrumental to other aspects of social equality, such as the absence of one or a group to have power and domination over another individual or group. Democratic political systems are often based on the principle of political equality, which is to say that a democratic political system is not the same as a democratic social system. Procedural equality usually includes just legal and political equality.

Equality in the USA and other liberal market economies, however, has generally tended to be conceived of in procedural terms. Procedural equality is critical to democratic society because it serves to secure another essential condition: personal freedom, which is also a necessary condition for individuals to function autonomously. In order for there to be freedom, certain political conditions must be met, and equality, particularly equality of opportunity or procedural equality, is one of them. Individuals are free to pursue their goals and objectives—that is, self-interests—so long as their pursuit does not interfere with others' ability to pursue their own goals and objectives. In a very basic sense, and certainly within the context of classical political thought, this is what it means to talk about personal independence or autonomy. Procedural equality is not usually concerned with how resources, wealth, and income are distributed but with how individuals stand in relation to one another. Individuals can have more than others so long as they are equal in terms of their legal and political standing.

A more substantive democratic theory, however, seeks to include both social and economic equality, in addition to legal and political equality, and would posit that equality in terms of standing, rights, access, and resources is the fundamental essence of democracy. This is the notion that unless resources in terms of wealth and income are equally distributed, democracy is at best partial—it is incomplete (Bowles and Gintis 1986; Dolbeare 1986). Full democracy requires that individuals enjoy the same rights in the economic realm that they do in the political. And yet, the notion of full democracy is really an ideal type. The closest to full democracy that some of the liberal democracies come are some of the social democracies in Europe where wage policies do exist in efforts to achieve a more egalitarian wage structure. A good example of this is France, where wage rates tend to be set in a more centralized fashion. Following World War II, the first national legal minimum hourly wage—the Minimum Interprofessional Guaranteed Minimum Wage (SMIG)—was introduced and indexed to inflation. In 1970 this was transformed into the SMIC—the interprofessional, indexed-linked growth minimum wage—and was automatically indexed to both inflation and particularly to real growth (Caroli and Gautie 2008). Although France has been characterized by higher rates of unemployment, it has also had much lower levels of low-wage work. Low-wage work in France is not identical to poverty. Rather, the minimum wage has played a key role in compressing the distribution of wages at the bottom. One of the key explanations for the smaller number of low-wage workers in France is the existence of the minimum wage. The minimum wage has also resulted in lower numbers of low-skilled, potentially labor-intensive activities (Caroli et al. 2008).

Sweden too has long been considered an example of a social democracy that may perhaps approximate a more full democracy. Sweden is governed by the "Swedish Model," which is predicated on an active labor policy. This active labor policy essentially has three components: full employment, a fair income distribution and higher standard of living, and higher efficiency and greater democracy in the economy. Fair income distribution and greater democracy revolve around what has come to be known as solidaristic wage policy (Wadenjso 2001). On one level, solidaristic wage policy implies equal pay for equal work regardless of the company's profitability. In effect, it is suggesting that a more democratic workforce in terms of equality is more important than a specific firm's profit. But on another level, the goal was to establish fair wage differentials rather than general wage equalization. Although wage difference between workers was to be expected, it was also believed that those differences should reflect objective differences in the working environment, responsibility, experience, and education as opposed to short-run profits or labor conditions.

Social democracy, or full democracy, is still a very different concept from the procedural democracy found in most Western liberal democracies, particularly the USA. By the procedural conception, a society is democratic if it affords political equality and equality of opportunity. Economic equality, however, is not essential to democracy. But as Tocqueville observed there cannot be real political equality without some measure of economic equality as well. Moreover, economic inequality could pose serious problems in a procedural democracy. Tocqueville also observed that a society with a great concentration of poor people would be dangerous as well. In every society the poor would be happy to tax the rich to provide benefit to themselves. This observation, as we have seen in Chap. 5, finds contemporary expression in the median voter theorem. In its initial formulation income distributions are skewed to the right, with the preferred amount of redistribution being a function of the relative position of the median voter on the income scale. The greater the distance between the median voter's income and society's average income, the greater the preferred amount of redistribution.

Why Income Inequality Is a Problem

Why, then, is there such a concern with inequality in liberal democracies? Procedural equality, which also stresses equal opportunity, would suggest that unequal outcomes arising from the choices that individuals had an equal opportunity to make unfettered are not really a problem. That is, it assumes that there were no obstacles to participation. Of course, if low-wage workers aren't able to effectively participate because they lack resources, compared to higher-wage workers who may have a wide range of options open to them, the outcomes are not likely to be fair. And yet, while procedural equality does not require equal outcomes for all, it does assume that there will be equal outcomes for a sufficiently large population in order to maintain stability; this sufficiently large population being defined as the middle class. So while procedural democracy does not explicitly require economic equality, it assumes a measure of it, as reflected in the presence of a broad middle class.

Unequal distribution of wealth and income, however, may adversely affect individuals' ability to participate in the democratic process on the same footing as equals. It may result in procedural inequality to the extent that those lacking in wealth and income may not enjoy the same access to political and policy officials as those who possess wealth and income may enjoy. With a greater concentration of wealth at the top, those at the top are in a better position to use their wealth toward the attainment of their political and other ideological objectives (Bachrach and Botwinick 1992, pp. 4–5). Those at the top of the distribution often enjoy inordinate power and are able to not only limit redistribution but shape the rules of the game in favor of those with more resources (Stiglitz 2012).

In studying the votes on minimum wage legislation, Larry Bartels (2008) found that members of Congress, both Republicans and Democrats, tended to be more responsive to affluent constituencies than to non-affluent constituencies. And in many cases, they were non-responsive to the views of those at the bottom of the income distribution. There is good reason to believe that the wealthiest Americans exert more political influence than the less fortunate citizens and that the wealthiest citizens also tend to be highly active in politics, far more so than the typical citizen. As an example, the gap between the policy preferences of the wealthy and those of other citizens are especially evident when it comes to job programs and income support. The wealthy give high importance to the problem of unemployment but overwhelmingly reject government action to help with jobs (Page et al. 2013). To the extent that is this true, it calls into question whether all groups really do have equal standing. This might then imply that a more equitable distribution could conceivably result in more responsiveness because members of Congress would no longer have incentives to favor the affluent over the less affluent or better-financed interest groups over poorly financed groups. Stiglitz attributes this to government policies that only reinforced the political power of those at the top of the distribution at the expense of those at the bottom and in the middle. The American political system has been more responsive to those with money, and as the distribution became more unequal it was only a foregone conclusion that policies pursued by elected officials would favor those at the higher end of the distribution (Bartels 2008; Bachrach and Botwinick 1992).

As much as inequality rose because of institutional decline, the rise in inequality also made it less likely that these institutions would be supported by legislative officials. And these very institutions were responsible for maintaining the middle class. The decline in institutions resulting in greater inequality has only made it a foregone conclusion that public policy will be oriented toward the interests of the very wealthy, whose interests may not be served by these institutions. Rising inequality has only left those at the top of the distribution with more ability to influence public policy, and in the direction that serves their interests at the expense of those at the bottom. This polarization, according to Nolan McCarty et al. (2008), has enabled those at the top of the income distribution to be able to devote more time and resources into supporting a political party strongly opposed to redistribution. Volscho and Kelly (2012) found that congressional shifts to the Republican Party along with declining union membership and lower top tax rates on top of a financial asset bubble did strongly contribute to the rise of the super-rich. As union membership decreased, a greater share of income shifted toward the top 1 percent between 1949 and 2008.

In measuring the relationship between policy preferences and policy outcomes, Gilens (2012) finds that the link between outcomes and preferences tends to be stronger for higher-income Americans than for the poor. At the same time the inequality in representation between the affluent and slightly less well-off also suggests that the political system is tilted much more in favor of those at the very top of the income distribution. According to Jacob Hacker and Paul Pierson (2010), rising American inequality is not mainly about the gap between the college educated and the rest, but the pulling away of the very top, which was facilitated by public policy. On the contrary, the failure to respond to market forces is in their view a deliberate policy choice. The absence of a government response to rising inequality can be regarded as a form of policy when it takes the form of "drift"—the deliberate failure to adapt policies to the shifting realities of a dynamic economy. One example of this is that intense opponents of the minimum wage have worked tirelessly and effectively to prevent it from being increased to prior levels or to be pegged to inflation. McCarty et al. (2008) note that minimum wage laws have always engendered liberal support and conservative opposition. Historically, minimum wage increases and expansive coverage generated a fair amount of bipartisan support. As polarization rose in the 1970s, bipartisanship disappeared. As a consequence of increasing Republican opposition in a period of polarization, there has been a dramatic decline in the real value of the minimum wage. These institutions gave voice to those in the middle; so the result was policy not favorable to the middle class.

Inequality, especially in its extreme form of poverty, does in the end deprive us of our capabilities, which are only requisite for autonomy. Those with more resources may be better positioned to pursue their goals and objectives, while those with fewer resources may find that their ability to pursue their goals and objectives is limited as a result. The ability to pursue goals and objectives is important to democracy for yet another reason. A democracy, especially as its legitimacy and power are derived from popular consent, assumes that individuals have the capacity to reason for themselves, that is, to deliberate in the public square and to act on that capacity in a responsible manner. They cannot effectively participate, whether it be in full policy discussions or selecting their own representatives, if they cannot deliberate in a rational manner. As democracy requires that individuals act on their agency, human agency must be protected. But this human agency also presupposes that basic material needs will have been met, which may be less likely with lower wages. Democracy also requires a measure of trust between people, and growing income inequality is said to threaten trust as various groups, mainly those at the bottom, experience political alienation and perceive the system not to be fair. As Joseph Stiglitz (2012) notes, social capital is the glue that holds society together. If individuals believe that the economic and political system is unfair, then the glue does not work and society does not function well. Eric Uslaner (2008) adds to this by noting that institutions effectively promote trust. A trusting population tends to be more cooperative, and governments with trusting populations tend to be less corrupt and function with less conflict and greater responsiveness.

Inequality may be partly responsible for a whole array of health and other related social problems. According to Richard Wilkinson and Kate Pickett (2010), the scale of income differences has a powerful effect on how we relate to each other. Looking at several different countries, they found that within each country people's health and happiness were related to their incomes. Rich people tended, on average, to be healthier and happier than poorer people in the same society. Poor health and violence are more common in unequal societies. One needs to feel valued, and capable human beings crave positive feedback and often react with anger to implied criticism. Social status carries the strongest messages of superiority and inferiority. Social mobility is widely viewed as a process by which people are sorted by ability. Greater inequality, then, appears to heighten people's social evaluation anxieties by measuring the importance of social status. We see social positions as a more important feature of a person's identity.

Greater inequality results in increased status competition. Inequality produces problems associated with social differences and divisive class prejudices that go along with them. It also weakens community life and increases violence.

The quality of social relations deteriorates in less equal societies. Our position in the social hierarchy affects who we see as part of the in-group and who is part of the out-group. Trust affects the well-being of individuals and also the well-being of civic society. Levels of social trust are connected to income inequality. In unequal countries, a much higher percentage of the population suffers from mental illness. Social status and social integration are now considered to be important determinants of population health. Inequality is now considered to be associated with lower life expectations, higher rates of infant mortality, shorter height, poor self and reported health, low birth weight, AIDS, and depression. Inequality affects other measures of societal well-being as well.

More unequal countries tend to have worse educational attainment, and greater inequality may affect children's development through its impact on family life and relationships. More unequal societies also tend to have more teenage birthrates and be more punitive. That is, they imprison more people and spend less of their wealth on the welfare of their citizens. Greater income inequality also reduces social mobility. Social mobility is lower and geographical segregation is greater in more unequal societies. Wilkinson and Pickett suggest that greater inequality actually increases downward social prejudices by inducing individuals to show their superiority to others, which is the way they maintain their social status. Finally, more unequal societies also have greater consumption which may be detrimental to the environment, and they also tend to be more belligerent internationally.

Impact of Inequality on Civic Participation

Income inequality not only distorts democracy in terms of how institutions and political actors respond to different levels of income, but it may have a profound effect on the development of social capital. Democracy requires the active participation of citizens in the affairs of their communities, which extends beyond mere voting. Citizens need to be civically engaged, and Robert Putnam (2000), for instance, has couched civic engagement in terms of social capital. Underlying social capital is the notion that civic virtue is most powerful when it is embedded in a dense network of social relations. American civil society has been defined by its associative life, in which Americans belong to voluntary organizations. And through these organizations, they participate in the affairs of their communities.

And yet, there is reason to believe that income inequality may lead to political anomie. As family income inequality increases, those families below the median are further from the social norm than before. Similarly, those at the top of the distribution see a larger gap between themselves and the rest of the population. Many fear that the growth in income disparities among families has had a variety of adverse consequences for both families and communities. Families at the bottom of the distribution may end up drifting further from the mainstream and thus may also experience greater alienation as those with greater resources may come to see them as both more distinct and undeserving. This may also have consequences for how citizens in turn view the potential role and functions of government (Haveman et al. 2004). Poor people tend to experience greater social alienation because their tendency to participate less means that they may be out of touch with common interests. But participation is also less likely because the alienation coming from social isolation will lead many to the conclusion that there really is no benefit from participation in the common project which they are part of. Less inclination to participate, then, isn't only a function of the absence of personal autonomy, but social alienation as well. Of course, these two may not be mutually exclusive, as one lacking in personal autonomy is likely to feel socially isolated because of the stigma attached.

The alienation may also have something to do with trust. Eric Uslaner and Mitchell Brown (2005), for instance, argue that greater equality and higher levels of trust are two pathways to participation. Inequality may actually depress participation, either directly or indirectly, through its effect on trust. Where inequality is higher, the poor may also feel powerless. Trust, in other words, rests on foundations of economic equality. When resources are unequally distributed, those at the top and the bottom might not see themselves as sharing the same fate. Consequently, they have less reason to trust people of different backgrounds. Where inequality is high, people may be less optimistic about being masters of their own fate. But it would also suggest that measures are necessary to strengthen institutions that have served to give people voice in the past like labor unions. Similarly, it would imply that other types of wage policy that give other workers a type of voice are also needed.

We might then postulate that the isolation resulting from inequality leads to political anomie—the absolute alienation of the individual from the political process. The most important individual and contextual factors influencing the extent to which one participates in the political system is the socioeconomic status (SES) model of participation, which stresses a strong association between political activities and an individual's income, participation, and especially education (Verba and Nie 1972). On the basis of Uslaner and Mitchell's (2005) argument, increasing inequality should have resulted in less participation because of declining trust.

Elsewhere (2013) in a study on the relationship between income inequality and civic engagement, I found that in 2008 individuals in households with different levels of income had different levels of civic engagement. Six measures of civic engagement were looked at: daily discussions of politics, daily reading of newspapers—which were intended to speak to one's knowledge about and interest in politics—involvement in protests, attendance at political meetings, visiting public officials, and participating in civic organizations. Participation was found to be greater on all measures of participation among those in households earning more than $100,000 a year than among those earning less than $30,000. Those at the highest end of the distribution were not necessarily more likely to be engaged than those between $30,000 and $99,999, but those in households between $30,000 and $59,999 were considerably more likely to be engaged than those in households below $30,000. Participation appeared to improve dramatically when one was in a household with income greater than $30,000.

These differences alone might suggest that entry into the middle class might result in greater levels of civic participation. This is important because the impact of a wage policy is bound to be felt more by those whom we would classify as being in the middle class. Moreover, logistical regressions found that those with higher incomes were more likely to be civically engaged and that those earning less than a minimum wage were least likely to be engaged. These findings might suggest a basis for inferring that a wage policy might result in more people being engaged, in part because they have greater capabilities. Although civic participation is generally in decline in the USA, it is still considered to be healthy relative to other countries (Howard 2006). And yet, civic involvement is generally lower in the USA, than in the Nordic countries where income inequality tends to be much lower (Center for Democracy and Civil Society 2007).

Personal Autonomy

A wage policy that might reduce the gap between the top and the bottom, or one that would enable individuals to move to higher-income ranges, may lead to greater participation. A wage policy, then, would be in keeping with the ends of democratic society because it may contribute to greater personal autonomy. A higher income, as Sen (1999) noted in the last chapter, would enable them to develop their capabilities, which are otherwise hindered by poverty.

Mark Rank (2004), for instance, suggests that poverty might be the most visible effect of income inequality, but because few people are affected by it, the connection between inequality and poverty might not be so readily apparent. And yet, poverty, just like income inequality, results from failings in economic and social structures. But it is self-perpetuating because to the extent that it deprives individuals of their capabilities, it effectively places them in the disadvantaged position that they will be unable to earn income sufficient to lift themselves out of poverty. Of course, it isn't only one's current status in poverty that determines whether one will remain in poverty or the extent to which one will be disadvantaged in the labor market.

Ultimately, however, wage policy is essential to democratic theory because through the personal autonomy it either confers or enhances, it serves as a bulwark against exploitation. Democratic theory, as I have been arguing, assumes a society of free, equal, and autonomous individuals. These individuals enjoy the same rights of citizenship as others and must enjoy their autonomy so that they can participate as full-fledged citizens in the democratic process. The greater their autonomy, the more likely they are to participate in the democratic process. This value of autonomy, which is ultimately a matter of human dignity, is considered to be an essential element in the complete attainment of democracy. One cannot participate as a full-fledged citizen if one isn't fully autonomous.

Bruce Kaufman (2005) suggests that democracy promotes self-development by giving people independence and autonomy, as well as opportunities to have voice in the political process. That voice, however, is meaningless if their personal autonomy is undermined because the low wages they earn in the marketplace renders them dependent on others and subject to exploitation. One of the arguments for a UBI is that a requisite for democracy is personal autonomy. Timothy Gaffaney (2000), for instance, maintains that a democratic polity operates on the premise that individuals will be politically autonomous—that they indeed will be citizens. A goal of democracy does not necessarily have to entail economic equality. But a democratic polity doesn't merely respect and ensure non-interference and non-coercion. It must also ensure that conditions for participation in that democracy are available to all individuals, for by doing so it guarantees a universal application of citizenship. In fact, the state must guarantee conditions for full citizenship. This ideally means that government provides the poor with the practical training and skills necessary for conducting democratic government. It might mean providing them the basis upon which they can achieve economic independence.

Amy Guttman and Dennis Thompson (1996) argue for autonomy on the basis of what they call a fair opportunity. In a deliberative democracy a basic opportunity principle secures citizens an adequate level of basic opportunity goods. Such opportunity goods include an adequate income level, defined as that which enables one to live a decent life according to society's current standards. By talking about opportunity to join the middle class, they in essence acknowledge the importance of the middle class to the maintenance of democracy. Their basic opportunity principle is within the context of welfare provision, but the same arguments could just as easily be applied to the minimum wage. A wage that enables workers to live with dignity is at the root of what it means to have a fair opportunity. The call for a fair opportunity, then, might really be seen as a response to the unequal opportunities that are the product of income inequality. By calling for fair opportunity, they are asserting that society has an obligation to redress the imbalance and ensure that each has the resources to participate.

If, however, we acknowledge that guaranteeing conditions of full citizenship would entail reversing income inequality, Wilkinson and Pickett (2010) concede that specialized policies and government programs that involve redistribution need not be the only approach. They may be the obvious answer but not necessarily the best. Rather, more equal societies appear to have strong trade union presence, which itself could be considered one form of wage policy. As modern inequality exists because democracy is excluded from the economic sphere, this needs to be dealt with by an extension of democracy into the workplace. Greater worker participation in the workplace might then lead to more worker voice with the result being less inequality. And yet, it would follow that if unions are in a state of decline, then a wage floor in the form of a minimum wage becomes essential. Workers can only achieve greater voice when the power imbalance, at least when it comes to negotiations, has been addressed.

Economic Development

Economic development has long been considered essential to democracy because it results in the generation of a broader middle class, in which there is relative equality of condition among its members. A successful democracy requires a minimum level of aggregate wealth, a certain degree of industrialization, urbanization, and a certain level of education that will result in fewer of its citizens living in poverty (Lipset 1959). But it also requires the maintenance of a middle class in order that the gap between the top and the bottom is not so wide that it leads to potential social unrest. To say that there cannot be wide disparities in wealth and income is to say that some measure of equality is necessary. And yet, to the extent that democracy requires economic development as a means of preventing wider disparities in wealth and income, it presupposes wage policy as part of that development. Development is ultimately about investing in people and their communities. As we saw in Chap. 3, wage policy in the form of a minimum wage, at least, would appear to have positive welfare effects that benefit the middle class in addition to assisting those at the bottom of the distribution.

For Sen (1999) development is about enabling individuals to enjoy more fully the freedoms that they have. Development, then, requires that the major sources of unfreedom be removed. These barriers include poverty as well as tyranny; poor economic opportunities as well as social deprivation; and neglect for public facilities as well as intolerance or overactivity of repressive states. Wage policy, then, needs to be seen as a measure that would remove at least two of these barriers in that it could also be about creating jobs. At a minimum, wage policy, as we have seen, will ensure that people who work will not become destitute, and it will also serve to maintain the middle class as part of a process of continued development. Moreover, it will enhance individual autonomy by enabling individuals to increase their capabilities. But because it will also have macroeconomic benefits it can be the basis of a jobs policy.

A wage policy in the form of a minimum wage, as we saw in Chap. 4, could result in job creation by allowing individuals to effectively demand more goods and services. A wage policy that bolstered the middle class might be a means by which individuals could be assured that they will continue to have purchasing power. Not only is this idea rooted in institutional economics but it is a fundamental tenet of macroeconomics. In current debates on the state of the economy, we constantly hear calls for economic growth and the need for wages to rise. The neoclassical economist assumes that through the laws of supply and demand wages will naturally grow on their own, especially as the economy experiences a labor shortage. But as we have seen, there is nothing natural about the market place. Rather these so-called natural forces are very much affected by the actions that those with power are able to take. The idea that the minimum wage could be used as a tool for restoring the middle class only underscores the need for a policy on behalf of the powerless to counteract the power of others.

Preventing Unrest?

A minimum wage in and of itself is certainly not going to make us equal, but if it slows down the growth in inequality, it could potentially stave off the potential for revolution. As we saw in Chap. 5, the minimum wage could be a viable response to the median voter theorem that understands redistribution to be the response to growing inequality. The basic argument in much of the public choice theory of democracy is that too much inequality will result in social strife and potentially lead to a violent revolution. Therefore, redistribution is seen as but one way of potentially staving off the revolution. And yet, it would also seem logical to conclude that any measure that potentially reduces income inequality can have the same effect. Moreover, a policy that serves to maintain the middle class would also be sufficient to stave off the potential revolution.

Carles Boix (2003) observes that democracy appears to prevail when either economic equality or capital mobility is high in a given country—when there is less inequality. Therefore, economic equality effectively promotes democracy because it effectively reduces the pressure for redistribution, which could occur as a by-product of mass revolution and the subsequent creation of an authoritarian regime. On the other hand, a decline in the specificity of capital—as costs of moving capital away from its country of origin decreases—curbs the redistributive pressures from non-capital holders. Authoritarianism, by contrast, tends to be prevalent in those countries in which both the level of inequality and the lack of capital mobility are high. The redistributive demands of the worse-off citizens on the wealthy are particularly intense in highly unequal societies. A political regime, after all, is merely a mechanism employed to aggregate individual preferences about the ideal distribution of assets among those individuals governed by this institutional mechanism. Since in a democracy all individuals are able to vote, increasing levels of economic equality will bolster claims of democracy, as individuals will use their democratic right to vote to pressure the legislature into guaranteeing a more equitable distribution. At the same time, a decline in the extent to which capital can either be taxed or expropriated as a result of its characteristics also fosters the emergence of a democratic regime, only in the sense that it is more attributable and responsive to the preferences of the people.

The problem would appear that Boix assumes that a truly democratic regime would not simply take away from the wealthy elite for the benefit of the masses. By redistributing from the rich to the poor, the equitable distribution may come at a cost to incentives and equality of opportunity that we expect democracies to foster. In other words, economic equality, or at least some measure of it, is essential to preserve the essence of procedural democracy. For if too much inequality results in increased redistributive pressure to the point that action is taken, the end result may well be a left-wing dictatorship whereby the poor now rule. But this does not make the regime any more democratic; rather one repressive regime—the traditional authoritarian one—has been replaced by another repressive regime that could be equally authoritarian.

Boix formally models an economy in which the population varies along two dimensions: the level of capital endowment of each individual and the extent to which capital is mobile and can actually be taxed. Those components underpinning the model are the structure of the economy with two types of individuals—rich and poor—and three types of political regimes—democratic, authoritarian, and communist. In an authoritarian regime, a right-wing dictatorship readily represses the poor, excluding them from the decision-making process. In a communist or left-wing dictatorship, the poor rule after expropriating all the wealthy's capital. And in a democracy, property is preserved and everybody votes on the tax rate. In a right-wing authoritarian regime the poor are excluded from the decision-making process. The cost of repression varies with organizational and technical means at the disposal of both the wealthy and the poor. The costs of repression, however, do increase when the lower classes are able to overcome their problems with collective action and organize in political parties and/or trade unions, and also where they live in very mountainous terrain which may breed the formation of guerilla movements.

Boix similarly assumes that both the rich and the poor are committed to their positions. If the rich opt to repress no one, a system of universal suffrage is then established in a peaceful manner. The poor will not rebel if the expected gain of revolting is smaller than the value of accepting an authoritarian regime. If the costs of repression are high, the wealthy then have no dominant strategy to follow. More unequal distribution of wealth increases the redistributive demands of the population and the ultimate level of taxes in a democratic system. In other words, demands for economic justice pose a challenge to individual liberties. And yet, some might hold that the push for redistribution is in effect a move toward instability because redistributive politics are bred from conflict. The less inequality, the less conflict. The implication would appear to be that democracy—especially a procedural one that protects property and individual liberties and guarantees equality of opportunity—is really a halfway medium between two authoritarian extremes. Maintenance of the balance, however, requires that both the people and the state continuously work at it.

According to Acemoglu and Robinson (2006), unrest is often a consequence of inequality. And yet, changes are more likely to occur in those societies with greater inequality between elites and citizens. The more equal the society, the less likely are the masses to demand democratization. Democratization actually requires that society be sufficiently unequal so that the threat of revolution is credible. Therefore, an elite may be willing to begin a transition by extending the right of franchise because it is in its interests to do so. The transition effectively preserves the status quo by staving off a threat of revolution, which in the end may preserve the power base of the elite. That the elite only democratizes to the degree necessary to stave off the threat of revolution might also explain why some societies opt for representative democracy over participatory or direct democracy. That is, because the former effectively limits the power of the majority by diluting popular pressure and undermining the power of the majority.

Although the public choice models posit that violence is the likely result of growing inequality, a revolution in the USA is highly unlikely largely because of the impact of the Hartz thesis. Echoing Tocqueville's observation that America was born free because, Louis Hartz (1955) argued that because we did not have the feudalistic baggage that old Europe had, there was no need for a revolution. In feudalistic Europe the only way out of a caste-like class structure was either through death or revolution. But in America there was upward socioeconomic mobility, which meant that nobody was limited by class and anybody could potentially make it. This meant that the type of revolution characteristic in Europe was most likely not going to occur here. But the Hartz thesis may also assume that there are still opportunities for upward mobility. It certainly assumes opportunities for earning middle-class wages. And yet, with globalization driving down wages, especially among the low-skilled, it would appear that those opportunities are vanishing.

Arguably nationwide protests over a variety of issues, including protests for a $15.00 an hour minimum, may be viewed as a low-level form of revolution. Certainly if such protests result in a change of policy, it might signal just the beginning of a transformation whose effect elevates the rights of some at perhaps the expense of others. On another level, however, it could serve to open a discussion of what are the minimum requirements for one to be truly autonomous in a democratic society. Clearly, political equality is a necessary condition, but it alone isn't sufficient. Although economic equality isn't required for democracy to flourish, democracy does require the presence of autonomous citizens. At a minimum, a $15.00 minimum wage forces us as a society to contemplate just how much income is necessary for individuals to be autonomous. At $15 an hour, one is earning over $30,000 a year. It is between $30,000 and $60,000 a year that the percentage of those civically engaged increased dramatically from the below $30,000 income threshold (Levin-Waldman 2013). It is in that vein that a $15 an hour minimum might be the beginning of a process that leads to greater democratization.

Policy for a Democratic Society

While a wage policy, especially in the form of a minimum wage, may be an essential ingredient in the maintenance of democracy, democratic society perhaps has an obligation to do more to foster greater participation among low-income workers. A wage policy that moves them into the middle class is certainly one way, but there are other things that could be done as well. We also know that in addition to those coming from high-income households and those with high levels of education are more likely to be civically engaged (Levin-Waldman 2013). At a minimum, they might be more engaged if they are assured of certain benefits in the future (Campbell 2002; Mettler 2002, 2007). A wage policy is not only confined to a minimum wage but can include unionization—another labor market institution designed to bolster wages by giving workers a voice. This could also involve more employee ownership options. Organizing workers, particularly low-wage workers, would be important for a variety of reasons. First of all, it would give them a form of voice, not only in the workplace through collective bargaining but in their communities as well. They certainly served as an important constituency for public policies that would benefit both low-wage workers and the middle class. Historically the minimum wage tended to be increased when unions, as its chief constituency, were supporting increases. And yet, as union membership declined, the constituency behind increases was no longer there, and Congress had less incentive to increase them (Levin-Waldman 2001). But unions also served another function: they provided their members with more social capital.

Union members have traditionally tended to be more involved in the civic affairs of their communities. Labor unions in particular provided the most common organizational affiliation among American working men. Among the traditional benefits to labor unions in terms of civic engagement is that they often got their members out, at a minimum, to vote, in part, because they could impress upon them the impact of electoral outcomes on policies of import to workers. Unions were on the front lines of every economic battle of the mid-twentieth century. During the 1960s, labor's influence was actually expected to grow. Hacker and Pierson (2010) note that as late as 1970, it was expected that union voter drives would actually transform the American electorate. As a result of declining union representation in the workplace, income inequality increased. Fewer union members meant that fewer union voters were motivated to get to the polls and vote for candidates favorable to organized labor. Moreover, societies where trade unions are stronger tend to be more equal. Although unions have been in decline, professional organizations have proliferated (Putnam 2000; Nissen 2010). But this is not necessarily an equal replacement as the two tend to represent different groups often at opposite ends of the income spectrum. Organizing low-wage workers, then, might serve to not only give them greater voice but also give a greater understanding of themselves as stakeholders.

Another important step that a democratic society could take to get low-wage workers involved is to invest more in worker education programs that could be provided through employers as on-the-job training. The literature on returns to education already makes it clear that increased education leads to higher wages presumably because education increases skill levels and thereby increases employee value to the employer (Levy and Murnane 1992; Tyler et al. 2000). In 2010, for instance,

American industry spent $171.5 billion on workforce education and development. On an individual employee basis, companies were spending an average of $1228 in direct expenditures per employee. And yet, 4 percent of the total expenditure was designated for "basic skills" and 7 percent for "interpersonal skills" (ASTD 2011). This would suggest that at least 11 percent or 18.9 billion was being spent on training low-wage workers. And yet, to the extent that these investments are being made in low-wage workers, it could be argued that such investment would also serve to develop social capital among them. Therefore, as a policy measure worker education training tax credits might be offered to firms to provide basic training for their workers—to develop their social capital. This approach has obvious connections to a wage policy approach and is by no means mutually exclusive of making greater efforts to organize low-wage workers.

Conclusion

Given the essential components of democratic theory, mainly equality and autonomy, a wage policy, to the extent that it furthers those components, can certainly be said to further the aims of achieving a more democratic society. Any policy that in any way enhances autonomy, by at a minimum conferring greater dignity on individuals, and more, which enables them to participate more fully as full-fledged citizens, is ultimately serving a democratic purpose. Wage policy is critical to the ends of democracy for the following reasons: First, through the additional security it affords workers through higher wages, especially at the bottom of the distribution, it enhances personal autonomy, and enhanced personal autonomy can allow for greater participation in the public sphere. Individuals who earn enough to live above the poverty line feel better about themselves and are more inclined to become more productive. They are more productive by virtue of their ability to better maintain themselves.

Second, to the extent that wage policy reduces income inequality, it results in less strife and threats to democratic society. Third, wage policy is part and parcel of economic development. Through the increased purchasing power it affords, individuals are able to demand more goods and services, which in time may fuel investment and economic expansion. Economic development is central because it is the basis for a broad middle class, which, in and of itself, militates against a dual distribution comprised of those at the very top and those at the very bottom. But economic development is also about developing and enhancing individual autonomy. As Sen (1999) has observed, it is the process by which the freedoms that people enjoy are improved, and individuals can only be free in a democratic society. Aside from wage policy itself, efforts to organize low-wage workers and the provision of worker education training credits could have the effect of developing the capabilities of low-wage workers, thereby making them more autonomous and better able to participate in a democratic society.

As much as a wage policy in the form of a minimum wage might be seen as a vehicle for achieving greater democracy as higher income might lead to greater civic involvement because individuals with higher income are more autonomous. It isn't inconceivable that those who oppose increases in the minimum wage because it may reduce employer control over workers would also be opposed to it because any measure that enhances democracy will be viewed as a threat to the political power of the most affluent. As already noted, the American political system is most responsive to those who are affluent and less responsive to simply the middle class. It is essentially non-responsive to the poor. The public choice theories of democracy generally maintain that elites will no doubt resist efforts to achieve greater democratization. In more authoritarian regimes, they will use the power of the state to quash efforts by the masses to achieve that end. In less authoritarian regimes, they can simply use the political process to achieve the same end result. Nobody is going to say in public discourse that greater democracy is bad for the body politic, but they will oppose the types of policies that can achieve that result, albeit it in an indirect way. By trotting out the argument that a higher minimum wage will result in disemployment effects because employers will either lay workers off or they will substitute machinery for workers, they can achieve the same end. That is the key reason why business interests have sought to localize the conflict by narrowing the scope of the political debate. And yet, because the minimum wage is in the end about the middle class, the conflict can finally be socialized as we view the minimum wage as a reference point for the larger low-wage labor market and see how wages in one contour of the distribution affect the wages of those in other contours. As the minimum wage comes to be understood as a middle-class issue, it will in the end achieve greater support.

Bibliography

Acemoglu, Daron, and James A. Robinson. 2006. *Economic Origins of Dictatorship and Democracy*. Cambridge/New York: Cambridge University Press.

ASTD Research. 2011. *2011 State of the Industry*. American Society for Training & Development.

Bachrach, Peter, and Aryeh Botwinick. 1992. *Power and Empowerment: A Radical Theory of Participatory Democracy*. Philadelphia: Temple University Press.

Bartels, Larry M. 2008. *Unequal Democracy: The Political Economy of the New Gilded Age*. Princeton: Princeton University Press.

Boix, Carles. 2003. *Democracy and Redistribution*. Cambridge/New York: Cambridge University Press.

Bowles, Samuel, and Herbert Gintis. 1986. *Democracy & Capitalism: Property, Community, and the Contradictions of Modern Social Thought*. New York: Basic Books.

Campbell, Andrea Louise. 2002. Self-Interest, Social Security, and the Distributive Participation Patterns of Senior Citizens. *American Political Science Review* 96 (3): 565–574.

Caroli, Eve, and Jerome Gautie. 2008. Low-Wage Work: The Political Debate and Research Agenda in France. In *Low-Wage Work in France*, ed. Eve Caroli and J. Gautie. New York: Russell Sage Foundation.

Center for Democracy and Civil Society. 2007. American Civic Engagement in Comparative Perspective: Key Comparative Findings from the U.S. 'Citizenship, Involvement, Democracy' Survey. Georgetown University.

Dolbeare, Kenneth M. 1986. *Democracy at Risk: The Politics of Economic Renewal*. Chatham: Chatham House Publishers.

Gaffaney, Timothy. 2000. *Freedom for the Poor: Welfare and the Foundations of Democratic Citizenship*. Boulder: Westview Press.

Gilens, Martin. 2012. *Affluence & Influence: Economic Inequality and Political Power in America*. New York/Princeton/Oxford: Russell Sage Foundation and Princeton University Press.

Guttmann, Amy, and Dennis Thompson. 1996. *Democracy and Disagreement*. Cambridge, MA: Belknap Press.

Hacker, Jacob S., and Paul Pierson. 2010. *Winner-Take-All Politics: How Washington Made the Rich Richer – And Turned Its Back on the Middle Class*. New York: Simon & Schuster.

Hartz, Louis. 1955. *The Liberal Tradition in America: An Interpretation of American Political Thought Since the Revolution*. New York: Harcourt Brace Jovanovich.

Haveman, Robert, Gary Sandefeur, Barbara Wolfe, and Andrea Voyer. 2004. Trends in Children's Attainments and Their Determinants as Family Income Inequality Has Increased. In *Social Inequality*, ed. Kathryn Neckerman. New York: Russell Sage Foundation.

Howard, Marc M. 2006. American Civic Engagement in Comparative Perspective. *Democracy & Society* 3 (2): 17–21.

Kaufman, Bruce E. 2005. The Social Welfare Objectives and Ethical Principles of Industrial Relations. In *The Ethics of Human Resources and Industrial Relations*, ed. John W. Budd and James G. Scoville. Champaign: Labor and Employment Relations Association.

Levin-Waldman, Oren M. 2001. *The Case of the Minimum Wage: Competing Policy Models*. Albany: State University of New York Press.

———. 2013. Income Inequality and Disparities in Civic Participation in the New York City Metro Area. *Regional Labor Review* 15 (2): 22–29.

———. 2013a. Income, Civic Participation, and Achieving Greater Democracy. *Journal of Socio-Economics* 43: 83–92.

———. 2013b. The Impacts of Recession on Civic Participation in the New York City Metro Area. *Regional Labor Review* 15 (Spring/Summer): 29–41.

Levy, Frank, and Richard J. Murnane. 1992. U.S. Earnings Levels and Earnings Inequality: A Review of Recent Trends and Proposed Explanations. *Journal of Economic Literature* 30 (3): 1333–1381.

Lipset, Seymour Martin. 1959. Some Social Requisites of Democracy: Economic Development and Political Legitimacy. *American Political Science Review* 53 (01): 69–105.

Manturuck, K., M. Lindblad, and R. Quercia. 2012. Homeownership and Civic Engagement in Low-Income Urban Neighborhoods: A Longitudinal Analysis. *Urban Affairs Review* 48 (5): 731–760.

McCarty, Nolan, Keith T. Poole, and Howard Rosenthal. 2008. *Polarized America: The Dance of Ideology and Unequal Riches*. Cambridge, MA/London: MIT Press.

Mettler, Suzanne. 2002. Bringing the State Back into Civic Engagement: Policy Feedback Effects of the GI Bill for World War II Veterans. *American Political Science Review* 96 (2): 351–365.

———. 2007. Bringing Government Back into Civic Engagement: Considering the Role of Public Policy. *International Journal of Public Administration* 30: 643–650.

Nissen, Bruce. 2010. Political Activism as Part of a Broader Civic Engagement: The Case of SEIU Florida Healthcare Union. *Labor Studies Journal* 35 (1): 51–72.

Page, Benjamin, Larry Bartels, and Jason Seawright. 2013. Democracy and the Policy Preferences of Wealthy Americans. *Perspectives on Politics* 11 (1): 51–73.

Putnam, Robert. 2000. *Bowling Alone: The Collapse and Revival of American Community*. New York: Simon & Schuster.

Rank, Mark Robert. 2004. *One Nation, Underprivileged: Why American Poverty Affects Us All*. Oxford/New York: Oxford University Press.

Sen, Amartya. 1999. *Development as Freedom*. New York: Anchor Books.

Stiglitz, Joseph E. 2012. *The Price of Inequality*. New York: W.W. Norton.

Tyler, John H., Richard J. Murnane, and John B. Willett. 2000. Estimating the Labor Market Signaling Value of the GED. *The Quarterly Journal of Economics* 115 (2): 431–468.

Uslaner, Eric. 2008. The Foundations of Trust: Macro and Micro. *Cambridge Journal of Economics* 32: 289–294.

Uslaner, Eric, and Mitchell Brown. 2005. Inequality, Trust, and Civic Engagement. *American Politics Research* 33 (6): 868–894.

Verba, Sidney, and Norman H. Nie. 1972. *Participation in America: Political Democracy and Social Equality*. Chicago: University of Chicago Press.

Verba, Sidney, Kay Lehman Scholzman, and Henry E. Brady. 2004. Political Equality: What Do We Know About It? In *Social Inequality*, ed. Kathryn Neckerman. New York: Russell Sage Foundation.

Volscho, Thomas W., Jr., and Nathan J. Kelly. 2012. The Rise of the Super-Rich: Power Resources, Taxes, Financial Markets, and the Dynamics of the Top 1 Percent, 1949–2008. *American Sociological Review* 77 (5): 679–699.

Wadenjso, Eskil. 2001. The Labour Market – Rehn or Rubbestad. In *Gosta Rehn, the Swedish Model and Labour Market Policies: International and National Perspectives*, ed. Henry Milner and Eskil Wadenjos. Aldershot/Burlington: Ashgate Publishing Co.

White, Stuart. 2007. *Equality*. Cambridge/Malden: Polity Press.

Wilkinson, Richard, and Kate Pickett. 2010. *The Spirit Level: Why Greater Equality Makes Societies Stronger*. New York/London: Bloomsbury Press.

Bibliography

Acemoglu, Daron, and James A. Robinson. 2006. *Economic Origins of Dictatorship and Democracy*. Cambridge/New York: Cambridge University Press.

Aglietta, Michael. 1979. *A Theory of Capitalist Regulation: The U.S. Experience*. London/New York: Verso.

Allegretto, Sylvia, Arindrajit Dube, and Michael Reich. 2011. Do Minimum Wages Really Reduce Teen Employment? Accounting for Heterogeneity and Selectivity in State Panel Data. *Industrial Relations* 50 (2): 205–240.

Autor, David H., Lawrence F. Katz, and Melissa S. Kearney. 2008. Trends in U.S. Wage Inequality: Revising the Revisionists. *The Review of Economics and Statistics* 90 (2): 300–323.

Bachrach, Peter, and Morton S. Baratz. 1962. Two Faces of Power. *American Political Science Review* 56: 947–952.

Bachrach, Peter, and Aryeh Botwinick. 1992. *Power and Empowerment: A Radical Theory of Participatory Democracy*. Philadelphia: Temple University Press.

Ball, Laurence. 1999. Aggregate Demand and Long-Run Unemployment. *Brookings Papers on Economic Activity* 2: 189–251.

Balleer, Almut, and Thija van Rens. 2013. Skill-Biased Technological Change and the Business Cycle. *The Review of Economics and Statistics* 95 (4): 1222–1237.

Bartels, Larry M. 2008. *Unequal Democracy: The Political Economy of the New Gilded Age*. Princeton: Princeton University Press.

Belman, Dale, and Paul J. Wolfson. 2014. *What Does the Minimum Wage Do?* Kalamazoo: W.E. Upjohn Institute for Employment Research.

Blanchflower, David G., and Alex Bryson. 2008. What Effect Do Unions Have on Wages Now and Would Freeman and Medoff Be Surprised? In *What Do Unions*

O. M. Levin-Waldman, *Restoring the Middle Class through Wage Policy*, Binzagr Institute for Sustainable Prosperity,
https://doi.org/10.1007/978-3-319-74448-3

Do?: A Twenty-Year Perspective, ed. James T. Bennett and Bruce E. Kaufman. New Brunswick: Transaction Publishers.

Boddewyn, J. 1961. Frederick Winslow Taylor Revisited. *The Journal of the Academy of Management* 4 (2): 100–107.

Boix, Carles. 2003. *Democracy and Redistribution*. Cambridge/New York: Cambridge University Press.

Bowles, Samuel, and Herbert Gintis. 1986. *Democracy & Capitalism: Property, Community, and the Contradictions of Modern Social Thought*. New York: Basic Books.

Braekkan, Kristian F., and Victoria "Tori" Sowa. 2015. Exploitation by Economic Necessity. *SAGE Open* 5 (4): 215824401561054.

Bridges, Amy. 1986. Becoming American: The Working Classes in the United States Before the Civil War. In *Working-Class Formation: Nineteenth-Century Patterns in Western Europe and the United States*, ed. Ira Katznelson and Aristide R. Zolberg. Princeton: Princeton University Press.

Brimmer, Arthur F. 1983. Monetary Policy and Economic Activity: Benefits and Costs of Monetarism. *American Economic Review* 73 (2): 1–12.

Brown, Christopher. 1992. Commodity Money, Credit, and the Real Balance Effect. *Journal of Post Keynesian Economics* 15 (1): 99–107.

Brown, Charles C. 1996. The Old Minimum-Wage Literature and Its Lessons for the New. In *The Effect of the Minimum Wage on Employment*, ed. Marvin H. Kosters. Washington, DC: AEI Press.

Brown, Charles, Curtis Gilroy, and Andrew Kohen. 1982. The Effects of the Minimum Wage on Employment and Unemployment. *Journal of Economic Literature* 20: 487–528.

Budd, John W. 2004. *Employment with a Human Face: Balancing Efficiency, Equity, and Voice*. Ithaca/London: ILR/Cornell University Press.

Burkhauser, Richard V., and T. Aldrich Finegan. 1989. The Minimum Wage and the Poor: The End of a Relationship. *Journal of Policy Analysis and Management* 8 (1): 53–71.

Campbell, Andrea Louise. 2002. Self-Interest, Social Security, and the Distributive Participation Patterns of Senior Citizens. *American Political Science Review* 96 (3): 565–574.

Card, David, and John DiNardo. 2002. Skill Based Technological Change and Rising Wage Inequality: Some Problems and Puzzles. Working Paper No. 8769. National Bureau of Economic Research, February.

Card, David, and Alan B. Krueger. 1995. *Myth and Measurement: The New Economics of the Minimum Wage*. Princeton: Princeton University Press.

———. 1998. A Reanalysis of the Effect of the New Jersey Minimum Wage Increase on the Fast-Food Industry with Representative Payroll Data. Working Paper No. 6386. National Bureau of Economic Research.

Card, David, Thomas Lemieux, and W. Craig Riddell. 2008. Unions and Wage Inequality. In *What Do Unions Do?: A Twenty-Year Perspective*, ed. James T. Bennett and Bruce E. Kaufman. New Brunswick: Transaction Publishers.

Caroli, Eve, and Jerome Gautie. 2008. Low-Wage Work: The Political Debate and Research Agenda in France. In *Low-Wage Work in France*, ed. Eve Caroli and Jerome Gautie. New York: Russell Sage Foundation.

Center for Democracy and Civil Society. 2007. American Civic Engagement in Comparative Perspective: Key Comparative Findings from the U.S. 'Citizenship, Involvement, Democracy' Survey. Georgetown University.

Clark, John Bates. 1913. The Minimum Wage. *The Atlantic Monthly* 112 (3): 289–297.

Cohen, Michael D., James G. March, and Johan P. Olsen. 1972. A Garbage Can Model of Organizational Change. *Administrative Science Quarterly* 17 (1): 1–25.

Collingnon, Stefan. 1999. Unemployment, Wage Developments and the Economic Policy Mix in Europe. *Empirica* 26: 259–269.

Congressional Budget Office. 2014. *The Effects of a Minimum Wage Increase on Employment and Family Income*. Congress of the United States, February. Downloaded from http://www.cbo.gov/publication/44995

Craypo, Charles, and David Cormier. 2000. Job Restructuring as a Determinant of Wage Inequality and Working-Poor Households. *Journal of Economic Issues* 34 (1): 21–42.

Currie, Janet, and Bruce C. Fallick. 1996. The Minimum Wage and the Employment of Youth. *Journal of Human Resources* 31 (2): 404–428.

Derksen, Maarten. 2014. Turning Men into Machines? Scientific Management, Industrial Psychology, and the 'Human Factor'. *Journal of the History of the Behavioral Sciences* 50 (2): 148–165.

DiNardo, John, and Thomas Lemieux. 1997. Diverging Male Wage Inequality in the United States and Canada, 1981–1988: Do Institutions Explain the Difference? *Industrial and Labor Relations Review* 50 (4): 629–650.

Dolbeare, Kenneth M. 1986. *Democracy at Risk: The Politics of Economic Renewal.* Chatham: Chatham House Publishers.

Drazen, Allan. 1986. Optimal Minimum Wage Legislation. *The Economic Journal* 96 (383):774.

Dube, Arindrajit, Suresh Naidu, and Michael Reich. 2007. The Economic Effects of a Citywide Minimum Wage. *Industrial and Labor Relations Review* 60 (4): 522–523.

Dube, Arindrajit, T. William Lester, and Michael Reich. 2010. Minimum Wage Effects Among State Borders: Estimates Using Contiguous Counties. *The Review of Economics and Statistics* 92 (4): 945–964.

Dubofsky, Melvyn. 1994. *The State & Labor in Modern America*. Chapel Hill: The University of North Carolina Press.

Dunlop, John T. 1957. The Task of Contemporary Wage Theory. In *New Concepts in Wage Determination*, ed. George W. Taylor and Frank C. Pierson. New York: McGraw-Hill Book Co.

Ehrenberg, Ronald G., and Robert S. Smith. 1997. *Modern Labor Economics: Theory and Public Policy*. 6th ed. Reading: Addison-Wesley.

Employment Act of 1946 ch. 33, section 2, 60 Stat. 23, codified as 15 U.S.C. § 1021.

Fairris, David. 1995. Control and Inefficiency in Capitalist Production: The Role of Institutions. *Review of Social Economy* 53 (1): 1–28.

———. 2003. *The Impact of Living Wages on Employers: A Control Group Analysis of the Los Angeles Ordinance*. Riverside: University of California. (April 11–12).

Figart, Deborah M., and June Lapidus. 1995. A Gender Analysis of U.S. Labor Markets for the Working Poor. *Feminist Economics* 1 (3): 60–81.

Figart, Deborah M., Ellen Mutari, and Marilyn Power. 2002. *Living Wages, Equal Wages: Gender and Labor Market Policies in the United States*. London/New York: Routledge.

Filene, Edward A. 1923. The Minimum Wage and Efficiency. *American Economic Review* 13 (September): 411–415.

Finegold, David. 1998. Is the Fair Labor Standards Act Fair to Welfare Recipients? *Journal of Labor Research* 19 (2): 245–262.

Foner, Eric. 1995. *Free Soil, Free Labor, Free Men: The Ideology of the Republican Party Before the Civil War*. Oxford/New York: Oxford University Press.

———. 1998. *The Story of American Freedom*. New York: W.W. Norton & Co.

Fortin, Nicole M., and Thomas Lemieux. 1997. Institutional Changes and Rising Wage Inequality: Is There a Linkage? *Journal of Economic Perspectives* 11 (2): 75–96.

Freeman, Richard B. 2004. What, Me Vote? In *Social Inequality*, ed. Kathryn Neckerman. New York: Russell Sage Foundation.

Freeman, Alida Castillo, and Richard B. Freeman. 1991. Minimum Wages in Puerto Rico: Textbook Case of a Wage Floor? NBER Working Paper No. 3759, June.

Freeman, Richard B., and James L. Medoff. 1985. *What Do Unions Do?* New York: Basic Books.

Fried, Barbara H. 1998. *The Progressive Assault on Laissez Faire: Robert Hale and the First Law and Economic Movement*. Cambridge, MA: Harvard University Press.

Friedman, Milton. 2002. *Capitalism and Freedom*. Chicago/London: University of Chicago Press.

Fry, Louis W. 1976. The Maligned F.W. Taylor: A Reply to His Critics. *Academy of Management Review* 1 (July): 124–129.

Gaffaney, Timothy. 2000. *Freedom for the Poor: Welfare and the Foundations of Democratic Citizenship*. Boulder: Westview Press.

Galbraith, James K. 1998. *Created Unequal: The Crisis in American Pay.* New York: The Free Press.

Gilens, Martin. 2012. *Affluence & Influence: Economic Inequality and Political Power in America.* New York/Princeton/Oxford: Russell Sage Foundation and Princeton University Press.

Glickman, Lawrence B. 1997. *A Living Wage: American Workers and the Making of Consumer Society.* Ithaca/London: Cornell University Press.

Gokcekus, Omer, and Edward Tower. 2003. An Efficiency Enhancing Minimum Wage. *Policy Reform* 6 (4): 247–259.

Goldfield, Michael. 1987. *The Decline of Organized Labor in the United States.* Chicago: University of Chicago Press.

Goldin, Claudia, and Lawrence F. Katz. 2008. *The Race Between Education and Technology.* Cambridge, MA/London: Belknap Press of Harvard University Press.

Gordon, Robert J. 1995. *Is There a Tradeoff Between Unemployment and Productivity Growth?* NBER Working Paper 5081, April.

Gordon, David M. 1996. *Fat and Mean: The Corporate Squeeze of Working Americans and the Myth of Managerial "Downsizing".* New York: The Free Press.

Gottschalk, Peter. 1997. Inequality, Income Growth, and Mobility: The Basic Facts. *Journal of Economic Perspectives* 11 (2): 21–40.

Gramlich, Edward M. 1976. Impact of Minimum Wages on Other Wages, Employment, and Family Incomes. *Brookings Papers on Economic Activity* 2: 409–451.

Guttmann, Amy, and Dennis Thompson. 1996. *Democracy and Disagreement.* Cambridge, MA: Belknap Press.

Haarlander, Lisa, and Sandra Tan. 2004. Minimum Wage Outlook: Opponents Say the Wage Will Force Price Hikes and Cuts in Staff and their Hours, While Supporters Say It Reflects the Reality of Businesses Today. *The Buffalo News*, December 11, p. A1.

Hacker, Jacob S., and Paul Pierson. 2010. *Winner-Take-All Politics: How Washington Made the Rich Richer – And Turned Its Back on the Middle Class.* New York: Simon & Schuster.

Hansen, Susan. 2006. *Globalization and the Politics of Pay: Policy Choices in the American States.* Washington, DC: Georgetown University Press.

Hardin, Garret. 1968. The Tragedy of the Commons. *Science* 162 (3589): 1243–1248.

Hartz, Louis. 1955. *The Liberal Tradition in America: An Interpretation of American Political Thought Since the Revolution.* New York: Harcourt Brace Jovanovich.

Hattam, Victoria C. 1993. *Labor Visions and State Power: The Origins of Business Unionism in the United States.* Princeton: Princeton University Press.

Haveman, Robert, Gary Sandefeur, Barbara Wolfe, and Andrea Voyer. 2004. Trends in Children's Attainments and Their Determinants as Family Income Inequality Has Increased. In *Social Inequality*, ed. Kathryn Neckerman. New York: Russell Sage Foundation.

Heilbroner, Robert L., and William S. Millberg. 1995. *The Crisis of Vision in Modern Economic Thought*. Cambridge/New York: Cambridge University Press.

Holzner, Charles A. 2007. The Poverty of Democracy: Neoliberal Reforms and Political Participation of the Poor in Mexico. *Latin American Political Society* 49 (2): 87–122.

Houseman, Susan N. 1998. The Effects of Employer Mandates. In *Generating Jobs: How to Increase Demands for Less-Skilled Workers*, ed. Richard B. Freeman and Peter Gottschalk. New York: Russell Sage Foundation.

Howard, Marc M. 2006. American Civic Engagement in Comparative Perspective. *Democracy & Society* 3 (2): 17–21.

Howell, David. 1999. Theory-Driven Facts and the Growth in Earnings Inequality. *Review of Radical Political Economics* 31 (1): 54–86.

Howell, David, and Friedrich Huebler. 2001. *Trends in Earnings Inequality and Unemployment Across the OECD: Labor Market Institutions and Simple Supply and Demand Stories*. Working Paper No. 23. Center for Economic Policy Analysis, New School University, May.

Howes, Candace. 2002. *The Impact of a Wage Increase on the Workforce Stability of IHSS Home Care Workers in San Francisco Country*. Working Paper. University of California Institute for Labor and the Economy and the University of California, Berkeley, Center for Education and Labor Research, November.

Jackson, William A. 1999. Basic Income and the Right to Work: A Keynesian Approach. *Journal of Post Keynesian Economics* 21 (4): 639–662.

Jacobs, Ken, Ian Perry, and Jennifer MacGillvary. 2015. *The High Public Cost of Low Wages*. University of California Berkeley Center for Labor Research and Education. Research Brief, April.

Johnson, Bob L. 1994. The Politics of Research-Information Use in the Education Policy Arena. *Education Policy* 13 (1): 23–36.

Juhn, Chinhui, Kevin Murphy, and Brooks Pierce. 1993. Wage Inequality and the Rise in Returns to Skills. *Journal of Political Economy* 101 (3): 410–442.

Kahn, Lawrence M., and Michael Curme. 1987. Unions and Nonunion Wage Dispersion. *The Review of Economics and Statistics* 69 (4): 600–607.

Katz, Michael B. 1989. *The Undeserving Poor: From the War on Poverty to the War on Welfare*. New York: Pantheon Books.

Katz, Lawrence, and Alan B. Krueger. 1992. The Effect of the Minimum Wage on the Fast-Food Industry. *Industrial and Labor Relations Review* 46 (1): 6–21.

Katz, Lawrence, and Kevin M. Murphy. 1992. Changes in Relative Wages, 1963–1987: Supply and Demand Factors. *Quarterly Journal of Economics* 107: 35–79.

Kaufman, Bruce E. 2003. John R. Commons and the Wisconsin School of Industrial Relations Strategy and Policy. *Industrial and Labor Relations Review* 57 (1): 3–30.

———. 2005. The Social Welfare Objectives and Ethical Principles of Industrial Relations. In *The Ethics of Human Resources and Industrial Relations*, ed. John W. Budd and James G. Scoville. Champaign: Labor and Employment Relations Association.

Kennan, John. 1995. The Elusive Effects of Minimum Wages. *Journal of Economic Literature* 33 (December): 1950–1965.

Kenworthy, Lane, and Jonas Pontusson. 2005. Rising Inequality and the Politics of Redistribution in Affluent Countries. *Perspectives on Politics* 3 (03).

Keynes, John Maynard. 1964. *The General Theory of Employment, Interest, and Money*. New York/London: Harcourt, Inc.

Kidwell, Roland E., Jr., and Philip M. Smith. 2001. Layoffs and the Ethical Implications Under Scientific Management, Quality Management and Open-Book Management. *Journal of Business Ethics* 29: 113–124.

Kingdon, John W. 1995. *Agendas, Alternatives, and Public Policies*. New York: Addison-Wesley Longmn Inc.

Konings, Jozef, and Patrick P. Walsh. 1993. Evidence of Efficiency Wage Payments in UK Firm Level Panel Data. *The Economic Journal* 104 (424): 542–555.

Kosters, Marvin H., ed. 1996. *The Effects of the Minimum Wage on Employment*. Washington, DC: AEI Press.

Kosters, Marvin H., and Finis Welch. 1972. The Effects of Minimum Wages on the Distribution of Change in Aggregate Employment. *American Economic Review* 62 (3): 323–332.

Lafer, Gordon. 2002. *The Job Training Charade*. Ithaca/London: Cornell University Press.

Lang, Kevin, and Shulamit Kahn. 1998. The Effects of Minimum-Wage Laws on the Distribution of Employment: Theory and Evidence. *Journal of Public Economics* 69: 67–82.

Leamer, Edward E. 1999. Effort, Wages, and the International Division of Labor. *Journal of Political Economy* 107 (6, Part 1): 1127–1162.

Lee, David S. 1997. Wage Inequality in the United States During the 1980ss: Rising or Falling Minimum Wage. *Quarterly Journal of Economics* 114 (3): 997–1023.

Lehrer, Susan. 1987. *Origins of Protective Labor Legislation for Women, 1905–1925*. Albany: State University of New York Press.

Lemieux, Thomas. 1998. Estimating the Effects of Unions on Wage Inequality in a Panel Data Model with Comparative Advantage and Nonrandom Selection. *Journal of Labor Economics* 16 (2): 261–291.

Lester, Richard A. 1946. Shortcomings of Marginal Analysis for Wage-Employment Problems. *American Economic Review* 36 (1): 63–82.

———. 1947. Reflections on the 'Labor Monopoly' Issue. *Journal of Political Economy* 56 (6): 513–536.

Levin-Waldman, Oren M. 2000a. The Minimum Wage Can Be Raised: Lessons from the 1999 Levy Survey of Small Business. *Challenge* 43 (2): 86–96.

———. 2000b. The Rhetorical Evolution of the Minimum Wage. *Rhetoric & Public Affairs* 3 (2): 131–153.

———. 2000c. Minimum Wage and Justice? *Review of Social Economy* 58 (1): 43–62.

———. 2001. *The Case of the Minimum Wage: Competing Policy Models*. Albany: State University of New York Press.

———. 2003. The Minimum Wage and the Cause of Democracy. *Review of Social Economy* 61 (4): 487–510.

———. 2004. The Living Wage Movement: Its Significance to Urban Politics and Citizenship. *Perspectives on Work* 8 (1): 40–42.

———. 2009. The Minimum Wage and Competing Ethical Conceptions. *Advances in Industrial and Labor Relations* 16: 181–210.

———. 2011. *Wage Policy, Income Distribution, and Democratic Theory*. London/ New York: Routledge.

———. 2013. Income Inequality and Disparities in Civic Participation in the New York City Metro Area. *Regional Labor Review* 15 (2):22–29.

Levy, Frank, and Richard J. Murnane. 1992. U.S. Earnings Levels and Earnings Inequality: A Review of Recent Trends and Proposed Explanations. *Journal of Economic Literature* 30 (3): 1333–1381.

Levy, Frank, and Peter Temin. 2010. Institutions and Wages in Post-World War II America. In *Labor in the Era of Globalization*, ed. Clair Brown, Barry Eichengreen, and Michael Reich. Cambridge: Cambridge University Press.

Lindbeck, Assar, and Denis Snower. 1988. *Long-Term Unemployment and Macroeconomic Policy*. AEA Papers and Proceedings, May, pp. 38–43.

Lindblom, Charles E. 1959. The Science of Muddling Through. *Public Administration Review* 17: 79–88.

Lipset, Seymour Martin. 1959. Some Social Requisites of Democracy: Economic Development and Political Legitimacy. *American Political Science Review* 53 (01):69–105.

Lowi, Theodore J. 1964. American Business, Public Policy, Case-Studies, and Political Theory. *World Politics* 16 (4): 677–715.

Lowi, Theodore J. 1996. *The End of the Republican Era*. Norman: University of Oklahoma Press.

Luebker, Malte. 2004. Income Inequality, Redistribution, and Poverty: Contrasting Rational Choice and Behavioral Perspectives. *Review of Income and Wealth* 60 (1): 133–154.

Machin, Stephen. 1997. The Decline of Labour Market Institutions and the Rise in Wage Inequality in Britain. *European Economic Review* 41: 647–657.

Manturuk, Kim, Mark Lindblad, and Roberto Quercia. 2012. Homeownership and Civic Engagement in Low-Income Urban Neighborhoods. *Urban Affairs Review* 48 (5):731–760.

McCarty, Nolan, Keith T. Poole, and Howard Rosenthal. 2008. *Polarized America: The Dance of Ideology and Unequal Riches*. Cambridge, MA/London: MIT Press.

McGregor, Douglas. 1960. *The Human Enterprise*. New York: McGraw-Hill.

Mead, Lawrence M. 1986. *Beyond Entitlement: The Social Obligations of Citizenship*. New York: The Free Press.

———. 1992. The New Politics of Poverty: The Nonworking Poor in America. New York: Basic Books.

Meltzer, Allan H., and Scott F. Richard. 1981. A Rational Theory of the Size of Government. *Journal of Political Economy* 89 (5): 914–927.

Mettler, Suzanne. 2002. Bringing the State Back into Civic Engagement: Policy Feedback Effects of the GI Bill for World War II Veterans. *American Political Science Review* 96 (2): 351–365.

———. 2007. Bringing Government Back into Civic Engagement: Considering the Role of Public Policy. *International Journal of Public Administration* 30: 643–650.

Meyer, Robert H., and David A. Wise. 1983. The Effect of the Minimum Wage on the Employment and Earnings of Youth. *Journal of Labor Economics* 1 (1): 66–100.

Michl, Thomas R. 2000. Can Rescheduling Explain the New Jersey Minimum Wage Studies? *Eastern Economic Journal* 26 (3): 265–276.

Minsky, Hyman P. 1986. *Stabilizing an Unstable Economy*. New Haven: Yale University Press.

Modigliani, Franco. 2003. The Keynesian Gospel According to Modigliani. *American Economist* 47 (1): 3–24.

Montgomery, David. 1993. *Citizen Worker: The Experience of Workers in the United States with Democracy and the Free Market During the Nineteenth Century*. Cambridge/New York: Cambridge University Press.

Moody, Kim. 1988. *An Injury to All: The Decline of American Unionism*. London/New York: Verso.

Murray, Charles M. 1984. *Losing Ground: American Social Policy, 1950–1980*. New York: Basic Books.

Murray, Charles. 2012. *Coming Apart: The State of White America 1960–2010*. New York: Crown Forum/Random House.

Nelson, Carnot E., Jeanne Roberts, Cynthia Maederer, Bruce Wertheimer, and Beverly Johnson. 1987. The Utilization of Social Science Information by Policymakers. *American Behaviorist Scientist* 30 (6): 569–577.

Neumark, David, and William Wascher. 1992. Employment Effects of Minimum and Subminimum Wages: Panel Data and State Minimum Wage Laws. *Industrial and Labor Relations Review* 46 (1): 55–81.

———. 2000. Minimum Wages and Employment: A Case Study of the Fast-Food Industry in New Jersey and Pennsylvania: Comment. *American Economic Review* 90 (5): 1362–1396.

Neumark, David, Mark Schweitzer, and William Wascher. 2004. Minimum Wage Effects Throughout the Distribution. *The Journal of Human Resources* 39 (2): 425–450.

Nissen, Bruce. 2010. Political Activism as Part of a Broader Civic Engagement: The Case of SEIU Florida Healthcare Union. *Labor Studies Journal* 35 (1): 51–72.

Page, Benjamin, Larry Bartels, and Jason Seawright. 2013. Democracy and the Policy Preferences of Wealthy Americans. *Perspectives on Politics* 11 (1): 51–73.

Palley, Thomas. 1995. Labor Markets, Unemployment, and Minimum Wages: A New View. *Eastern Economic Journal* 21 (3): 319–326.

———. 1998. *Plenty of Nothing: The Downsizing of the American Dream and the Case for Structural Keynesianism*. Princeton: Princeton University Press.

Partridge, Mark D., and Janice S. Partridge. 1999. Do Minimum Wage Hikes Raise U.S. Long Term Unemployment? Evidence Using State Minimum Wage Rates. *Regional Studies* 33 (8): 713–726.

Petit, Philip. 1997. *Republicanism: A Theory of Freedom and Government*. Oxford/ New York: Oxford University Press.

Piketty, Thomas. 2014. *Capital in the Twenty-First Century*. Cambridge, MA/ London: Belknap Press of Harvard University Press.

Piore, Michael J. 1995. *Beyond Individualism*. Cambridge, MA: Harvard University Press.

Pontusson, Jonas. 2005. *Inequality and Prosperity: Social Europe v. Liberal America*. Ithaca/New York: Cornell University Press.

Power, Marilyn. 1999. Parasitic Industries Analysis and Arguments for a Living Wage for Women in the Early Twentieth-Century United States. *Feminist Economics* 5 (1): 61–78.

Prasch, Robert E. 1995. Toward a 'General Theory' of Market Exchange. *Journal of Economic Issues* 29 (3): 807–828.

Putnam, Robert. 2000. *Bowling Alone: The Collapse and Revival of American Community*. New York: Simon & Schuster.

Randall Wray, L. 2000. The Employer of Last Resort Approach to Full Employment. *SSRN Electronic Journal*. Working Paper No. 9, University of Missouri-Kansas City: Center for Full Employment and Price Stability, July.

Rank, Mark Robert. 2004. *One Nation, Underprivileged: Why American Poverty Affects Us All*. Oxford/New York: Oxford University Press.

Rawls, John. 1971. *A Theory of Justice*. Cambridge, MA: Harvard University Press.

Reagan, Michael D. 1961. The Political Structure of the Federal Reserve System. *American Political Science Review* 55: 64–76.

Reich, Robert B. 1997. *Locked in the Cabinet*. New York: Alfred E. Knopf.

Reich, Michael. 2010. Minimum Wages in the United States: Politics, Economics, and Econometrics. In *Labor in the era of Globalization*, ed. Clair Brown, Barry Eichengreen, and Michael Reich. Cambridge/New York: Cambridge University Press.

Reich, Michael, Peter Hall, and Ken Jacobs. 2003. *Living Wages and Economic Performance: The San Francisco Airport Model.* Institute of Industrial Relations. University of California, Berkeley, March.

———. 2005. Living Wage Policies at the San Francisco Airport: Impacts on Workers and Businesses. *Industrial Relations* 44 (1): 106–138.

Report of the Minimum Wage Study Commission. 1981. Vol. 1. Washington, DC: Government Printing Office.

Rodgers, Daniel T. 1978. *The Work Ethic in Industrial America 1850–1920*. Chicago: University of Chicago Press.

Rowley, Charles K. 1984. The Relevance of the Median Voter Theorem. *Journal of Institutional and Theoretical Economics* 140: 104–126.

Sabia, Joseph J., and Richard V. Burkhauser. 2010. Minimum Wages and Poverty: Will a $9.50 Federal Minimum Wage Really Help the Working Poor? *Southern Economic Journal* 76 (3): 592–623.

Sandler, Manfred, and Rudiger Wapler. 2004. Endogenous Skill-Biased Technological Change and Matching Unemployment. *Journal of Economics* 81 (1): 1–24.

Schacter, Hindy Lauer. 1989. Frederick Winslow Taylor and the Idea of Worker Participation. *Administration & Society* 21 (1): 20–30.

Schattschneider, E.E. 1960. *The Semisovereign People: A Realist's View of America*. New York: Holt, Rinehart.

Schmitt, John. 1996. *Cooked to Order*. American Prospect, pp 82–85, May–June.

Schneider, Anne, and Helen Ingram. 1993. Social Constructions and Target Populations: Implications for Politics and Policy. *American Political Science Review* 87 (2): 334–347.

Schram, Sanford F. 1995. *Words of Welfare: The Poverty of Social Sciences and the Social Science of Poverty*. Minneapolis: University of Minnesota Press.

Sen, Amartya. 1999. *Development as Freedom*. New York: Anchor Books.

Shapiro, Carl, and Joseph Stiglitz. 1984. Equilibrium Unemployment as a Worker Discipline Device. *American Economic Review* 74 (3): 433–444.

Shefter, Martin. 1986. Trade Unions and Political Machines: The Organization and Disorganization of the American Working Class in the Late Nineteenth Century. In *Working-Class Formation: Nineteenth-Century Patterns in Western Europe and the United States*, ed. Ira Katznelson and Aristide R. Zolberg. Princeton: Princeton University Press.

Simler, N.J. 1964. Long-Term Unemployment, the Structural Hypothesis, and Public Policy. *American Economic Review* 54 (6): 985–1001.

Smith, Adam. 1976. In *An Inquiry into the Nature and Causes of the Wealth of Nations*, ed. Edwin Cannan. Chicago: University of Chicago Press.

Smith, Hendrick. 2012. *Who Stole the American Dream?* New York: Random House.

Spriggs, William E., and Bruce E. Klein. 1994. *Raising the Floor: The Effects of the Minimum Wage on Low-Wage Workers.* Washington, DC: Economic Policy Institute.

Stigler, George. 1946. The Economics of Minimum Wage Legislation. *American Economic Review* 36 (June): 358–365.

———. 1986. The Goals of Economic Policy. In *The Essence of Stigler*, ed. Kurt Leube and Thomas Moore. Stanford: Hoover Institution Press.

Stiglitz, Joseph E. 2012. *The Price of Inequality.* New York: W.W. Norton.

Stone, Deborah. 2002. *Policy Paradox: The Art of Political Decision Making.* New York/London: W.W. Norton & Co.

Swan, Kyle. 2012. Republican Equality. *Social Theory and Practice* 38 (3): 432–454.

Taylor, Frederick Winslow. 2013. 1911. *The Principles of Scientific Management.* Amazon/CreateSpace.

Tyler, John H., Richard J. Murnane, and John B. Willett. 2000. Estimating the Labor Market Signaling Value of the GED. *The Quarterly Journal of Economics* 115 (2): 431–468.

Uslaner, Eric. 2008. The Foundations of Trust: Macro and Micro. *Cambridge Journal of Economics* 32: 289–294.

Uslaner, Eric, and Mitchell Brown. 2005. Inequality, Trust, and Civic Engagement. *American Politics Research* 33 (6): 868–894.

Van Parijs, Philippe. 1992. Basic Income Capitalism. *Ethics* 102(3):465–484.

———. 1995. *Real Freedom for All: What (If Anything) Can Justify Capitalism?*

Verba, Sidney, and Norman H. Nie. 1972. *Participation in America: Political Democracyand Social Equality.* Chicago: University of Chicago Press.

Verba, Sidney, Kay Lehman Scholzman, and Henry E. Brady. 2004. Political Equality: What Do We Know About It? In *Social Inequality,* ed. Kathryn Neckerman. New York: Russell Sage Foundation.

Vivarelli, Marco. 2014. Innovation, Employment and Skills in Advanced and Developing Countries: A Survey of Economic Literature. *Journal of Economic Issues* 48 (1): 123–154.

Volscho, Thomas W., Jr., and Nathan J. Kelly. 2012. The Rise of the Super-Rich: Power Resources, Taxes, Financial Markets, and the Dynamics of the Top 1 Percent, 1949–2008. *American Sociological Review* 77 (5): 679–699.

Volscho, Thomas W., Jr. 2005. Minimum Wages and Income Inequality in the American States, 1960–2000. *Research in Social Stratification and Mobility* 23: 347–373.

Wadenjso, Eskil. 2001. The Labour Market – Rehn or Rubbestad. In *Gosta Rehn, the Swedish Model and Labour Market Policies: International and National Perspectives*, ed. Henry Milner and Eskil Wadenjos. Aldershot/Burlington: Ashgate Publishing Co.

Wagner, Richard E. 1996. *Economic Policy in a Liberal Democracy*. Cheltenham/Brookfield: Edward Elgar Publishing.

Wagner-Tsukamoto, Sigmund. 2007. An Institutional Economic Reconstruction of Scientific Management: On the Lost Theoretical Logic of Taylorism. *Academy of Management Review* 37 (1): 105–117.

Wallerstein, Michael. 1999. Wage-Setting Institutions and Pay Inequality in Advanced Industrial Societies. *American Journal of Political Science* 43 (3): 649–680.

———. 2008. Centralized Bargaining and Wage Restraint. In *Selected Works of Michael Wallerstein: The Political Economy of Inequality, Unions, and Social Democracy*, ed. David Austen-Smith, Jeffrey A. Frieden, Miriam A. Golden, Karl Ove Moene, and Adam Przeworski. Cambridge/New York: Cambridge University Press.

Waltman, Jerold L. 2008. *Minimum Wage Policy in Great Britain and the United States*. New York: Algora Publishing.

Webb, Sidney. 1912. The Economic Theory of a Legal Minimum Wage. *The Journal of Political Economy* 20 (10): 973–998.

Weber, Max. 1947. *The Theory of Social and Economic Organizations*. Trans. A.M. Henderson and Talcott Parsons. New York: Free Press of Glencoe.

Weintraub, Sidney. 1972. Incomes Policy: Competing the Stabilization Triangle. *Journal of Economic Issues* 6 (4): 105–122.

Welch, Finis. 1974. Minimum Wage Legislation in the United States. *Economic Inquiry* 12 (3): 285–318.

———. 1978. *Minimum Wages: Issues and Evidence*. Washington, DC: American Enterprise Institute for Public Policy Research.

White, Stuart. 2003. *The Civic Minimum: On the Rights and Obligations of Economic Citizenship*. Oxford/New York: Oxford University Press.

———. 2007. *Equality*. Cambridge/Malden: Polity Press.

Wilkinson, Richard, and Kate Pickett. 2010. *The Spirit Level: Why Greater Equality Makes Societies Stronger*. New York/London: Bloomsbury Press.

Wood, Gordon S. 1993. *The Radicalism of the American Revolution*. New York: Vintage Books.

Wray, L. Randall. 2007. *The Employer of Last Resort Programme: Could It Work for Developing Countries?* Economic and Labor Market Papers, International Labour Ofice, Geneva Employment Analysis and Research Unit, Economic and Labour Market Analysis Department, International Labour Organization, August.

Zatz, Noah D. 2009. The Minimum Wage as a Civil Rights Protection: An Alternative to Antipoverty Arguments? *The University of Chicago Legal Forum*. Downloaded from http://www.lexisnexis.com/ex-proxy.brooklyn.cuny.edu:2048/Inacui2api/delivery/PrintDoc

Index

O. M. Levin-Waldman, *Restoring the Middle Class through Wage Policy*, Binzagr Institute for Sustainable Prosperity,
https://doi.org/10.1007/978-3-319-74448-3

The manufacturer's authorised representative in the EU is Springer Nature Customer Service Centre GmbH, Europaplatz 3, 69115 Heidelberg, Germany. If you have any concerns regarding our products, please contact ProductSafety@springernature.com

Printed and bound by CPI Group (UK) Ltd, Croydon, CR0 4YY

30/09/2026

02225660-0008